The Universal Adversary

The history of bourgeois modernity is a history of the Enemy. This book is a radical exploration of an Enemy that has recently emerged from within security documents released by the US security state: the Universal Adversary.

The Universal Adversary is now central to emergency planning in general and, more specifically, to security preparations for future attacks. But an attack from who, or what? This book – the first to appear on the topic – shows how the concept of the Universal Adversary draws on several key figures in the history of ideas, said to pose a threat to state power and capital accumulation. Within the Universal Adversary there lies the problem not just of the 'terrorist' but, more generally, of the 'subversive', and what the emergency planning documents refer to as the 'disgruntled worker'. This reference reveals the conjoined power of the contemporary mobilisation of security and the defence of capital. But it also reveals much more. Taking the figure of the disgruntled worker as its starting point, the book introduces some of this worker's close cousins – figures often regarded not simply as a threat to security and capital but as nothing less than the Enemy of all Mankind: the Zombie, the Devil and the Pirate. In situating these figures of enmity within debates about security and capital, the book engages an extraordinary variety of issues that now comprise a contemporary politics of security. From crowd control to contagion, from the witch-hunt to the apocalypse, from pigs to intellectual property, this book provides a compelling analysis of the ways in which security and capital are organized against nothing less than the 'Enemies of all Mankind'.

Mark Neocleous is Professor of the Critique of Political Economy at Brunel University, UK.

The Universal Adversary

Security, Capital and 'The Enemies of
All Mankind'

Mark Neocleous

Routledge
Taylor & Francis Group
a GlassHouse Book

First published 2016
by Routledge
2 Park Square, Milton Park, Abingdon, Oxon, OX14 4RN

and by Routledge
711 Third Avenue, New York, NY 10017

a GlassHouse book

Routledge is an imprint of the Taylor & Francis Group, an informa business

© 2016 Mark Neocleous

British Library Cataloguing in Publication Data
A catalogue record for this book is available from the British Library

Library of Congress Cataloging-in-Publication Data
A catalog record for this book has been requested

ISBN: 978-1-138-95515-8 (hbk)
ISBN: 978-1-138-95516-5 (pbk)
ISBN: 978-1-315-66654-9 (ebk)

Typeset in Baskerville by
by FiSH Books Ltd, Enfield

MIX
Paper from responsible sources
FSC® C013604

Printed and bound by CPI Group (UK) Ltd, Croydon, CR0 4YY

Contents

Figures

Acknowledgements

The argument in this book was developed initially for a paper presented at a plenary session of the Critical Legal Conference held at the University of Sussex in September 2014. It was then presented in a slightly different form as a keynote paper at the Critical Terrorism Studies Annual Conference held at Nottingham Trent University later that same month. The argument has moved on a great deal since those talks, but I am nonetheless grateful to Tarik Kochi and Kimberley Brayson for the opportunity to talk at Sussex, and to Charlotte Heath-Kelly, Christopher Baker-Beall and Lee Jarvis for the opportunity to talk at Nottingham Trent. Thanks are due to Tyler Wall for reading and commenting on an early and undeveloped version of the manuscript and to Colin Perrin for supporting the project as commissioning editor. For support throughout the whole project and more, including the shared recognition that 'Zombies have issues too', I am grateful as always to DB, KK, PC and LL.

Introduction

As Anger causeth heat in some parts of the Body, when we are awake; so when we sleep, the over heating of the same parts causeth Anger, and raiseth up in the brain the Imagination of an Enemy.

(Thomas Hobbes, *Leviathan*, 1651)

Bourgeois modernity is oriented around the imagination of an Enemy. This is so because the fear of some kind of Enemy is a fundamental feature of the supreme concept of bourgeois society: security. Thomas Hobbes understood this connection well. 'The Passion to be reckoned upon, is Fear', he comments in *Leviathan*. The state of nature which he so famously describes in that book is a state of 'continuall feare' in which life is 'poore, nasty, brutish, and short', and a condition of war in which 'every man is Enemy to every man'. In such a state 'there can be no security'.[1] The reason for creating the mighty Leviathan state and offering it our obedience is for the security the state provides. Yet that barely begins to tell the whole story.

In the purported state of nature, the fears we are assumed to have are entirely obvious and rational, based on our fear of death. But Hobbes is also aware that the security obtained within the Leviathan and the feeling of protection that then ensues in the newly created Commonwealth produces in turn a new kind of Enemy: a 'common enemy'. 'The Multitude sufficient to confide in for our Security, is not determined by any certain number, but by comparison with the Enemy we feare'. Thus despite giving up the condition of war that is the state of nature, there must still be a common Enemy which the members of the Commonwealth fear and which binds them together. 'When there is no common enemy', Hobbes says, men 'make warre upon each other, for their particular interests'.

Nor is it enough for the security, which men desire should last all the time of their life, that they be governed, and directed by one judgement, for a limited time; as in one Battell, or one Warre. For though they obtain a Victory by their unanimous endeavour against a forraign enemy; yet afterwards, when either they have no common enemy, or he

that by one part is held for an enemy, is by another part held for a
friend, they must needs by the difference of their interests dissolve, and
fall again into a Warre amongst themselves.[2]

Fear of other humans drives us initially into the security and protection
offered by the state, but the *ongoing* project of security is produced through
an *imagination of a new Enemy* said to be an Enemy of all the members of that
state and a threat to the very existence of the state itself. Hobbes is on to
something: security is very much dependent on the fabrication of the
Enemy; security will always find security threats.

Yet Hobbes is on to something else as well. A key theme in *Leviathan* is
the question of what Hobbes variously calls 'Powers Invisible', 'Invisible
Powers', 'Spirits Invisible', 'Invisible Agents' and 'Invisible Spirits', which
give fear another dimension.[3] Humans, claims Hobbes, are also 'enclined
to suppose ... severall kinds of Powers Invisible; and to stand in awe of their
own imaginations; and in times of distresse to invoke them'. He makes this
point partly in order to challenge the superstitious fears concerning 'the
power of Witches ... Fayries, Ghosts, and Goblins'. 'This Feare of things
invisible', he says, 'is the natural Seed of that, which every one in himself
calleth Religion'. But at the same time, Hobbes wants to make a political
point, which is that such fears are a mechanism through which political
leaders can exercise secular power, especially when people believe that
such 'Invisible Agents' have a 'Kingdom on Earth also'.[4]

> This seed of Religion, having been observed by many; some of those
> that have observed it, have been enclined thereby so to nourish, dresse,
> and forme it into Lawes; and to adde to it of their own invention, any
> opinion of the causes of future events, by which they thought they
> should best be able to govern others, and to make unto themselves the
> greatest use of their Powers.[5]

In other words, the fear of 'Invisible Agents' and 'Powers Invisible' has
been a mechanism 'to keep the people in obedience'.[6] Order and security
might be a product of the rational fear of death, but might also be
produced by a far less rational fear of 'Invisible Powers' thought to be at
large.

This book concerns imagination and fear in the world of contemporary
security and capital. It takes as its starting point an 'Invisible Power' that has
recently been conjured up within the security state and which now permeates the whole problematic of security but which also, as we shall see,
connects to the problematic of the Enemy as a whole. In Hobbesian terms,
it is a Power that is as awesome as it is fearsome, and which has come to the
fore in a particular 'time of distress', namely the contemporary war on
terror and the contemporary crisis of capital. The 'Invisible Power' with

which this book is concerned goes by the name of 'The Universal Adversary'.

'The Universal Adversary' is a category that has been invented by the project for US homeland security. We will explore some of its origins in Chapter 1, but here we can simply note that at a certain point in the project for homeland security the unknown enemies that might generate an attack became singular, pushed together into one in Emergency Planning Scenarios and united as a singular for reasons of state. As the Homeland Security Council puts it: 'Because the [future] attacks could be caused by foreign terrorists; domestic radical groups; state-sponsored adversaries; or in some cases disgruntled employees, the perpetrator has been named, the Universal Adversary'.[7]

The *Universal Adversary*? It is a fantastic phrase, conjuring up a complex set of images and conflating a host of disparate subjects under a blanket conceptual term. Yet despite this, and despite the extent to which the Universal Adversary is referred to within the project of homeland security, the category has not really been picked up in critical commentaries on security. One easy interpretation has been to think of the Universal Adversary solely as the terrorist. Speaking in memoriam for Norman O. Brown, James Clifford asks: 'what would he say about today's universal adversary, "the terrorist"?', an equation repeated by Joseba Zulaika in his work on contemporary terrorism.[8] But to think of the Universal Adversary simply as another word for 'terrorist' tells us little, ignores the other aspects of the definition provided by the Homeland Security Council and barely touches the surface of what might be going on, not least because 'terrorist' is itself a 'non-existent substance, an empty name'.[9]

Another interpretation which comes just a little too easy is to pass it over as the kind of strange idea generated by bureaucracy. Commenting on the various 'universals' that have been used to organize imperial taxonomies, Ann Laura Stoler connects these to the war on terror.

> Unreason organized the political grammar of empire at the beginning – and in so far as it has been concentrated in rationales for torture in the name of curbing violence, it re-emerges in the 'standard operating procedures' of the US presence in Iraq, and in the US Department of Homeland Security's billion-dollar initiatives to identify people's propensities for 'Violent Intent' (prior to any act) with 'non-invasive brainscans' and by calculating the tautness of their posture and body temperatures. It takes privileged shelter in colonizing Zionist reason that underwrites relentless Israeli incursions on Palestinian land, in the continued singling out of French citizens whose parents may be of North African origin, and in the US State Department's surreal endeavour to identify the attributes of a 'Universal Adversary'.[10]

Stoler is surely right to connect the Universal Adversary to the violent practices of the war on terror and she is absolutely spot on in connecting this
back to the violence of imperialism. But the term she uses when she comes
to the Universal Adversary (namely, 'surreal') is, aside from being one of
the most overused and misused words in the English language, a word
which usually nowadays tells us nothing more than that something seems a
little bit strange. There is of course much that is strange about the phrase
'Universal Adversary', but leaving it at that tells us not very much at all. So
what might we make of the idea?

In their account of the global state of contemporary war, Michael Hardt
and Antonio Negri comment that for such war to continue requires the
'constant presence of an enemy and threat of disorder' in order to legitimate the violence taking place. But the Enemy 'is no longer concrete and
localizable'. Rather, it has 'now become something fleeting and ungras-
pable'. The Enemy is now 'unknown and unseen and yet ever present,
something like a hostile aura. The enemy appears in the haze of the future
and serves to prop up legitimation where legitimation has declined. This
enemy is in fact not merely elusive but completely abstract'. Making the
same point in a slightly different way, Carlo Galli comments that 'Global
War is certainly not waged against identified enemies, but against "nebu-
las", adversaries who have no face, but instead are spectres onto which we
can project our own spectres'. Slavoj Žižek suggests that 'the enemy is by
definition, always – up to a point, at least – *invisible*', and this invisibility
gives it an auratic, ghostly, abstract quality.[11] And indeed, a spectral presence is precisely how the Enemy has been described time and again by the
security state, with its claims about a 'ghost enemy', a 'ghostly presence', a
'faceless phantom', a 'phantom menace'. (Such talk might also explain why
it is that when the security documents discuss the supposed links between
piracy and terror, about which we will have much more to say in Chapter 4,
they speak of 'phantom ships', and might also explain the names of strategies employed against the Enemy, such as such as 'Operation Phantom
Thunder', 'Operation Phantom Strike' and 'Operation Phantom
Phoenix'.)

This book proceeds on the basis that the abstract ghostly emptiness is
important. On the one hand, it leaves the category of the Enemy open to
endless modification, and the modification is always conducted by those
who claim the power to pronounce on what the Enemy is, where it can be
found and how it behaves. The function and status of that perennial prop-
agator of banalities, the 'security expert', is thereby reinforced, as is the
modern take on the idea of 'mystery of state', namely the secrecy that
surrounds security. The emptiness also allows those same people to name
and rename the Enemy: hence 'the perpetrator has been named, the
Universal Adversary'. On the other hand, the abstract ghostly emptiness of
the Enemy would also appear to demand the permanent ghostly presence

of the police power, that all-pervasive power that lies at the heart of the state.[12] The ghostliness of this power underpins what is obviously being demanded by the threat posed by a so-called Universal Adversary: the existence of a Universal Police Power, acting in the name of all and claiming power over all in its permanent war against the Adversary in question.

Thus rather than ask 'what is the Universal Adversary?', this book explores the kind of work that the concept 'Universal Adversary' might be performing for the state. But the question concerning what kind of work the 'Universal Adversary' might be performing for the state raises a related but necessary question: what kind of work might the concept 'Universal Adversary' be performing for capital? First, however, a more pressing question arises: *why* has the perpetrator been named the 'Universal Adversary'?

'Adversary' is clearly a word designed to avoid using 'Enemy'. It is well known that in the years following the attacks on 11 September, 2001, the US had been searching for a way to capture the 'new kind of enemy' it understood itself to be facing. Document after document made the point of saying that the kind of Enemy faced in the Cold War is gone and that the security strategy employed against that Enemy must now also change. 'The United States is under attack from a new kind of enemy', as George W. Bush put it in the original planning document for the Department of Homeland Security.[13] One procedure was to see this new Enemy precisely *not* as a genuine Enemy at all but as some kind of figure transcending the traditional categories of war: 'terrorist', 'militant' and 'insurgent' but also, less obviously, 'evildoers' or 'pirates' (two categories we explore in chapters to follow). Another procedure was to start talking of 'the Adversary'. Shortly after his appointment as US Secretary of Defense, for example, Robert Gates commented that success in future war 'will be less a matter of imposing one's will and more a function of shaping behaviour – of friends, adversaries, and most importantly, the people in between'.[14] Gone is the long-standing 'friend-enemy' distinction, he claimed, and in its place comes 'friend-adversary'. That Gates was speaking about success in non-military terms is also important, because the recent rethinking of counterinsurgency strategy has also relied on the idea of the Adversary rather than Enemy.[15] At the same time, much of the 'cultural intelligence' and 'anthropological knowledge' being developed in support of the new counterinsurgency also speaks of 'adversaries' rather than 'enemies', not least because of the growing military and security interest in programs such as the Human Terrain Systems (HTS). For Montgomery McFate, perhaps the leading 'security expert' in this field, the issue of 'cultural knowledge of adversaries' is connected to the changing form of war in which 'adversaries neither think nor act like nation-states'. The language of 'Adversary' rather than 'Enemy' has been reinforced by others who stress the cultural aspects of war and HTS.[16] The language has also proliferated throughout military intelligence and the war power in general: one finds, for example, discussions about the 'networked insurgency' articulated in terms of the Adversary,[17] air power explained as a police power to 'frustrate the adversary's opportunity for the close fight',[18] and the Marine Corps described as gathering intelligence about and controlling the population of the Adversary.[19] Speaking about the launch of the Gorgon Stare drone, Major General James O. Poss, the US Air Force's Assistant Deputy Chief of Staff for intelligence, commented in 2011 that 'Gorgon Stare will be looking at a whole city, so there will be no way for the adversary to know what we're looking at, and we can see everything'.[20] The reconfiguration of the war on terror as a global manhunt has also played on this idea that the war power is now engaged in 'adversary manhunting activities' in which what is being hunted is less an 'enemy' and more an 'Adversary'.[21] To put it bluntly: the Enemy has become the Adversary.

Why 'Universal' Adversary? 'Universal' serves as a powerful image of a projected threat: its lack of specific content means that the Enemy can be presented as possessing infinite scope and capability, qualities which render it somehow 'Universal'. 'Universal' also plays on the story we are told time and again: that the Enemy is anywhere and everywhere, that the theatre of war is universal. 'Universal' also implies that the enemy is a threat to the whole world or all people, and here it plays on a very old theme in the politics of enmity which will run through this book, namely the ways in which the Enemies of Order and Capital ('security threats') have been interpolated as the Enemy of Humanity as a whole. What I want to do here is to therefore explore the ways in which the *Universality* of this Adversary is a very contemporary take on an old trope in bourgeois ideology: of thinking about the Enemy of capitalist order as some kind of Enemy of Humanity. The *Universality* of the Universal Adversary is constituted by its supposed enmity to all things considered as good and proper in the mind of the ruling class and which that class wishes to impose on the whole of mankind: law and order, peace and security, private property and police power. Bourgeois modernity is oriented around the imagination of an Enemy, then, but it also tends to present this Enemy as the *Enemy of All Mankind*. In trying to mobilise something called 'humanity', nothing works better than to talk of one's enemy as being the 'Enemy of All Mankind', or, as it now appears, the 'Universal Adversary'.

In his book on homeland security, Christos Boukalas suggests that the Universal Adversary 'is an abstraction referring to an overall enemy against which homeland security is mobilised'.[22] Building on this observation, this book reads the Universal Adversary in terms of the *mobilisation of security*, a form of total mobilisation in the name of the war power. But mobilised against what, exactly? How does one combat an aura, wage war on a spectre or defeat an abstraction?

'There is something monstrous in this abstract, auratic enemy', Hardt and Negri comment. Or as Galli puts it, 'the enemy cannot be a *iustus hostis*, a legitimate enemy; it must be a monster existing outside humanity'. Both comments pick up on the truism that mobilising people against an Enemy is made easier if the Enemy be thought of as existentially different or alien.[23] Now, to render something as 'monstrous', 'alien' or 'demonic' is perhaps the most extreme form of enmity, in that it enables a class of people to be represented as not just an Enemy to be feared but as a threat to the very existence of the polity and even to humanity as a whole.[24] The interpellation of something as monstrous, alien, or demonic, as somehow outside nature as well as outside law, is crucial to the political construction of fear and has long been a feature of political demonology, not least because the idea of an abstract sinister force that seeks to undermine and destroy a way of life helps call forth the police power, from the most mundane security measures to all-out war.[25] The security imaginary is riddled with demons, which is one reason why security talk often strikes a decidedly Manichean tone.

One such demon is perhaps the oldest enemy of all: the Devil. It will come as no surprise that in these deeply theological times – 'what is there today that is not "theology" (apart from theological claptrap)?'[26] – the Devil looms large in the mobilisation of security. The accusation that one's Enemy is in league with the Devil is 'the theological version of the accusation of being in league with the international conspirators against the polity', notes Rodney Barker.[27] But talk of the Devil is always as political as it is theological. The Devil was a political invention, as we will see, and in Chapter 3 we will have cause to connect the Devil that was said by many to have been at work on 11 September, 2001, with the Devil who, with the help of his rebellious army of followers, was a key figure in the rise and consolidation of the ideology of security and order during the development of capitalist modernity. Refining the view which holds that the concept of 'international terror' is a secular version of the ancient enemy,[28] we shall consider the Universal Adversary in terms of the role of the Devil as the original Enemy of All Mankind. And yet speaking of demons, ghosts, phantoms and the Devil always leaves security with a problem. The problem, which is in effect the task of security's struggle, lies in not only denouncing the Enemy as a demon but in simultaneously offering a recognizable image of the Enemy: to render visible the Invisible Power; to generate the belief that despite its phantom quality the Enemy nonetheless also possesses a physical presence; to 'despectralise' it and so to transform the Enemy's ghostly presence into a more material and fleshy thing.[29] Talk of the Devil, for example, historically became the basis for talk of the Devil's agents, none more so than the Witch. And as we shall also see in Chapter 3, it is through the figure of the Witch that many of the practices the state calls 'security measures' have been formed, and it is the same figure that provides the ideological foundation of that archetypal security practice, the 'witch-hunt'.

This need to 'despectralise' the Enemy and transform it into a more material and fleshy thing is further explored in the shape of two further figures which have come to the fore in these days of heightened security consciousness: the Pirate and the Zombie.

The Pirate is widely regarded as the original Enemy of All Mankind. Piracy was historically interpellated as a *crime* so terrible that the whole of mankind must wage *war* against it. The Pirate's status as Criminal-cum-Enemy has a long and complicated history, much of which is connected to the rise of capitalism and its imperialist expansion and which we will explore in Chapter 4. Throughout this history the Pirate has been an ambiguous figure. As Gerry Simpson notes, 'at different times he is glamorous, transgressive, dangerous, a former ally and a possible adversary'. Such ambiguity is partly what lies behind the lack of a stable legal definition of piracy. What we end up with when we explore the history and legal status of the Pirate 'is a figure who is sharply demarcated in much of the field's judicial and doctrinal work as an enemy of mankind, and fluid and ambiguous in our politics and in some of our legal practice as enemy, ally, proxy, privateer and combatant (legal and illegal)'.[30] What we also end up with is a figure present at the birth of capital and at the inception of the project of security, but which also remains at the heart of the contemporary world of security and capital.

Alongside the centuries-old figure of the Pirate there has appeared another figure: the Zombie. Compared to the Pirate's much longer history, the Zombie is a relatively recent invention, and yet they share some common characteristics, not least given the Zombie's emergence out of the violence of capitalist imperialism. Chapter 2 considers this history in order to unravel why it is that the Zombie has become such a prevalent force not just in popular culture but in mainstream security politics too. When the United Nations launches an App for its 'Model UN' events in which it suggests '60-minute lesson plans' on key issues such 'climate change, poverty eradication, and the Zombie Apocalypse',[31] it is clear that the Zombie is being made to do some serious political work. Might this work lie in the fact that a Zombie apocalypse is the emergency situation writ large? Might it lie in the fact the Zombie appears to kill all humans indiscriminately, with no apparent political cause, making it seem like an Enemy of us all? Or might it lie in the fact that the Zombie apocalypse is presented to us as a time of violent lawlessness, in which we are encouraged to imagine ourselves taking the powers of war and police into our own hands in order that we ourselves might kill zombies in an equally indiscriminate fashion?

The Zombie, the Pirate, the Witch, the Devil: such figures might appear to be marginal to mainstream political discourse. But what appears marginal often turns out to have heuristic value when examined closely in the wider order of things.[32] As we shall see, the Pirate, the Zombie, the

Witch and the Devil are figures around which law and violence coalesce, drawing lines across which norms are policed and the war power exercised. By embodying a certain kind of problem for *capital* which must be dealt with by the *state* and which is articulated as a problem for *humanity*, such figures are integral to the mobilisation of security. And we must never forget that it is precisely the *mobilisation* of security that is the key to its success as a political power.[33]

In the series of lectures at the Collège de France delivered in 1975 and 1976, and published as *'Society Must be Defended'*, Michel Foucault comments that if we concentrate on the techniques of power and show what kinds of political utility or economic profit might come from them, then we have a better chance of understanding their more general role.

> The bourgeoisie doesn't give a damn about the mad, but ... the procedures used to exclude the mad produced or generated a political profit, or even a certain economic utility. The bourgeoisie is not interested in the mad, but it is interested in power over the mad; the bourgeoisie is not interested in the sexuality of children, but it is interested in the system of power that controls the sexuality of children. The bourgeoisie does not give a damn about delinquents, or about how they are punished or rehabilitated, as that is of no economic interest. On the other hand, the set of mechanisms whereby delinquents are controlled, kept track of, punished, and reformed does generate a bourgeois interest that functions within the economico-political system as a whole.[34]

We might say, following this, that the bourgeoisie is not interested in the Zombie, Witch, Pirate or Devil, but in the system of power that can be used to control, persecute or punish them, and thus, as we shall see, in a system of power to control, persecute or punish the Universal Adversary *per se*. Which is way of saying that the bourgeoisie is interested in how this system of power might help constitute the political subjectivity of those who are to be prepared and mobilised to fight the enemies of mankind in the name of security. Moreover, the bourgeoisie is interested in these things not simply because of that mythical entity called 'security' but also because they have what Foucault coyly calls an 'economic utility' about which we can be a little more categorical: they are mechanisms used in the defence of capital.

On this basis, we will be dealing with a figure far less marginal than the Zombie, Pirate, Witch and Devil, one which constitutes the focus of Chapter 1 but which also appears throughout the other chapters because it is around this figure that the other more seemingly marginal figures often circulate: the Worker. As the definition of Universal Adversary cited above makes abundantly clear: 'foreign terrorists; domestic radical groups; state-sponsored adversaries; [and] disgruntled employees', all grasped together as the Universal Adversary. Here, alongside the foreign terrorist and state-sponsored adversaries are domestic radical groups and *disgruntled workers*. As Boukalas notes, although much has been made about the ways in which during the war on terror the lines between terrorism, subversion, dissent and protest have become blurred (for the state, conveniently so), the Enemy is finally identified and the object of security finally defined.[35] The disgruntled Worker is bundled together with the foreign Terrorist. In the 'Universal Adversary', then, the war on terror coincides with the class war.

At one point during the revolutionary days of 1848, Engels made an astute observation about the class war: 'the bourgeoisie declares the workers to be not ordinary enemies who have to be defeated but enemies of society who must be destroyed'.[36] The bourgeoisie sees itself as the guardian of civilisation and democracy, law and order, peace and security. But it also likes to present itself as guardian of the whole of humanity. As such, it likes to regard its enemies, including and especially the proletariat and most notably when that class looks to be organising as a revolutionary force, as the Enemy of Humanity. This book proceeds on the basis that the bringing together of the Terrorist-Enemy, Criminal-Enemy, Political-Enemy and (Disgruntled) Worker-Enemy under the label 'Universal Adversary' is by no means a side issue or a momentary lapse by the movers and shakers within the security state. Rather, this bringing together of such figures is at the very heart of the mobilisation of security and the defence of capital against what we are encouraged to believe is nothing less than the Enemy of All Mankind.

The chapters which follow thus explore a series of diverse strands of thought, mobile metaphors, allusions and tropes that arise from and are connected to the idea of the Universal Adversary. As should be clear from this introduction, a book which takes as its starting point a critique of a concept which very few people have noticed and which uses this critique to engage in a discussion of plagues of Zombies, hordes of Pirates and minions of the Devil is a book that is itself going to have to perform some imaginative leaps and bounds, not least in an attempt to keep up with the kinds of imaginative leaps and bounds now being made under the banner of security; contemporary security wars are nothing if not wars of the imagination. The chapters therefore frequently veer away from the Universal Adversary itself in order to move across political ideas about friend and enemy, cultural conceptions of the normal and the abnormal, and legal assumptions about order and disorder. The point is not to try and explain what the Universal Adversary is[37] but, rather, to explore how security and capital operate when the Enemy is conceived as Universal.

It might seem a little odd to organise a book around a term that few people have heard of and which might at very best be said to be merely a loose allusion to a vague and unspecified Enemy. To that, I can suggest only that we take note of a point sketched out many years ago by Gilles Deleuze and Félix Guattari in their account of the war machine. 'Doubtless, the present situation is highly discouraging', they comment:

> We have watched the war machine grow stronger and stronger, as in a science fiction story; we have seen it assign as its objective a peace still more terrifying than fascist death; we have seen it maintain or instigate the most terrible of local wars as parts of itself; we have seen it set its sights on a new type of enemy, no longer another state, or even another regime, but the 'Unspecified enemy'.[38]

The characteristics of the Unspecified Enemy include being multiform, manoeuvrable and omnipresent, but also being inherently subversive of the social and economic order.

Paraphrasing Deleuze and Guattari we might say that despite appearing solely in the Emergency Planning Scenarios of the American state, the Universal Adversary is in fact axiomatic in official and unofficial texts on national security, international law and police powers.[39] So axiomatic is it that despite being a term of which few people have heard, the Universal Adversary may in fact be a lived reality for most of us, in the sense that part of its very 'universality' inculpates each of us, as a disgruntled Worker, as part of the Universal Adversary. *De te fabula narrator!* ['this tale is told of you!'], as Marx put it to the readers of *Capital.*[40] Security is ranged against us. But if today the world wants to be deceived, it wants to be deceived in the name of security. It wants to be deceived about the conceptual concoctions of the security industry, the new terms and concepts which continue to bamboozle and mystify while peddling fears and pandering to engrained cultural assumptions about figures we think we know. The Universal Adversary does all of these things and more.

Chapter 1

'The perpetrator has been named the Universal Adversary': on the disgruntled Worker

The future teaches you to be alone,
The present to be afraid and cold.
(Manic Street Preachers, 'If You Tolerate This
Your Children Will Be Next', 1998)

Shouldn't call 'em pigs
The most oppressed species is a pig.
(Sole and DJ Pain 1, 'Fire the Police', 2014)

The future

Contemporary security is structured around imagining the unimaginable and planning for the unexpected. Imagining emergency, preparing for emergency, managing emergency: these are the key terms of contemporary state power.

A few months after the attacks of 11 September, 2001, it was announced that US security strategy was to be reoriented around preparing for the future.

> *Preparing for the future* will require us to think differently and develop the kinds of forces and capabilities that can adapt quickly to new challenges and to unexpected circumstances … *Surprise and uncertainty are the defining characteristics of our new security environment.* During the Cold War, we faced a fairly predictable set of threats. We came to know a great deal about *our adversary*, because it was the same one for a long period. We knew many of the capabilities they possessed, and we fashioned strategies and capabilities that we believed we needed to deter them. And they were successful. It worked.
>
> …
>
> The challenges of a new century are not nearly as predictable as they were during the Cold War. Who would have imagined only a few months ago that terrorists would take commercial airliners, turn them

into missiles and use them to strike the Pentagon and the World Trade Towers, killing thousands? But it happened.

And let there be no doubt, in the years ahead, it is likely that we will be surprised again by *new adversaries* who may also *strike in unexpected ways.*
...

Our challenge in this new century is a difficult one. It's really to *prepare to defend our nation against the unknown, the uncertain and ... the unexpected.* That may seem on the face of it an impossible task, but it is not. But to accomplish it, we have to put aside the comfortable ways of thinking and planning, take risks and try new things so that we can prepare our forces to *deter and defeat adversaries...*
...

To *prepare for the future,* we [have] also decided to move away from the so-called threat-based strategy that had dominated our country's defense planning for nearly a half-century and adopt what we characterized as a capability-based strategy, one that focuses less on who might threaten us or where we might be threatened, and more on how we might be threatened and what we need to do to deter and defend against such threats. Instead of building our armed forces around plans to fight this or that country, *we need to examine our vulnerabilities,* asking ourselves, as Frederick the Great did in his great General Principles of War, *what design would I be forming if I were the enemy,* and then fashioning our forces as necessary to deter and defeat those threats.[1]

So: the security state must now deal with 'the unknown, the uncertain and ... the unexpected' and must constantly ask itself what design any new Adversary might be forming. Hence the 'one percent doctrine': 'even if there's just a one percent chance of the unimaginable coming due, act as if it is a certainty'.[2] The logic is: we don't know what the enemy might be planning, but let's try to imagine it; let's try to imagine the unimaginable – even if there's just a one percent chance of the unimaginable coming due, we should prepare for it as though it is a certainty.

Without pandering to the view that holds that on 11 September 2001 *everything changed* – after all, the leading politicians behind these ideas had been arguing for some time that what was needed was 'some catastrophic and catalyzing event' which could be used to galvanise a new strategy for both security and capital[3] – the outcome of such claims has been the development of a logic of security rooted in the uncertain but hypothetical, the unknown but imaginable; in effect, an intensification of the politics of fear driven by the imagination of the future as one of crisis and disaster.

Crisis and disaster are the major tropes of our time. States now spend a huge amount of time, money and energy on the threat of the future:

terrorists threaten an attack, societies threaten to collapse, populations threaten to explode, currencies threaten to plummet, national economies threaten to crash. The threat level is always severe, an attack is always imminent, a crisis is coming, disaster is round the corner.[4] The state demands that we imagine the threat and the attack, the crisis and the disaster, and then reimagine them, and then imagine our response to them and then reimagine that response, and then go through the whole thing again and again. Preparation is thus the order of the day: preparation to prevent, to pre-empt, to short-circuit and to recover from disaster. Such a drive underpins what security documents call 'all-hazards preparedness',[5] where 'all hazards' includes literally anything that could go wrong. This morphing of the national security state into the disaster-security state is organised through the fear of what *might* happen in order to be better prepared for it. And it is not just the state that is to be prepared, but the whole social order, as witnessed by the proliferation of the discourse of 'resilience' in which citizens are to now be trained. Resilience requires us to imagine how we might prepare to recover or 'bounce back' from crisis or disaster. Resilience both engages and encourages a culture of preparedness for a terrorist attack and all sorts of other unknown disasters – social, political, personal, systemic – driven by what we might call the security *of* resilience and a certain kind of security *in* resilience.[6]

The whole range of 'contingency planning', 'crisis preparation' and 'disaster management' that now exists is captured under the label 'emergency'. Implicit in the logic of preparation is the idea that although the emergency cannot be properly brought into the realm of everyday political administration, it is nonetheless imperative that political administration plans for the emergency, which in turns means that political administration has become obsessed by the emergency itself. Thinking through emergency has been constituted as political reason. Emergency is now an industry. Emergency is the new normal. One no longer shows one's obedience through an acceptance of the security offered by the state but, rather, through one's preparation to defend that security when the state of emergency is declared. What else is emergency but mobilisation? The motto which has underpinned the whole history of security within bourgeois modernity, *Protego ergo Obligo* (Protection, therefore Obedience), needs to be supplanted by a new motto: 'Protection, therefore Preparation'. Security is now nothing without its allies: preparation and emergency.

The narrative of emergency underpins the apocalyptic tone which is so present today and about which we will have more to say in Chapters 2 and 3. Here we need only note that this tone ratchets up the fundamental tensions that underpin the whole politics of (in)security.[7] The events of intense insecurity imagined by today's security fetishists are often captured in the form of Emergency Planning Scenarios. These have been developed by the core institutions of the security state in the US, from the Department of Homeland Security, to the Homeland Security Council and on to the Fusion Centres. Such Scenarios are based on the question 'What If...?' 'In scenario analysis, researchers posit a "what if" framework and examine how various factors might interact to generate a sequence of events – i.e., "What if such and such happened next?"'.[8] What if terrorists are planning x? What if subversives could pull off y? What if z were possible? 'What if...?' is the question asked of us as our entry ticket into the world of security, which is precisely why the same 'What if...?' dominates the cultural imagination of (in)security.[9]

The Introduction to the Homeland Security Council document called *National Planning Scenarios* opens as follows:

> The Federal interagency community has developed 15 all-hazards planning scenarios (the National Planning Scenarios or Scenarios) for use in national, Federal, State, and local homeland security preparedness activities. The Scenarios are planning tools and are representative of the range of potential terrorist attacks and natural disasters and the related impacts that threaten our nation.[10]

Of the 15 Scenarios listed, 3 involve 'natural' emergencies such as an influenza pandemic, and the other 12 are all instigated by a terror attack, such as through the use of chemical weapons, explosives, biological contamination, nuclear weapons, and cyber-attacks.

That some Scenarios are presented as 'natural' disasters should not be misconstrued. There is no such thing as a 'natural' disaster, of course, but the more telling point now is that what are *called* 'natural' disasters are now understood by the state largely in terms of national security.[11] Thus an event such as the 2001 anthrax attacks reinforced concerns over 'bioterrorism' (that particular attack was a key rationale for the Public Health Security and Bioterrorism Preparedness and Response Act, 2002), while the 2003 SARS epidemic and the 2009 H1N1 flu pandemic facilitated the development of 'disease surveillance networks' by the Department of Homeland Security. Such events underpin the research into what the Epidemic Intelligence Service unit of the Centers for Disease Control (CDC) calls 'intentional epidemics'. The whole process brings medical power and police power together: what if the flu strain or virus is part of a biological attack? What if a seemingly 'natural' emergency such as a forest fire was started by terrorists? The Scenarios thus combine national security and national ('natural') disaster under the general rubric of 'emergency'.

The emergency scenario is a device of power. 'Scenario' has its roots in the 'sketch of the plot of a play', from the Latin *scenarius* meaning 'stage scenes', a reminder that 'a great part of politics and law is always theatre'.[12] The theatre of power is nowhere clearer than in the history of the national security state, which has always involved a certain kind of 'staging': a staging of politics in general and a staging of disaster in particular. Hence the first recorded use of 'scenario' to describe an 'imagined situation' was in 1960, in the context of a Cold War nuclear attack.[13] In the emergency scenario we therefore witness a certain kind of *performance* – of emergency, of chaos, of disaster, of catastrophe – as part and parcel of the wider theatre of security. (Some contemporary manifestations of this theatrical theme are widely known, such as the fact that film directors have been used as advisors on anti-terrorist exercises; others are less widely known, such as the fact that the White House calls its list of targeted killings a 'playbook'). The dramaturgy offers scenes in which the sovereign power can appear as sovereign: under threat, in crisis, but always reasserting itself in spectacular fashion as sovereign and thus as legitimate in its sovereignty. The performance of emergency is part and parcel of the rationalisation of domination. Hence the *performance of emergency* is expected to close with an *exhibition of the sovereign power to reconstitute order*. This is the spectacle of security: statecraft as stagecraft.

Statecraft as stagecraft always benefits from the existence of an Enemy, and in the chapters to follow we will meet a cast of characters who have appeared on the historic stage to perform this role: the Zombie, the Pirate, the Witch and the Devil. But it is in the Emergency Planning Scenarios that we first meet a new character, with whom the Zombie, Pirate, Witch and Devil will turn out to be related: the Universal Adversary.

> The scenarios have been developed in a way that allows them to be adapted to local conditions throughout the country. Although certain areas have special concerns ... every part of the country is vulnerable to one or more major hazards.
>
> Because the attacks could be caused by foreign terrorists; domestic radical groups; state-sponsored adversaries; or in some cases disgruntled employees, the perpetrator has been named, the Universal Adversary.[14]

With this comment, a new Enemy appeared in the theatre of emergency, a new Invisible Power entered the performance of security. The Universal Adversary took centre stage.

A 'Universal Adversary Program' was originally proposed with Senate Report 106–404 in September 2000, which required Top Officials (TOPOFF) exercises to include a realistic threat model. But it was during the TOPOFF 3 Full-Scale Exercise (FSE) in March and April 2005 (the exercise began in March with simulated intelligence activities, prior to the full exercise in April) that the Universal Adversary became a crucial component of the first-ever use of real-world intelligence systems in a domestic counterterrorism exercise.[15] A Department of Homeland Security Review of TOPOFF 3 from later that year noted that 'the opponent was fictionalized but based upon real world terrorist groups to influence player actions, create decision-making avenues, and provide participants with an opportunity to exercise against a realistic and adaptive adversary'. The footnote to this comment then adds that 'for the TOPOFF 3, the opponent is generally referred to as the Universal Adversary', and it goes on to say that 'the Universal Adversary is a data source ... that replicates the actual terrorist networks in extreme detail and includes dossiers down to names, photos and drivers' license numbers'.[16] In other words, the Universal Adversary provides 'fictionalized intelligence products required by the U.S. Department of Homeland Security (DHS), Federal Bureau of Investigation (FBI), and State, local, and tribal (SLT) analysts while ensuring that these products were realistic, accurate, and sophisticated enough to challenge intelligence analysts'. This Universal Adversary Program has expanded beyond it roots since TOPOFF 3 and now 'serves as a real-world tool for analysts and law enforcement personnel'.[17]

The Planning Scenarios document went through various drafts and shifts in title, with the final one (Version 21.3) issued as *National Planning Scenarios* and dated March 2006.[18] Where Version 2.0, from July 2004, is just over 50 pages, the final version of March 2006 is over 3 times longer and, more importantly, refers to the Universal Adversary far more frequently. The documents treat the Universal Adversary as an abstract entity used solely for purposes of simulation, to help imagine future emergencies.[19] Hence the documents outline various Scenarios with the view that teams will be trained in how to cope with the emergency in question. In other words, preparedness training now almost always includes something along the lines of a 'description of the Universal Adversary' as part of the training (and so, completely unsurprisingly, the Universal Adversary concept is now a huge business for the security industry),[20] from which flows certain expectations and demands on the teams put together to deal with the attack. Let me offer here five examples from different sources.

The first is from is from 'National Planning Scenario #11' produced by the Office of the Assistant Secretary for Preparedness and Response, in the US Department of Health and Human Services. The Scenario imagines an explosion with 180 fatalities and 270 injuries, and the contamination of 36 city blocks. The Scenario is introduced as follows: 'In this scenario the Universal Adversary (UA) purchases stolen cesium chloride (CsCL) to make a radiological dispersal device (RDD), or dirty bomb'. It is simply taken as read that anyone attending will already know what the phrase 'Universal Adversary' means (Figure 1.1).[21]

The second example is the 'Course Description' of the State Preparedness Training Center of the New York State Division of Homeland Security and Emergency Services. It is a description of a two-day event which ran on 9–10 August, 2014, which was a training session on 'Indicators

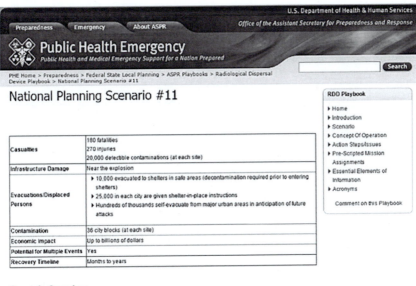

Figure 1.1 The National Planning Scenario # 11, including the Universal Adversary

of the Terrorist Attack Cycle – Advanced'. The topics covered, listed as bullet points, include:

- The Terrorist Attack Cycle
- Target Selection, Planning, Surveillance, and Elicitation
- Rehearsal Phase
- Attack Phase
- Escape/Evasion/Exploitation Phase

And listed there as one of this series is a bullet point which simply reads:

- Description of the Universal Adversary.

Again, it is simply taken as read that people will know what is being referred to by the term 'Universal Adversary' (Figure 1.2).[22]

Indicators of the Terrorist Attack Cycle – Advanced

August 9 - 10, 2014

Course Description:

The *Indicators of the Terrorist Attack Cycle: Advanced* course is intended to provide the law enforcement and counter-terrorism communities with an opportunity to enhance observational skills that could help, when coupled with appropriate and timely information sharing and other appropriate interdictions, prevent a terrorist attack on a domestic target. The two-day, instructor-led course, which is designed at the performance level and is scenario-based, actively engages students in interactive discussions and activities.

The course utilizes "red team" group activities as a means for increasing students' understanding of the planning, surveillance, attack, and escape/evasion/exploitation actions commonly found among terrorist attacks. Students in each class will be organized into three teams. Each team will be assigned a specific target within a scenario community. As the class progresses through the key phases of a terrorist attack, each team will assume the roles of terrorist cell operatives. The team will design surveillance and rehearsal plans, work through the attack phases, and ultimately, plan the escape/evasion/exploitation efforts. The design of the group activities is such that as the students move through each phase, they will ultimately see the evolution of the various phases across three different targets. Thus, students will gain significant insight into potentially observable terrorist actions and behaviors.

An essential element of the course is the discussion and reinforcement of the need for timely and appropriate information sharing with government and law enforcement agencies through field intelligence officers (or similar positions), Joint Terrorism Task Forces, and related systems. Students will also have an opportunity to discuss potential interdiction strategies as the phases evolve.

The course is taught at an unclassified level but relies heavily upon information that is designed as For Official Use Only (FOUO) and/or Law Enforcement Sensitive (LES).

Course Provider: This course is being taught by a team of instructors from the National Center for Security & Preparedness and the State Preparedness Training Center.

Topics Include:

- The Terrorist Attack Cycle
- Description of the Universal Adversary
- Target Selection, Planning, Surveillance, and Elicitation
- The Rehearsal Phase
- The Attack Phase
- The Escape/Evasion/Exploitation Phase
- Selected Case Studies
- Information Sharing in Support of Intelligence Operations and Fusion Centers

Times:

August 9, 2014
Registration and Check-In: 7:30 AM – 8:00 AM
Course: 8:00 AM - 5:00 PM
The course will begin **promptly** at 8:00 AM

August 10, 2014
Registration and Check-In: 7:30 AM – 8:00 AM
Course: 8:00 AM- 5:00 PM
The course will begin **promptly** at 8:00 AM

For more information: Contact DHSES, State Preparedness Training Center at (315)-768-5689
email SPTC@dhses.ny.gov   website http://www.dhses.ny.gov/sptc/

© NYSDHSES/NCSP   1

Figure 1.2 New York State Preparedness Training Center training course, including the Universal Adversary

Third example: in 2008 the Army, Marine Corps, Navy and Air Force co-produced a 'multi-service' publication called *Multiservice Tactics, Techniques, and Procedures for Chemical, Biological, Radiological, and Nuclear Consequence Management Operations*, intended to provide commanders, staffs, agencies and military members a 'key reference for planning and conducting management strategies' for attacks of the kind listed in the title. It refers to the Universal Adversary as instigator of the attacks in question.[23]

As a fourth example we can cite a PowerPoint presentation on 'Terrorism Prevention Exercise Program (TPEP)' by Michael J. McMullen, Program manager at the Department of Homeland Security, which details the centrality of the Universal Adversary Program (UAP) as 'an analytical framework for planning, training, and exercising against potential criminal and terrorist adversaries'. There is no further information about the nature of 'criminal' here – it is simply taken as read that criminal activity is on par with terrorist activity in a way which renders criminals part of the Universal Adversary. The presentation communicates with bullet points:

- Mission – the UAP mission is to enhance the homeland security community's understanding of the current and emerging threat environment and potential terrorist adversaries, and strengthen national preparedness capabilities through exercise support.
- The UAP level of support can be customized and scaled to support any exercise. The UAP offers a variety of products and services.[24]

The products and services include a Resource Library of dynamic threat assessments, dossiers and an analytic notebook link analysis; Exercise Scenario Assessments, Customized Adversaries, and Simulation Cell Support.

A final example comes from the summer of 2012 when the US army went about practicing its *Vibrant Response 13 FTX*. This is an Exercise Plan to prepare for the Scenario of a 10-kiloton nuclear attack without warning on a major US city. The Exercise, one of the largest ever, involved FEMA, DHS and the Joint Task Force Civil Support unit, had approximately 9,000 service members participating in 200 training events lasting 19 days, and took place on a 1,000 acre site, complete with buildings including a hospital, industrial plants, residential homes, car parks, trailer parks, schools, and 9 miles of roads and streets. The in-built assumptions were that buildings were damaged to a distance of 3 kilometres, 100,000 fatalities occurred in the same area, 200,000 evacuees would be on the move, and looting would very quickly occur. And the final assumption: that the nuclear device would be launched by the Universal Adversary.[25]

Despite their variety, the Emergency Scenarios all *presuppose an Enemy attack*. Amidst all the unknowns, uncertainties and unexpected events, one thing is clear: 'the Universal Adversary will attack'.[26] This assumption of an attack is why the various Planning Scenarios are run along certain lines: 'Scenario 1: Nuclear Detonation', 'Scenario 4: Biological Attack – Plague', 'Scenario 5: Chemical Attack – Blister Agent', and so on. In each case the attack is launched by the Universal Adversary: 'terrorist members of the Universal Adversary group … plan to assemble a gun-type nuclear device'; 'members of the Universal Adversary disseminate plague via an agricultural sprayer while driving through a metropolitan city'; 'the Universal Adversary uses a light aircraft to spray chemical agent Yellow into a packed college football stadium'.[27] If permanent emergency is sustained through endless war against an invisible Enemy, then its normalisation is achieved in part through endless preparation for an attack by the Enemy in question. This is where the new logic of *pre-emption* which purports to prevent terror attacks from happening coincides with the new logic of *preparation* which purports to nurture a readiness for terror attacks. These two logics merge through the idea of the Universal Adversary and, in particular, the idea that the Universal Adversary will attack.

To grasp the significance of the possible attack, let us return to the passage from the Homeland Security Council document, *Planning Scenarios: Executive Summaries*, which we have already cited and in which the perpetrator is 'named':

> Because the attacks could be caused by foreign terrorists; domestic radical groups; state-sponsored adversaries; or in some cases disgruntled employees, the perpetrator has been named, the Universal Adversary.

This latter passage, appearing under the heading 'General Considerations for the Scenarios', disappears from Version 20.2 issued in April 2005, and remains off of the final version of March 2006 which refers simply to 'the perpetrator, the "Universal Adversary" (UA)'.[28] It is also an advance on other documents which merely cite the usual 'threat groups'.[29] But the passage is surely interesting. For here, alongside the security problem posed by the terrorist and the radical one finds part of the problem: the *disgruntled Worker*.

It is a noticeable feature of much of the scholarly literature on emergency in general that workers rarely appear, whether disgruntled or not; their non-appearance is indicative of the fact that in this literature questions of capital and class rarely get a look in.[30] This is no doubt because the same scholarly literature tends to repeat the same assumption: the Cold war is over, replaced with the 'war on terror'; the problem of the Worker at the heart of the war on communism has been replaced with the problem of the Terrorist at the heart of the war on terror. But as I have argued at length elsewhere, to fully grasp the concept of emergency, especially as it pertains to the politics of security, we must grapple with the ways in which emergency works with and for capital.[31] And here, in the Emergency Planning Scenarios and in the definition of the Universal Adversary around which those Scenarios are organised, lies capital's perennial problem: the disgruntled Worker. These workers will have a major role to play in this book, though as we shall see they often appear not directly as themselves but in a variety of forms. In the stagecraft of statecraft they are forced to don masks, appearing as various characters, from Zombies to Witches, from Pirates to the Devil, all of which will appear in the chapters to follow. First however, let us take the Emergency Scenarios at their word and consider the Worker purely in terms of the short character description offered to us: as disgruntled.

The pigs

It is an interesting word, 'disgruntled'. Let's be honest, it is a word that appears to very easily describe most of us: the disgruntled employed, the disgruntled unemployed, the disgruntled under-employed. It is a word that captures the fact that although management in capitalist regimes rarely have to deal with mass industrial unrest any longer, they increasingly have to deal with employees who are unmotivated, uncommitted, apathetic, unfocused, discontented, and who are regularly and also suspiciously absent through physical or mental illness. It is a word that therefore unsurprisingly appears time and again in contemporary literature on the workplace.[32]

The *Oxford English Dictionary* has 'disgruntled' as connoting 'moody, discontent' (with the comma, though one wonders if they were tempted to leave out the comma and run it as 'moody discontent'), with earliest references in the late-nineteenth century to 'Partisans' 'wandering aimlessly about' in 'disgruntlement'. But with its roots in 'grunt', there might be even more to say. 'To gruntle' is a phrase that emerged in the sixteenth century to refer to uttering a low groan or grunt. We refer to people grunting as expressing disgruntlement, where it is close to groaning. But a grunt is also a low guttural sound usually associated with pigs.

To refer to 'disgruntled' workers is thus a reminder of the long history in which the working class were associated with pigs. If we go back to the first extended polemic against revolutionary change, Edmund Burke's *Reflections on the Revolution in France*, we find various reasons articulated for resisting the kind of revolution being carried out in France, including the idea that the revolution was tearing apart the established order, destroying national traditions and undermining what Burke liked to think of as 'organic' communities. Such things happen, according to Burke, when those seeking change get taken up with abstract ideas such as liberty and equality. Here is one passage from the *Reflections*, cited here for its famous final sentence:

When antient opinions and rules of life are taken away, the loss cannot possibly be estimated. From that moment we have no compass to govern us; nor can we know distinctly to what port we steer ... We are but too apt to consider things in the state in which we find them, without sufficiently adverting to the causes by which they have been produced and possibly may be upheld. Nothing is more certain, than that our manners, our civilization, and all the good things which are connected with manners, and with civilization, have, in this European world of ours, depended for ages upon two principles; and were indeed the result of both combined; I mean the spirit of a gentleman and the spirit of religion. The nobility and the clergy, the one by profession, the other by patronage, kept learning in existence, even in the midst of arms and confusions, and whilst governments were rather in their causes than formed. Learning paid back what it received to nobility and to priesthood; and paid it with usury, by enlarging their ideas, and by furnishing their minds. Happy if they had all continued to know their indissoluble union, and their proper place! Happy if learning, not debauched by ambition, had been satisfied to continue the instructor, and not aspired to be the master! Along with its natural protectors and guardians, learning will be cast into the mire and trodden down under the hoofs of a swinish multitude.[33]

Burke elsewhere describes the multitude as 'unthinking', 'licentious', 'ferocious', 'savage', 'frantic', 'drunken' and, above all, as monstrous,[34] but it is the idea that the multitude is 'swinish' that was the one noticed by most people. It was a truly 'epochal indiscretion', as E. P. Thompson calls it.[35] Why?

Burke was by no means the first to suggest the image. He would have known, for example, of the Biblical story told by Matthew in which Jesus is confronted with some demons and casts them out into a herd of swine (Matthew, 8:28–32; Mark, 5:9–13); he would have been aware of the wider Biblical discourse in which the pig was associated with sin; he would surely have been alert to the cultural connections made between swine and bad manners; he would probably have known of Samuel Johnson's comment that the masses 'must be treated like pigs'; he would have certainly known of the entry for 'swine' in Johnson's *Dictionary of the English Language* (1755), which defines it as 'a creature remarkable for stupidity and nastiness' and which in another entry elsewhere cites a comment from King Charles linking swine with rebellion ('as swine are to gardens and orderly plantations, so are tumults to parliaments'); and he might well have been in a position to know of Martin Marprelate's attack on 'the swinish rabble'.[36] Nonetheless, despite not being the first person to come up with the epithet, Burke's phrase was one for which he very quickly became (in)famous.

Sensing what was at stake in Burke's epochal discretion, radicals at the time made a great deal of Burke's phrase. 'By vividly defining a large part of the population as brutish and inarticulate, Burke provoked them into speech', notes Olivia Smith. 'The insult that embodied their social status as inadequate thinkers became the chosen mode for disproving the accusation by engaging in the act of writing'.[37] Pamphleteers offered numerous satirical variations on Burke's theme: Thomas Spence's *Pigs' Meat* was a series of essays published in cheap weekly editions, including pieces by Voltaire and Godwin but also satirical pieces such as 'The Rights of Swine'. It also included a poem in parody of Burke, called 'Edmund Burke's Address to the Swinish Multitude':

Ye Swinish Multitude who prate,
What know ye 'bout the matter?

The chorus then runs:

Then hence ye Swine nor make a rout,
Forbearance but relaxes;
We'll clap the muzzle on your snout,
Go work, and pay your taxes.

The essays were eventually collected into volumes such as *Pigs' Meat; or, Lessons for the Swinish Multitude* (1794) and *Pig's Meat; or, Lessons for the People. Alias (According to Burke) The Swinish Multitude* (1795; Figure 1.3).[38]

Other periodicals published at around the same time include *Politics for the People*, subtitled *A Salmagundy for Swine*, including an essay in 1793 called 'Remonstrance of the Swinish Multitude, to the Chief and Deputy Swineherds of Europe', and another the same year with the title 'Address to the Numerous Herd of Tradesmen, Mechanics, and Labourers, And Others, Comprized under the Appellation of the Swinish Multitude'. Other essays and articles were written under pseudonyms such as Brother Grunter, Gregory Grunter, Porkulus, Liberty Pig, Young Pig, Learned Pig, and so on. In 1793 there also appeared James Parkinson's *Address to the Hon. Edmund Burke: From the Swinish Multitude*, accusing Burke of being 'blest with a snug corner, in the warmest part of the stye, for grunting libels against THE SWINISH MULTITUDE'. It went on: 'Whilst ye are … gorging yourselves at troughs filled with the daintiest wash; we, with our numerous train of porkers, are employed, from the rising to the setting sun, to obtain the means of subsistence, by … picking up a few acorns'.[39]

It was by no means only intellectuals and radical writers who picked up on Burke's phrase. In November 1792 the people of Sheffield took to the streets in support of France and its developing revolution, and they displayed an effigy of Burke riding a pig. Two months later, in January

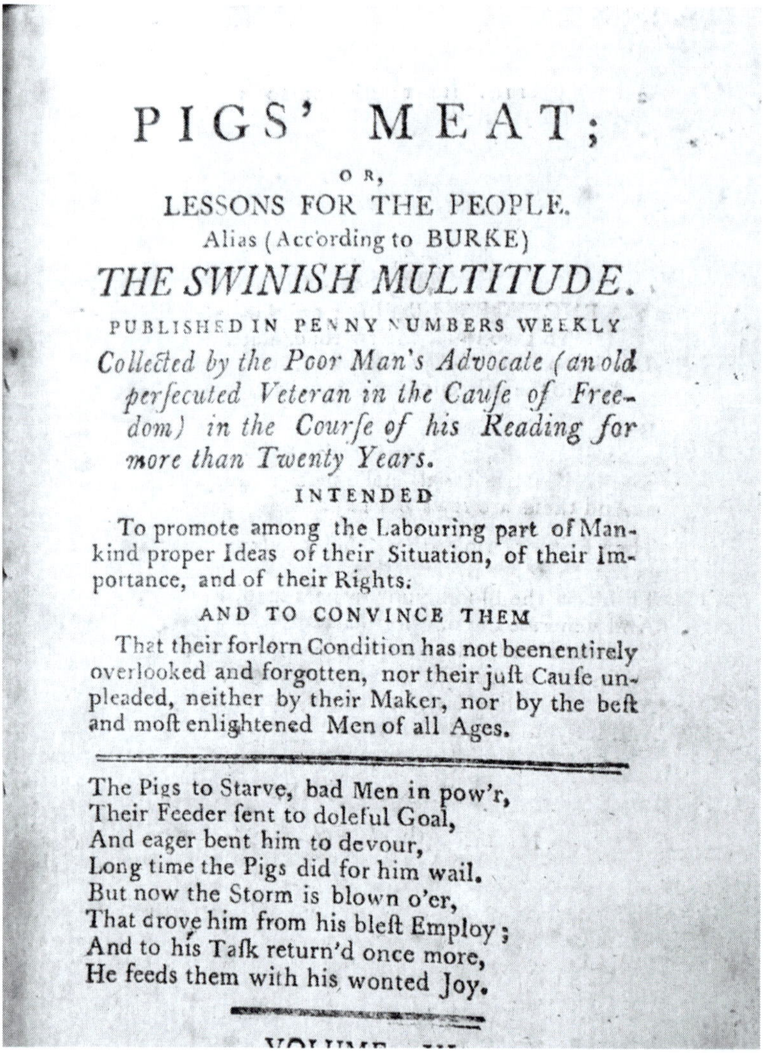

PIGS' MEAT;

OR,

LESSONS FOR THE PEOPLE.

Alias (According to BURKE)

THE SWINISH MULTITUDE.

PUBLISHED IN PENNY NUMBERS WEEKLY

Collected by the Poor Man's Advocate (an old perfecuted Veteran in the Caufe of Freedom) in the Courfe of his Reading for more than Twenty Years.

INTENDED

To promote among the Labouring part of Mankind proper Ideas of their Situation, of their Importance, and of their Rights.

AND TO CONVINCE THEM

That their forlorn Condition has not been entirely overlooked and forgotten, nor their juft Caufe unpleaded, neither by their Maker, nor by the beft and moft enlightened Men of all Ages.

The Pigs to Starve, bad Men in pow'r,
Their Feeder fent to doleful Goal,
And eager bent him to devour,
Long time the Pigs did for him wail.
But now the Storm is blown o'er,
That drove him from his bleft Employ;
And to his Tafk return'd once more,
He feeds them with his wonted Joy.

VOLUME ...

Figure 1.3 Front cover of Thomas Spence's *Pigs' Meat* (1795)

1793, an effigy of Burke was burned just south of Sheffield, with the crowd toasting 'The Swinish Multitude'. A jug produced in the early 1790s and now held in Brighton museum in the UK has a figure of Burke on one side (Paine is on the reverse) addressing a herd of pigs, holding in one hand a paper with 'Thoughts on French Revolution'. From his mouth comes a speech bubble with the verse: 'Ye pigs who never went to college, You must not pass for pigs of knowledge' (Figure 1.4).

Figure 1.4 Creamware jug with Burke and swinish multitude

Source: © Royal Pavilion and Museums, Brighton & Hove, UK

In 1795 a popular song called 'Wholesome Advice to the Swinish Multitude' was widely sung, and in the same year a hairdresser was prosecuted for posting a sign in his shop reading 'Citizen Shaver to the Swinish Multitude'.

So well known was the phrase that cartoonists such as Gillray could depict the idea without comment. Gillray's cartoon called 'Presages of the Millennium', 1795, has the Prime Minister Pitt as the figure of Death riding a White Horse of Hanover (a white horse is also ridden by Death in the book of Revelations), the Prince of Wales kissing his arse, followed by several demons. One of the demons, the winged snake, is meant to be Burke. The image also shows a swinish multitude trodden on the ground along with those leaders who had urged peace with France. The inscription at the bottom has 'And e'er the Last days began, I looked & beheld a White Horse, & and his name was Death, & Hell followed after him... And I saw under him the Souls of the Multitude, those who were destroy'd for maintaining the word of Truth, & for the Testimony' (Figure 1.5).

Later in 1795 Gillray produced an image called 'Substitutes for Bread', with the starving poor at the window holding 'Petitions from Starving Swine' (1795 being a year of famine, and also the year of Burke's essay 'Thoughts and Details on Scarcity' in which he argues against relief for the poor).

Two decades later radicals such as William Cobbett were still referring to the term: 'with what indignation must you hear yourselves called the Populace, the Rabble, the Mob, the Swinish Multitude', Cobbett commented to the journeymen and labourers in 1816. 'The insolent hirelings call you the *mob*, the *rabble*, the *scum*, the *swinish multitude*, and say

Figure 1.5 James Gillray, *Presages of the Millennium* (4 June, 1795)

Source: © The Fitzwilliam Museum, Cambridge, UK

that your voice is nothing; that you have no business at public meetings; and that *you* are, and ought to be, considered as nothing in the body politic!'. Perhaps, Cobbett wondered, 'as some have called you the swinish multitude, would it be much wonder if they were to propose to serve you as families of young pigs are served?'[40] And a few years later the radical journal *Black Dwarf* was still imagining a working class insurrection in the form of a rising of swine: 'some little grunter may creep into a royal cradle in the midst of the confusion; and the stalls of the bishops, deans, and prebends, be metamorphosed into genuine pig-sties, and be polluted by popular swine. The "HIGHER ORDERS" of animals are quite alarmed'.[41] Indeed, some thirty-five years after Burke's death, letters written by radicals to journals were still signed off as being written by people such as 'One of the Swinish Multitude'.[42]

On the one hand, then, radicals used the phrase against Burke and against the whole culture, ideology and attitude of the ruling class. On the other hand, the ruling class and its ideologues adopted the term as a political invective against workers. 'Look there – behold the swinish multitude', commented *Blackwood's Edinburgh Magazine* in May 1831. It was making a decision to embrace Burke's terminology. Four months earlier, in January 1831, as the demand for reform intensified in England and as that country's ruling class feared that if they did not reform they might be subject to far worse, the same magazine had discussed 'that many-mouthed Monster, the Swinish Multitude' which threatened to destroy English liberties under 'bestial feet'.[43] In the May issue it was extending the point:

> Look at their tails contorted in desperate obstinacy, that will neither be led nor driven – and telling as plainly as tails can tell, that it is an equal chance whether the bestial herd will make a charge upon women and children, or higglety-pigglety go headlong, in demoniac suicide, into the sea. Look, we beseech you, at their eyes – their small red eyes so fiery with greed and lust! Their snouts scenting all the airts for garbage, and their tusks stone-whetted and sharp as the mower's scythe – their hoofs – say rather their cloots … raking the mire fore and aft! And their hides horrid from nape to rump with angry bristles, at once the terror and delight of cobblers; and if you still have your doubts whether or no these be indeed such reformers as you would choose either to send you to, or represent you in Parliament, why you only have to solicit their voices – their most sweet voice – and your wavering mind will be settled by one unanimous grunt from the old boars and sows, and by a multifarious and multitudinous bubble-and-squeak from all the infant schools of piggies, on recovering from which, if you are a Christian, you will exclaim in soliloquy, 'The voice of the swine is the voice of the devil'.[44]

The magazine did not let up in its reiteration of Burke's phrase: three years later it held that Burke 'had only proclaimed a truth acknowledged by every rational understanding' in calling them the 'swinish multitude'.[45] And it was clear that despite Burke's attempts at identifying subtle but important differences between English and French subjects (the former are quiet, tame and domesticated while the latter are dangerous, wild and rampaging), most of these writers simply worked on the basis that 'they're all pigs in the end'.[46]

Symbolically base animals often appear less central to human order than other animals. Yet 'what is socially peripheral is so frequently symbolically central', as Peter Stallybrass and Allon White note. And as they also suggest, nowhere is this clearer than in the figure of the pig.[47] The use of terms such as 'swinish multitude' and 'pigs' by the ruling class to describe the working class played on the fact that the pig had long been associated in the ruling class mind with the revolutionary mob and unruly crowd. To link the pig to the Worker was thus a way of hinting at social insubordination and the threat of democracy.[48] But it also played on the fact that pigs had long been an ordinary part of working class life, straddling the line between the domestic and the wild, the rural and the urban, order and disorder, liberty and confinement.[49] 'Pigs were *almost*, but not quite, members of the household and they *almost*, but not quite, followed the dietary regimes of humans'.[50] This was true even in the city and continued well into the nineteenth century and well after most common land had been enclosed. There was, for example, about one pig for every five people in Manhattan in 1820, and around 3 pigs to every one person in the slums of North Kensington, London, in 1850.[51]

One reason for this was that the pig was a major component of the subsistence economy for the working class. 'One of the few possibilities for a limited self-sufficiency still accessible to labouring people was the keeping of a pig – or even two'.[52] It was a common family animal, used to clear up the dross and refuse, treated almost as pet and yet destined to be killed and eaten. Pigs appear time and again in reports on the working class and cities in the nineteenth century. In *The Moral and Physical Condition of the Working Classes* (1832) and *Report on the Sanitary Condition of the Labouring Population of Great Britain* (1842), for example, James Kay-Shuttleworth, Edwin Chadwick and their teams of advisors note how common the keeping of pigs is among working class households. Frederick Engels picked up on this fact in his report on the *Condition of the English Working Class* in 1844. One finds 'piggery repeated at every twenty paces', Engels comments. 'In the district now under discussion' says Engels about one of the areas in England, one feature 'is the multitude of pigs walking about in all the alleys, rooting into the offal heaps, or kept imprisoned in small pens'. Engels also notes how official reports into the condition of the working class fed into the rhetoric of class hatred and disgust in the work of figures such as Thomas Carlyle (in *Chartism*): in their 'rags and laughing savagery' workers live in 'any pig-hutch or dog-hutch' and thus become 'the ready-made nucleus of degradation and disorder'. Likewise, in Chapter 25 of *Capital*, Marx cites one police officer's report to the *Children's Employment Commission* that 'they live like pigs'. The very same observations were made about American cities.[53] It is not too much of an exaggeration to say that the pig was, in effect, part of the working class.[54]

The pig has therefore been at the heart of class conflict. The closeness of the pig to the Worker encouraged the ruling class view that the line between the 'respectable working class' and the 'criminal class' was impossible to draw. It was widely believed that keeping a pig meant that a Worker was likely to steal in order to sustain the pig. Police reformer Chadwick noted in his *Report* that keeping a pig 'furnishes a temptation to dishonesty', and those offering local information to Chadwick for his Report suggested that 'it is well known that a pig cannot be profitably fed by a poor person in a town by honest means', as James Sym put it in his report to Chadwick. For this reason employers often sought to prohibit their workers from keeping pigs because they feared that the Worker would be tempted to steal anything that might be used to feed it.[55] Attempts to criminalize the keeping of pigs in cities therefore intensified through the nineteenth century.

For the ruling class, then, the urban pig was a problem for all sorts of reasons: it created the possibility of a Worker having some form of subsistence without the wage, it was an indicator of slum conditions, it led to bad hygiene, it was symbolic of an absence of civilised life, and it generated a propensity to commit crimes against property. More than anything, the closeness of the pig to its urban working class owner appeared to the bourgeoisie as evidence of the Worker's own swinishness. 'To have nothing in common with pigs – was that not the aim of every bourgeois subject – to get as far away from the smell of the pigsty as possible?'[56] This aim meant that the bourgeoisie and its police power came to share the dream of a pig-free city.[57] Turning the dream into reality meant clearing pigs from the city in what was an all-out war – in New York the police and sanitary officers were described as an 'army of expulsion' and their working class opponents as the 'pork army' – to produce a city in which the *swinish multitude was itself brought under control*. Which is to say: it was a war to produce a city in which disgruntled workers were well-policed; a city, that is, in which working class 'beastliness' was well-managed.

The beast, as a creature outside the law, has long been a key figure in the sovereign imagination. The beast has underpinned many of the fears on which sovereignty is founded, for which the police power is exercised, and against which security is expected.[58] The beast has also played a prevalent ideological role in the history of capital. As such, the beastliness of the lower orders is a common theme in the history of mainstream western political thought. Grotius, Locke, Vattel, Tocqueville, a whole host of colonisers and imperialists and large swathes of the ruling class have time and again described workers and, along with them, Indians, Africans, Arabs, criminals and paupers, as beasts. The beast in general is a lawless creature 'with whom men can have no society nor security', as John Locke puts it in Chapter 2 of the *Second Treatise*. If the beast performs for the sovereign the role of being sufficiently outside the law to allow certain practices of violence against it, then this applies equally to those humans designated 'beastly'. The category 'beast' is a discursive political resource rather than a zoological designation, as recent work in critical animal studies suggests and for which we find evidence time and again when the security of bourgeois order is an issue, from the systematic colonisation of land occupied by beastly Indians through to the worry expressed by liberals and conservatives about the noxious beasts who transgress the law and threaten revolution. The Worker, as beast, is taken to be a threat to the social order of the bourgeois; the beast, as inhuman, is taken to be a threat to the social order of the human. Unless the beast can be tamed, that is. Beyond the idea of the general 'beastliness' of the lower orders (a threat to the bourgeois/human), it has also often been the case that the idea of particular animals has played a more prominent role. The pig is one such animal.

Foxes, wolves, lions and tigers have long played a certain kind of role in political rhetoric, along with many other animals which have also appeared: sharks, snakes and vultures; apes, monkeys and gorillas; donkeys, sheep and (scape-)goats;[59] cockroaches, rats and dogs. Each of these resonates for us in different ways. Each is a way of dehumanizing an enemy or opponent, of demonizing them and justifying a certain kind of treatment, usually akin to the way in which the animal in question is itself treated: exterminate them like rats, crush them like roaches, cage them like dogs, herd them like sheep. A term such as 'pig' and related terms such as 'swinish multitude' or 'grunt' are dehumanizing in a very specific way. The terms suggest a visceral contempt of lowly, disorderly and dirty creatures. The dirt is important here. As John Stuart Mill puts it, cleanliness is the 'quality which forms the most visible and one of the most radical of the moral distinctions between human beings and most of the lower animals' and which 'more than of anything else, renders men bestial'.[60]

Dirty, then, but also impure, insensitive, fat, ugly, stupid, selfish, greedy and obstinate: the pig is all of these things and more. And for all of these things the pig was associated with poverty. As such, 'pig' has long been a basic signifier of disgust and contempt and a metaphor for a gross and degraded human lacking in civilised manners and social graces. The fact that pigs survive in the conditions in which they live 'simply helps to confirm the suspicion that they are, indeed, debased', just like the workers with whom they are associated.[61]

The pig's mode of finding food, for example, was traditionally known as 'foraging'. When applied to humans the idea of 'foraging' became the basis of 'scrounging' (as in 'we scrounged around for something to eat'). Scrounging was originally connected to the practice of gleaning but later took on the implication of 'acquiring something by irregular means' and is thus closely associated with begging. The word developed new connotations with the emergence of the 'welfare scrounger' or 'benefits scrounger': a member of the working class who lives off the state rather than engage in wage labour. Hence those who seek to avoid wage labour by either begging or living off of benefits came to have the epithet 'scrounger' attached to them, aligning them closely with the main activity of the pig. At the same time, terms such as 'pig' or 'swinish multitude' offer a threat to those same subjects about what will happen to them should they dare to step out of line or try to do something about their disgruntlement. That was the insight behind Cobbett's comment cited above – 'as some have called you the swinish multitude, would it be much wonder if they were to propose to serve you as families of young pigs are served?' – but it extends well beyond nineteenth century England. As Boria Sax notes, those who wish to brutalize and slaughter other people usually find it a lot easier psychologically if they think of their victims as swine.[62]

'Of all the animals commonly eaten in the Western world, the pig is without doubt the most intelligent', notes Peter Singer. 'It is possible to rear a pig as a pet and train it to respond to simple commands much as a dog would'.[63] Such intelligence might explain why pigs in the machine for mass slaughter known as 'the meat industry' suffer from Porcine Stress Syndrome. It might also explain why the pig was the animal to suffer most in the long history of the criminal prosecution and capital punishment of animals, a process by which animals were put on a par with humans and tried for various misdemeanours; it is estimated that pigs account for around half of the animal executions. It might also explain why the pig had long been associated with paganism and thus devil-worship, itself long thought to be the basis of criminality.[64] This is the basis of the connections cited above between swine and demons in the Biblical book of Matthew, Martin Marprelate's link between the human swine and the Antichrists, and the choice of 'cloots' for 'hoofs' by *Blackwood's Edinburgh Magazine* – both 'cloots' and 'hoofs' refer to cloven feet but the former had long been associated with the Devil.[65] We are getting close here to the view that fighting the swinish multitude is equivalent to fighting the Devil – 'The Beast' – and that the multitude might possess some kind of demonic power, though we shall hold on to that discussion until later Chapters.

Bear in mind, as well, that in the twentieth century 'grunt' became a slang term to describe labourers, low-level workers, unskilled industrial assistants and those engaged in laborious work in general. In the later-twentieth century, in the US in particular, the grunt also became slang for low-level (that is, working class) infantry soldiers. Infantrymen in Vietnam were the 'grunts'. *The Times* in May 1970 discussing the American war on Vietnam noted that the 'luckless victims of the American military machine are known as "grunts"', and the *Oxford English Dictionary* offers this as one of the early uses. (In Canadian military slang, these 'grunts' were known as 'Zombies', an issue we shall take up in the next chapter.) The grunts are the cannon fodder, expendable and disposable, just like the pigs that are so widely used in military experiments.

'The idea is to work with live tissue', commented one soldier about such experiments.

> You get a pig and you keep it alive. And every time I did something to help him, they would wound him again. So you see what shock does, and what happens when more wounds are received by a wounded creature. My pig? They shot him twice in the face with a 9-millimeter pistol, and then six times with an AK-47 and then twice with a 12-gauge shotgun. And then he was set on fire. I kept him alive for 15 hours. That was my pig.[66]

We are often told that this is to work with live tissue that is closest to human tissue, just as the soldier reports, but one cannot help wonder if it is to allow the war power to practice on the animal that is most closely associated with the workers who make up the military machine: if the injured soldiers are grunts, we may as well practice on the animal that grunts, that shares its history with the Worker, and that will scream and bleed just like the workers we will send off to war. Yet the most obvious reason for the use of the term 'grunts' is because of the continual moaning and groaning – in other words, the *disgruntlement* – of the working class soldiers.

The grunts, then, are the low-level members of both the industrial army and the military machine, or the military army and the industrial machine. If the 'grunts' are the low-level members of both the industrial army and military machine then the disgruntled are, in turn, members of the working class who need to be managed, maintained, controlled and eventually devoured, just as grunting pigs are managed, maintained, controlled and eventually devoured, but with this key difference: the disgruntled might be on the verging of allowing their grunting to get the better of them, infecting others with their disgruntlement (disgruntlement is contagious and contagion is now a major problem in emergency planning documentation, as we shall see in the chapter to follow) and thus might come to rebel against their condition and status. They might, in the contemporary parlance of state power, be a security threat and a future problem for which plans and preparations must be made. A preparation which will, where necessary, lead to their eventual destruction; 'like pigs to the slaughter', as the English phrase has it.

All of which might sound a little odd given the widespread use of the term 'pigs' to describe police officers. To describe the police as 'pigs' appears to work given the historical function of the pig as an interstitial animal, with the 'police-pig' occupying a position similar to the 'house-pig': situated between ordered domestic society and the wild criminal and expected to clear up the dirt and refuse identified as such by its masters.[67] And yet on this issue we might make two observations. First, despite some references to the use of 'pig' to describe the police in the early nineteenth century – the *Lexicon Balatronicum* of 1811 cites 'pig' as used to describe a police officer – the term only really took off in this way when student protestors and countercultural radicals began calling police officers 'pigs' in America in the 1960s. As Andrew Levinson notes, this was widely seen as a form of class elitism:

> The popularity of the word 'pig' as an epithet for policemen among students in the sixties was a fascinating example of the class prejudice which is still very real in America. Although most student 'radicals' in the sixties would deny that they were engaging in middle-class elitism against all workers by using that term, workers clearly recognized it for what it was.
>
> ...
> The word 'pig' ... is an insult that an elitist will use to refer condescendingly to the lack of education and 'culture' of the classes below.[68]

This is perhaps reinforced by the fact that the *Lexicon Balatronicum* was in fact a 'Dictionary of University Wit' as the subtitle has it, and aimed at 'young men of fashion', as the Preface comments, and thus had more than a touch of class power about it.[69] Second, as Sole and DJ Pain 1 suggest in the passage cited as an epigraph to this chapter, it is a more than a little odd to name the police after one of the most violently oppressed and abused animals in the world.

The point, then, is that in the recycling of Burke's reference to the 'swinish multitude' we see the capacity of a single image or phrase to take on a life of its own, as David Duff puts it,[70] in this case running through the centuries as a well-known derogatory term in the kind of class war conservatism first articulated by Burke and then developed by the ruling class as a means of projecting its power. So when the Emergency Planning Scenarios of the twenty-first national security state refer to 'disgruntled' workers, the term should not be passed by too quickly. The use of 'disgruntled' plays heavily on the kind of insult long used by the ruling class to deride the poor and hint at their general swinishness: living in filth, eating rubbish, being fat from an excess of carbohydrates, scrounging and grunting just like pigs, but also pointing to their fundamentally *unruly* condition and *disorderly* status. Read with a sense of the historical and ideological

connotations at stake, the reference to 'disgruntled' workers is an important rhetorical device with huge implications for what is going on in the
documents in question. And if we reopen the documents with those historical and ideological connotations in mind, it turns out that the disgruntled
Worker is central to virtually all the imagined security crises of the future.
In one sense, this should be no surprise, for ever since security was recast
as 'social security' in the early 1930s and then 'national security' in the late-
1940s, the problem of the *disloyal* worker has been at its very core, as
witnessed by the loyalty tests which people had to take to show that they
were not communists and which were applied most aggressively to workers.[71] What we have now is the re-casting of the *disloyal* Worker as a
disgruntled Worker and a concerted attempt to imagine what such workers
might actually do to threaten security.

The idea that the actions of a disgruntled Worker might be behind any
terror attack is thus more or less a running assumption in the documents.
The terror attack in the Emergency Planning Scenarios rarely comes from
an isolated terrorist or violent group with no connections within the body
politic, but more often than not *relies on a disgruntled Worker from somewhere
within the system*. Workers therefore appear in these documents time and
again. One Scenario, 'Biological Attack – Food Contamination', begins by
pointing out that any such attack would require familiarity with a specific
production site: 'A UA operative who is a worker at a meat processing plant
obtains liquid anthrax and uses it to contaminate meat at the plant'.[72] In
other Scenarios equipment is obtained from a worker within the chemical
industry in order the help build a dirty bomb, a worker in the shipping
industry is used for information, equipment is obtained entirely legally
from workers within the relevant industries, fire department or emergency
service vehicles are obtained via contacts with workers in those fields. A
great deal hangs on phrases such as 'the UA delivers liquid anthrax to pre-
selected terrorist plant workers'.[73] Who are these workers? Why would they
become susceptible to such activities? Are they disgruntled?

Might it be, then, that at the heart of the Universal Adversary is the very
thing that was at the heart of the fear of the Communist Menace: the
disloyal and disgruntled worker? If so, then maybe what is at stake in the
Universal Adversary is long standing issue: class war? And if it is, what might
this then mean for our understanding of security? Of emergency? Of
preparation? And what might it imply for our understanding of capital as
well as security? More to the point: what does it do for our understanding
of the dream of capital: 'Let there be workers!', and in particular workers
who are not disgruntled, or who at least are undergoing the requisite training to manage their disgruntlement, who have perhaps signed up to the
'happiness agenda', who have had their 'resilience training', and about
who capital can say: 'they work faithfully; they're not afraid of long hours'.

Chapter 2

'They work faithfully; they're not afraid of long hours': on the Zombie

Wild, dark times are rumbling toward us, and the prophet who wishes to write a new apocalypse will have to invent entirely new beasts, and beasts so terrible that the ancient animal symbols of St. John will seem like cooing doves and cupids in comparison.

> (Heinrich Heine, *Lutetia*, 1842)

He asked, 'What does "apocalypse" mean, Daddy?', and his father pressed pause and told him, 'It means that in the future, things will be even worse than they are now'.

> (Colson Whitehead, *Zone One*, 2011)

Could anything have dissolved so thoroughly the illusion of progress ... as an outbreak of the walking dead?

> (Bennett Sims, *A Questionable Shape*, 2014)

In 2011 an Emergency Planning document appeared suggesting that planners who had attended a training session at the Joint Combined Warfighting School [JCWS] realized that emergency planning always had to accommodate the political fallout that occurs if the general public mistakenly believes that a fictional training scenario is actually a real plan. Rather than risk such an outcome the document opted 'to use a completely-impossible scenario that could never be mistaken as a real plan'. What was the 'completely-impossible scenario'? The long title of the Scenario in question is 'CDRUSSTRATCOM CONPLAN 8888-11 COUNTER-ZOMBIE DOMINANCE OPERATIONS'. The shorter title simply uses the first half of the long one, 'CONPLAN 8888-11', though we might suggest that it is the latter part of the full title that would have offered a much better abbreviated form: Counter-Zombie Dominance Operations.

Conplan 8888 contains a 'disclaimer': 'This plan was not actually designed as a joke'. It goes on:

> During the summers of 2009 and 2010, while training auginentees from a local training squadron about the JOPP, members of a USSTRATCOM component found out (by accident) that the hyperbole involved in writing a 'zombie survival plan' actually provided a very useful and effective training tool.

That is, rather than confusing the situation and misleading the public by referring to 'Tunisians' or 'Nigerians' or anyone else, the intention was to imagine the Universal Adversary as a creature with which they (wrongly) thought no-one would want to identify: the Zombie.

Established to offer defensive and offensive operations against 'the system of Zombie Conditions (Z-CONS or ZOMBIECONS)', the Scenario offers a variety of political, military and legal tactics and techniques, which it develops by citing a series of diverse texts, from the *National Security Strategy* to Max Brooks's *World War Z: An Oral History of the Zombie War*, and from the *Joint Strategic Capabilities Plan* to Roger Ma's *Zombie Combat Manual: A Guide to Fighting the Living Dead*. Through engaging these texts and thinking through the various techniques, Conplan 8888 presents a Scenario in which the Universal Adversary attacks in the form of a Zombie War. The Scenario thus deals with the attack itself by such 'foreign' agents but also the chaos that ensues within the social order as more and more of the population succumb to 'zombieism'. It goes on to say that:

> Zombies are horribly dangerous to all human life and zombie infections have the potential to seriously undermine national security and economic activities that sustain our way of life. Therefore having a population that is not composed of zombies or at risk from their malign influence is vital to U.S. and Allied national interests. While the U.S. currently enjoys several asymmetric advantages in against zombie infections originating in the Eurasian landmass, these advantages can easily be negated by air and sea traffic that could transport the source of a zombie infection to North and South America. Further, asteroids and nuclear space radiation that can convert people into zombies can affect any landmass or population on earth. Given the rapidity at which zombie outbreaks spread, decisive, overwhelming, and possibly unilateral military force may be required to negate the zombie threat.

In other words, zombies come from outside, but the threat from outside turns into a threat from within as more and more of the population becomes zombified.

There seem to be two points that are being made with the Scenario: zombies might *live among us* and are *contagious*. Thus a major problem is the fact that zombies can and will operate throughout both civil society and the state, including the health system, law-enforcement, and power supplies. As regards the health system, for example, the Report notes that:

> Zombie interactions will create human casualties who will eventually become zombies depending upon the source of the zombieism. In cases where zombieism manifests slowly, injured humans will likely seek out medical care in hospital and local clinics. These locations will ultimately become sources of zombieism in and of themselves as victims mutate. Not only will this render hospitals useless, it will likely cause irreparable casualties among medical professionals and members of the chaplain corps who will be necessary to combat zombie dominance. Additionally, zombies in hospitals will deny healthy humans access to medical equipment, medicines and blood/tissue/organ banks necessary for survival ... Further, damage to medical infrastructures will likely degrade the abilities of healthy human populations to purify potable water sources.[1]

The point of all this, according to the Scenario, is to learn how to 'prepare to preserve the sanctity of human life and conduct operations in support of any human population', to eradicate sources of zombieism and deter 'potential adversaries'. The figure of the Zombie, in other words, helps generate a form of political rationality through which the state and its subjects can learn how to prepare for an emergency.

Félix Guattari once commented that should some form of extra-terrestrial life land on earth tomorrow, the one thing of which we could be sure is that 'there would be experts, journalists, and all sorts of specialists to explain that there is nothing so extraordinary about it, that there were already plans for it, that a special committee has been dealing for a long time with the subject'. Above all, there would be plenty of people saying that 'there is nothing to get upset about, because the government is there to take care of these things'.[2] The Zombie is a figure which allows the state to let us know that it is prepared. But is also does much more, in a way which goes beyond Guattari's point that the message will be 'the government has been preparing for this'. For what it also does is seek to *prepare the population itself* for the emergency in question.

A month after the release of Conplan 8888, the Centers for Disease Control and Prevention (CDC) issued a press release and blog called 'Preparedness 101: Zombie Apocalypse':

> There are all kinds of emergencies out there that we can prepare for. Take a zombie apocalypse for example. That's right, I said z-o-m-b-i-e a-p-o-c-a-l-y-p-s-e. You may laugh now, but when it happens you'll be happy you read this, and hey, maybe you'll even learn a thing or two about how to prepare for a *real* emergency.

Note the point: this is a joke about a '*real* emergency' that is also clearly not a joke as it is meant to encourage the population to think about what to do in a real emergency.

> The word zombie comes from Haitian and New Orleans voodoo origins. Although its meaning has changed slightly over the years, it refers to a human corpse mysteriously reanimated to serve.
>
> ...
>
> If zombies did start roaming the streets, CDC would conduct an investigation much like any other disease outbreak. CDC would provide technical assistance to cities, states, or international partners dealing with a zombie infestation. This assistance might include consultation, lab testing and analysis, patient management and care, tracking of contacts, and infection control (including isolation and quarantine). It's likely that an investigation of this scenario would seek to accomplish several goals: determine the cause of the illness, the source of the infection/virus/toxin, learn how it is transmitted and how readily it is spread, how to break the cycle of transmission and thus prevent further cases, and how patients can best be treated. Not only would scientists be working to identify the cause and cure of the zombie outbreak, but CDC and other federal agencies would send medical teams and first responders to help those in affected areas.
>
> To learn more about what CDC does to prepare for and respond to emergencies of all kinds, visit: http://emergency.cdc.gov/cdc/orgs_progs.asp. To learn more about how you can prepare for and stay safe during an emergency visit: http://emergency.cdc.gov/.[3]

The CDC, which despite its name is in fact an organisation at the core of American security strategy and practice, issued this with the idea that the population would 'Get a Kit, Make a Plan, Be Prepared' (the title of its campaign), a graphic novel on preparing for the Zombie War, and with links to its own preparedness advice. The Office of Public Health continues to run a 'Zombie Preparedness Campaign' through the CDC,[4] and other large organisations and nations have followed suit (Figures 2.1, 2.2 and 2.3).

This idea became so prevalent among emergency planning that it is now commonplace. As *Emergency Management Magazine* put it in 2011, 'preparing for a zombie attack requires the same planning as emergencies like natural disasters – from putting together a disaster kit to creating an emergency plan'.[5] Hence, for example, Kansas declared October 2014 to be 'Zombie Preparedness Month'. Under the strapline 'If you're prepared for zombies, you're prepared for anything', it encourages Kansans to be prepared and advises on how much water, dried and tinned food, batteries, flashlights, tools and pet food to stock: 'Build a Kit, Make a Plan, Be Prepared!'[6] (Figure 2.4).

Figure 2.1 CDC Zombie preparation
            sticker

Source: © The US Government Centers for
        Disease Control and Prevention.
        Reproduced with permission of the
        CDC

Figure 2.2 CDC Preparedness 101 graphic novel

Source: © The US Government Centers for Disease Control and Prevention. Reproduced with
        permission of the CDC

Figure 2.3 Emergency preparation sticker, British Columbia, Canada.

Source: EmergencyInfoBC.

Figure 2.4 Kansas Zombie Preparedness Month sticker

Source: Photo by Devan Tucking. Reproduced courtesy of The Adjutant General's Department, Kansas, US

Many other states have enacted the same emergency plans, as the figure of the Zombie is used time and again to encourage citizens to imagine emergency, prepare for emergency and thereby learn their role in the mobilisation of security.

The idea has also been taken up by the United Nations (UN). As we noted in the Introduction, the Model UN App features '60-minute lesson plans' on what it now sees as the big issues facing international organisation today: 'climate change, poverty eradication, and the Zombie Apocalypse'.[7] This has filtered down into the Model UN meetings in which students have traditionally gone to learn about diplomacy, international relations and conflict resolution, but which they now attend to learn about how to deal with a Zombie attack. Take, as just one example, the Model UN run by The High School for Enterprise, Business & Technology, in Brooklyn, New York. The School hosts what it calls WHIS-MUN (short for 'World Humanitarian Improving Society Model United Nations'). Its 2014 Model UN, on 7–8 February 2014, operated the following simulation:

> In addition to the real world parallels, however, this committee will also turn the real world on its head somewhat, countries that typically dominate international diplomacy, such as the UK and France, will suddenly find themselves in positions of relative weakness, as their remaining populations are besieged by zombies. Other countries fortunate enough to be distant from the zombie plague will now be called on to provide aid to these countries, forcing them to balance domestic needs with the overall fight to contain the zombie threat.

Among the 'Questions to Consider' were:

- How much has your country been affected by zombies?
- Are they at a near term risk of the zombie threat?
- What resources can your country commit to the effort to stop the zombies?
- Does your country believe that treating the zombies or stopping the zombies is more important?[8]

Similar exercises have taken place at University campuses elsewhere, either as part of a Model UN exercise, such as at the University of Chicago or Minnesota State University,[9] or sometimes just independently, such as at the University of Rhode Island.[10]

Survivalists also now use a possible Zombie attack as part of their survivalist training. Zombie Squad, for example (see www.zombiehunters.org), 'an elite zombie suppression task force ready to defend your neighborhood from the shambling hordes of the walking dead', offers workshops, seminars, training and merchandise to prepare for the forthcoming zombie attack, and concentrates its energies on 'emergency preparation' (Figure 2.5).

A Channel 4 documentary shown in the UK on 31 July, 2014, called 'Kids and Guns', showed some survivalists teaching their children how to shoot, but the more 'traditional' methods of aiming at targets on trees or fences has been replaced by going on a 'zombie hunt'. Forming themselves as 'Zombie Response Teams', they would shoot at images of zombies that had been placed outdoors, including one image of Osama Bin Laden mocked up as a zombie. With survivalist discourse epitomising more or less the same logic that underpins the discourse surrounding the Universal Adversary, namely preparedness and emergency planning for the attack of the Other, the survivalist in general and the Zombie Squad in particular epitomise the very grassroots activism advocated by the national security state.[11]

What is at stake in this developing interest in the zombie? And why has this interest coincided with the rise of the idea of 'the Universal Adversary'?

When the use of the Zombie by the CDC and other public bodies first became public it was the source of either some annoyance ('why are they wasting public money?'), some frivolity ('let's all laugh at the ridiculous idea of a zombie outbreak') or, for the Zombie fanatics, a little too much seriousness ('here at last is the confirmation we need: zombies do exist'). Leaving those responses aside, the first thing to note is the wider Zombie zeitgeist, for the Zombie is without doubt *the* monster of our time.

Zombies trundled along as a relatively minor interest for a long time, but 'then came the terrorist attacks of 9/11 and the national fear of a face-less horde of enemies slavishly obedient to their objective of dishing out

Figure 2.5 Zombie preparedness paraphernalia

extreme violence'.[12] 'People have apocalypse on the brain right now', noted Max Brooks, author of the bestselling *World War Z*. 'It's from terrorism, the war, natural disasters like Katrina'. Zombies, he suggests, 'are the perfect goblin for such times, in part because they suggest broad social collapse, when anyone — a policeman, a nurse, a friend — can turn into a force of evil'.[13] By roughly 2006, zombies were everywhere. 'Back from the dead', noted *The Guardian* newspaper of the Zombie in January 2006. 'Zombies are back', noted the *New York Times* two months later. 'In films, books and video games, the undead are once again on the march, elbowing past were-wolves, vampires, swamp things and mummies to become the post-millennial ghoul of the moment'.[14] 'We're really seeing the day of the zombie', noted one executive editor of a publisher specialising in horror titles in 2006. 'Until three years ago [that is, 2003] they were really unseen. Then they just seemed to pop up everywhere. As a monster, it's speaking to people'.[15] 'Zombies Spreading Like a Virus', it was noted in *Publishers Weekly* in the same year.[16] The Zombie film genre proliferated so much that it spawned a series of sub-genres: Zombie westerns, Zombie porn, Zombie romantic comedy ('Zom Rom Com'), Zombie musicals, Zombie Nazi films and Zombie terrorist films. The last of these sub-genres includes *Flight of the Living Dead* (2007), which has zombies hijacking an aeroplane, taking over the cockpit, crash-landing the plane and then making their way towards the city; *Osombie* (2012), which has Osama Bin Laden and his henchmen as Zombies; and *ZMD: Zombies of Mass Destruction* (2010), which plays on the main rationale offered for the war on terror. The TV series *The Walking Dead* became one of the most popular television programmes ever. Literary classics were rewritten Zombie-style, such as *Pride and Prejudice and Zombies* (2009).

The interest spread beyond film and publishing. 'Zombie chic' took to the catwalks[17] and Zombie walks became common in cities across the world. Intellectuals started talking about 'zombie categories' ('"living dead" categories which govern our thinking but are not really able to capture the contemporary milieu') in an attempt to peddle what we can assume they thought of as their own 'living ideas'.[18] One major international publisher of academic books started publishing a new 'Shortcuts' series of 'concise, accessible introductions to some of the major issues of our time': included in the major issues are Climate Change, Global Finance, Food and Zombies.[19] Scientists have also started exploring the issue: the book *Infectious Disease Modelling Research Progress* contains a chapter called 'When Zombies Attack! Mathematical Modelling of an Outbreak of Zombie Infection', and the *Journal of Clinical Nursing* has published an article on the role of nurses in dealing with a Zombie epidemic.[20]

So there is clearly something in the zeitgeist that may have prompted the security state's interest in using the figure of the Zombie as the basis for emergency planning. Yet maybe there is more to be said. For as Yari Lanci notes, there is a sense in which despite all the recent flurry of interest in the Zombie, the real critical potential of the figure has perhaps not really been appreciated.[21] This critical potential requires us to uncover a little of the Zombie's history, conveniently forgotten by many in this recent zeitgeist – domination's first priority being to eradicate historical knowledge[22] – and which points to what the Zombie narrative seems to be saying about security and capital.

In relation to capital, commentators have made three broad claims, although these sometimes overlap. The first is that for some time the Zombie has been treated as a figure of 'consumer-society'. The classic instances of this are those film scenes in which the zombies converge on a shopping mall to continue to enact the rituals of a rapacious consumerism gone mad by satiating their hunger for human flesh, such as in some of the films of George Romero; 'for Romero, shopping is our farcical resurrection'.[23] The contemporary concept of the Zombie within the wider capitalist culture is heavily dominated by this kind of Zombie-ghoul, where the emphasis is on the ghoulishness and – when read politically – the ghoulishness as metaphor of consumption. A second claim connects the Zombie to capitalism more generally, with the category quickly becoming a way of trying to describe what was happening during the economic crisis: 'Zombie banks', 'Zombie debt', 'Zombie brands', 'Zombie firms', 'Zombie households' and 'Zombie politicians' have all recently been invoked as the reason why capital is in crisis.[24] A third claim treats the flurry of interest in the Zombie in terms of the increased speed of contemporary zombies in the media as representative of the speed that *homo œconomicus* must adopt in order to survive in the neoliberal market, combined with much broader fears about subjectivity in a globalized and highly mobile world in which politics, economics and infectious diseases all appear to be spiralling out of control under the pressure of 'globalisation', 'displaced persons' and 'pathologized humans' with contagious infections.[25]

There is much that is useful in these analyses, but I want here to explore a little more of the history of the Zombie and, in particular, the ways in which it seeped into the western cultural consciousness, because it is through this connection that we can start making sense of the figure of the Zombie in contemporary emergency planning, the mobilisation of security and the history of capitalist violence. For just as we noted in the Introduction, we need to ask not so much 'what is a Zombie?' but, rather, 'what does the figure of the Zombie allow, in terms of techniques of power?'. Asking this question takes us to the point at which the Zombie and security come together; the point, that is, at which the Zombie becomes a mechanism for the mobilisation of security and connects us back to the Universal Adversary. At the same time, however, if we *were* to ask the question 'what is a Zombie?', what answer could we offer other than that the Zombie is a *disgruntled Worker*? We will develop this answer through the chapter, but we might note the simple recognition of this fact in the way that business management journals now like to advise the ruling class on how to deal with Zombie-Workers in their organisations.[26] And if we do read the figure of the Zombie as a disgruntled Worker, what does this then tell us about the contemporary mobilisation of security against this creature? The flurry of interest in the Zombies since 2001 may well be because they have 'become phantasmal stand-ins for Islamist terrorists, illegal immigrants, carriers of foreign contagions, and other "dangerous" border crossers',[27] but why are *workers* not also on this list? After all, is not the figure of the disgruntled Worker at the heart of the Emergency Planning Scenarios?

If we read the Zombie in terms of its entry point into western culture and consciousness, we find that it appears as a Worker in the context of the pacification of the colonies, under the combined forces of capital, colonialism and the war power. The figure of the Zombie therefore invites a materialist analysis linking it to both capital and security and, in so doing, it allows us to think of the Zombie in terms of its appearance as some kind of Enemy of All Mankind.

Myth I: work

The first flurry of Zombie film and literature occurred towards the end of the 1920s and in the early 1930s, with most accounts pointing to William Seabrook's book *The Magic Island* (1929) as the work which introduced the Zombie myth to the West and the text on which early films such as *White Zombie* (1932) were based. The timing is important, coming towards the end of the two decades in which the US had sought to pacify Haiti (the 'magic island' in Seabrook's title). To understand its importance we need to backtrack just a little.

The Haitian 'Zombi' ('zombie' was an Anglicization introduced by Seabrook in *The Magic Island*)[28] came from Africa. In an extensive survey of the origins of the Zombie concept, Hans-W. Ackerman and Jeanine Gauthier note that 'all components of the zombi concept ... are African in origin'.[29] To speak of the Haitian zombie is to speak of 'a process by which the African, as he became Haitian, was able to retain the essential nature of his heritage and at the same time renew it'.[30] Part of that 'essential nature' was the belief that it is other human beings rather than God who brings about man's death and, relatedly, the belief that the deceased is never really separated from his living relations but continues to live. As the Zombie moved from Africa to the West Indies and other colonies this idea of the dead continuing to live was retained, but underwent an important political development reflecting the new colonial situation rather than the precolonial spirit world.[31]

According to the *Oxford English Dictionary* (*OED*), the word 'zombi' first appeared in an English-language publication in 1819, in Robert Southey's *History of Brazil*, in which Southey uses the word in two senses: first, to refer to a Chief, from the Angolan word 'Nzambi', the word for Deity, and thus connoting a kind of living god or divine power with political force; second, to refer to a living dead creature set to work. Ann Kordas notes that the word appears in a fictional story called 'The Unknown Painter', which first appeared in *Chambers Edinburgh Journal* and was then reprinted in an 1838 edition of an Ohio newspaper called *The Alton Telegraph*. In the story, 'zombi' is the name given to a spirit who appears to a young African slave and which is said by the slave to have altered the canvases of the slave's master and his apprentices. Similar stories appeared elsewhere. Hence through the nineteenth century the word 'zombi' was in the English-speaking world associated with a creature of African origin that worked for white masters and thereby connoted the condition of slavery in general and, in particular, the idea that slavery somehow strips someone of their personhood.

The way to understand the Zombie myth as it emerges in Haiti is to therefore link it to the fact that the Haitians are former Africans, transported to America by slave-traders and forced to work for masters. As Alfred Métraux puts it following his extended research on Haitian voodoo, 'the zombi's life is seen in terms which echo the harsh existence of a slave'. He goes on: 'the *zombi* is a beast of burden which his master exploits without mercy, making him work in the fields, weighing him down with labour, whipping him freely and feeding him on meagre, tasteless food'.[32] The mute nature of the figure of the Zombie reflects this by reminding us of the fact that slaves and other forms of servile labour often had their tongues cut out as a punishment.[33] The original concept of the Zombie as a powerful creature therefore exists not because the Zombie is a figure of malevolence but, rather, because it is a form of Worker: a living dead slave-labour, an alienated person robbed of their will and controlled by a master-sorcerer. Laroche notes:

> A man becomes a zombi when … a spell is cast over him by an individual possessing supernatural powers. But the reasons for transforming a man into a zombi appear natural indeed to the individual who casts the spell: he wants to possess a being who will serve him, work his fields and constitute a truly low-cost work force. To put it bluntly, he wants cheap labour.[34]

As pointed out by George Romero, perhaps the most famous maker of zombie films of all time, if we return to the origins of the Zombie we discover nothing less than workers out picking sugar cane.[35] Why sugar cane?

Romero's comment is a reference back to Seabrook's *Magic Island*, in which zombies are 'dead men working in the cane fields', as Seabrook has it in the crucial chapter of the book. At the heart of that novel's treatment of the Zombie is the idea that the dead can still be put to use in way that renders them somehow not quite dead.

> The *zombie*, they say, is a soulless human corpse, still dead, but taken from the grave and endowed by sorcery with a mechanical semblance of life – it is a dead body which is made to walk and act and move as if it were alive. People who have the power to do this go to a fresh grave, dig up the body before it has time to rot, galvanize it into movement, and then make of it a servant or a slave, occasionally for the commission of some crime, more often simply as a drudge around the habitation or the farm, setting it dull heavy tasks, and beating it like a dumb beast if it slackens.[36]

In other words, in the moment in which the Zombie enters into western consciousness and culture, we discover a mythic symbol of slavery and the spectre of colonialism, alienation and exploitation. We discover, that is, the figure of a self dispossessed and reduced to being a mere source of slave labour. This is also why the Zombie as a 'monster' is so different to many other monsters: the real dread of encountering a Zombie is less being *harmed* by them than of *being made into one*; in effect, it is the dread of becoming nothing but a mindless slave.

Yet there is more to be said and the wider context of the US occupation of Haiti in 1915 is important here. Over nearly two decades the US occupation instituted a pacification programme in which it dissolved or replaced key Haitian political institutions, installed a puppet regime under a new constitution ('I wrote Hayti's constitution myself', claimed Franklin D. Roosevelt)[37] suppressed fundamental liberties, abolished what it called 'undemocratic' clauses in the constitution that barred foreign companies (i.e., American capital) owning property in Haiti, took over the National Bank, established the police power as a force against any resistance by the Haitian population and killing somewhere between 15,000 and 30,000 Haitians in the process (some of whom were killed in their attempt to resist the occupation, but many were killed in their attempt to flee from the forced labour being reintroduced), tortured many others, and imposed Jim Crow racial segregation. Most importantly, the occupying forces expropriated land, created new plantations and reinstituted *corvée* labour to facilitate the capitalist colonisation of the island. Thus in the interest of creating roads, for example, the occupation reinstated a law from 1864 stating that peasants could be forced to work on road construction in lieu of paying a road tax. This was a system rooted in the *corvée*, a process through which peasants were forced to engage in unpaid labour for their Lords and which many colonial powers revived in their pacification programmes. As always, the law of labour and the reign of terror in the name of security go hand-in-hand.[38]

In the pacification of Haiti the horror of re-enslavement – or the horror of a *new form of enslavement* – became apparent. As Haitians were forced to build roads and rebuild their nation under the model of capital accumulation imposed on them by the US, and as thousands of peasants were massacred and their resistance violently crushed in the process, tales of zombies proliferated, not just in Haiti but in the United States as well.[39] The emergence of the Zombie fantasy in the US during this period is thus in some sense a cultural recognition that the pacification of Haiti was based on a new kind of slavery and colonisation: '*the history of colonisation is the process of man's general zombification*', as René Dépestre puts it.[40] In the western cultural unconscious the emergence of the Zombie is connected to the colonisation of the world by capital, to unpaid slave labour and to the violence of empire.

Now, it is true to say that 'colonialism does not always call forth zombies, and zombies are not always associated with colonialism', as Jean Comaroff and John Comaroff note. But as they also add, once we make the connection between the Zombie and colonialism we are forced to associate zombieism more broadly with the conditions of work under contemporary capitalism.[41] And once we do so we realise that the (postmodern) Zombie's capacity to consume flesh is far less relevant than the (original) Zombie's capacity for mindless labour as living death. As a dead body put to work, and put to work forever, the Zombie is thus emblematic of a fate truly worse than death: of being brought back to life and then kept alive *in order to be made to work forever*. This is why Frantz Fanon would write in *The Wretched of the Earth* that the Zombie is in many ways more terrifying than the colonial settlers.[42]

'Europeans, you must open this book and enter into it', writes Jean-Paul Sartre in his Preface to Fanon's book. He goes on:

> After a few steps in the darkness you will see strangers gathered around a fire; come close, and listen, for they are talking of the destiny they will mete out to your trading centers and to the hired soldiers who defend them. They will see you, perhaps, but they will go on talking among themselves, without even lowering their voices. This indifference strikes home: their fathers, shadowy creatures, *your* creatures, were but dead souls; you it was who allowed them glimpses of light, to you only did they dare speak, and you did not bother to reply to such zombies. Their sons ignore you; a fire warms them and sheds light around them, and you have not lit it. Now, at a respectful distance, it is you who will feel furtive, nightbound, and perished with cold. Turn and turn about; in these shadows from whence a new dawn will break, it is you who are the zombies.[43]

You who are the zombies? *We* who are the zombies? How so?

One of the significant features of Seabrook's novel *The Magic Island* is that he recognises that although zombies are 'dead men working in the cane fields', the cane fields are themselves part and parcel of capital as a whole. The production process in the novel is distinctly modern and industrial. One of the characters in Seabrook's novel makes the point that zombies are found not only in the countryside, but in the cities and the factories. 'Close even to the cities there are sometimes zombies', the character notes, adding: 'Perhaps you have already heard of those that were at Hasco?' The narrator is confused: 'Hasco is perhaps the last name anybody would think of connecting with either sorcery or superstition'. Why? Because 'the word is American-commercial-synthetic, like Nabisco, Delco, Sony. It stands for the Haitian-American Sugar Company – an immense factory plant, dominated by a huge chimney, with clanging machinery, steam whistles, freight cars. ... It is a modern big business, and it sounds it, looks it, smells it'.[44] HASCO was in fact a real company, one which was at the heart of American commercial activity on the Island and which during the occupation generated huge profits: from being in a state of receivership in 1921 it had by 1928 tripled its sugar production and by the 1930s was employing over 1,000 workers, a success almost entirely dependent on the low labour-costs of workers achieved through the pacification program.[45] But if we allow HASCO to stand for capital in general then the implications are clear: the dead men working in the cane fields are systematically connected to the other fields and then to the sugar factories and on to the whole production and circulation of commodities through the capitalist system. Central to these different sites and moments in the production of commodities are the 'poor dead creatures' who 'toil day after day dumbly in the sun', 'dead bodies walking, without souls or minds'. They 'continue dumbly at work', 'plodding like brutes, like automatons', 'nothing but poor ordinary demented human beings, idiots, forced to toil in the fields' with eyes 'like the eyes of a dead man, not blind, but staring, unfocused, unseeing'.[46] The Zombie, as the living dead, is to be made good for work not just in the fields but also in the factories and thus within capital as a whole.

As a figure in Western culture the Zombie thus started life deeply enmeshed in capitalist production and the exchange of labour and commodities. It is this very understanding that seeps into Western culture in general. For example, Zora Neale Thurston, a popular American novelist and anthropologist specialising in folklore, explored the 'meaning' of the Zombie in *Tell My Horse* (1938), offering an eye witness account ('I know there are Zombies in Haiti') but also a notably political analysis. As well as noting that Zombies are 'bodies without souls' and 'the living dead', the point she makes is that Zombies form almost a class of beings in what is more or less a modern slave system. The Zombie 'will work ferociously and tirelessly without consciousness of his surroundings and conditions and without memory of his former state'. She gives the example of 'A': he 'was awakened [from death] because somebody required his body as a beast of burden. In his natural state he could never have been hired to work with his hands, so he was made into a Zombie because they wanted his services as a labourer'. This is a class issue, she notes.

> The upper class Haitians fear too, but they do not talk about it so openly as do the poor. But to them also it is a horrible possibility. Think of the fiendishness of the thing. It is not good for a person who has lived all his life surrounded by a degree of fastidious culture, loved to his last breath by family and friends, to contemplate the probability of his resurrected body being dragged from the vault … and set to toiling ceaselessly in the banana fields, working like a beast, unclothed like a beast, and like a brute crouching in some foul den in the few hours allowed for rest and food.[47]

The same image of the Zombie as deeply enmeshed in capitalist production is found in the early films. The Bela Lugosi film *White Zombie*, directed by Victor Halperin and based loosely on Seabrook's novel, has Lugosi playing Murder Legendre, a Haitian sugar cane factory owner who raises the dead to work like slaves in the factory, and contains scenes of mechanized, gaunt, alienated workers. 'They work faithfully; they're not afraid of long hours', notes Legendre. At one point in the film one of the zombies falls into the machinery, capturing the ways in which workers are killed day in and day out in and through the process of production. Despite this corporate killing in the workplace, the other Zombie-Workers in the film carry on working. Marina Warner comments that it is as though the film is saying to its Western viewers, 'Don't look now. Don't ask where your money is coming from: you will not be able to bear it if you find out'.[48] But it is also as if the film is saying 'Don't look now, because you might also see just what capital thinks of you'. In this regard it is also notable that despite the 'White Zombie' in the title of the film often being interpreted as the character of the vulnerable white female virgin who is threatened by black sexual power, the 'White Zombie' in the title might also be taken as a reference to the fact that some of the zombies in the factory are white; and even the white female virgin becomes an unpaid domestic servant once she becomes a Zombie. Part of the 'horror' here lies in the fear of racial levelling, and thus the horror of a common degradation in which whites as well as blacks are degraded, exploited and alienated as workers. It turns out that just like 'trash' and 'slave', the 'Zombie' can also be white.[49]

Extrapolating from its origins in Haiti, then, we might say that it is not just that the Zombie is a sign of the effect of American capital on Haiti, or even the effect of American capital anywhere else. And it is also not that the Zombie is meant to be some kind of critique of consumerism. The point of the Zombie is that it is a creature brought back from the dead in order to work. We might comment here on the old story told about the hard-working and committed 'company man' or 'organisation man' who works all his life, spends little time with family or friends, and develops no interest in things outside work, who retires and then dies shortly after. The moral we are expected to take away from this 'horror story' is to develop a life outside work. But the figure of the Zombie offers an alternative horror story: of the hard-working and committed worker who works all his or her life, spends little time with family or friends and so on, who retires, dies, and then immediately finds themselves brought back to life in order to continue working, only this time forever. What horror is worse than the horror of spending the whole of one's life working? Spending the whole of one's death doing the same thing.

At the heart of the Zombie myth is thus not the Zombie-*ghoul* engaged in *consumption* (of human flesh), but the Zombie-*labourer* engaged in *production* (of commodities): the living dead Worker under the permanent power of another and used by the Other in their pursuit of perpetual accumulation. The more recent deployment of the flesh-eating Zombie-consumer has short-circuited this older and far more politically telling vision of the Zombie-labourer.[50] The focus on consumerism derails the focus on labour, especially its coerced nature, and which is registered even in the contemporary security and emergency documentation cited above, which notes that the Zombie is a human corpse mysteriously reanimated to serve.

The horror of the Zombie, then, is the horror of the effects of capital per se, the logical end of the process of systematic colonisation, of being once more a form of slave despite or perhaps even because of one's 'freedom' from earlier forms of slavery. This is the process in which the term 'living dead' can be read as the *not-fully-dead status of the living Worker* as much as the 'brought back to life to work' status of the dead: kept alive but in a state of mindless subordination, a dead person working in fields and factories, enslaved as a dehumanized capitalist subject, an automaton in the machine of accumulation and the systematic colonization of the world by capital, a 'mindless' bureaucrat administering the system – 'dehumanization' is the *sine quo non* of bureaucracy',[51] as Max Weber notes – or even a Worker in one of those occupations previously looked up to with awe but which have more recently been stripped of their halo and turned into just another form of wage labour, such as University teaching.[52] Under the power of capital, we are all zombies.[53]

This idea that we the people are all zombies is highlighted in one of the major themes in the Zombie genre when one of the characters in a film, novel or TV series asks the obvious question about who or what these creatures 'really' are. The answer comes time and again: 'They're us', as Peter puts it in Romero's *Dawn of the Dead* (1978). 'They are us', a character in

Day of the Dead (1985) states.[54] *Land of the Dead* (2005) opens two with characters watching some zombies:

A: They're trying to be us.

B: They used to be us. They're learning how to be us again.

A: Those things are walking but there's a big difference between us and them. They're dead. It's like they're pretending to be alive.

B: Isn't that what we're doing? Pretending to be alive.

'WE ARE THE WALKING DEAD', as the lead character Rick Grimes puts it in the graphic novel *The Walking Dead*, repeated in the TV series based on the novel.[55] When not stated so directly, the point is still alluded to, as for example in *Shaun of the Dead* (2004) where the zombies turn out to be most of the characters in the film, looking like ordinary working people going about their normal lives. 'A zombie was once someone like you and me', notes Marina Warner.[56] *Once* someone like you and me? Perhaps. But the point also being made in the genre is that you and me are a bit like Zombies. Perhaps the central motif of the Zombie genre is that zombieism is in some fundamental way about the living death of being a worker in capitalism. 'The shock of meeting a zombie is thus not the shock of encountering a foreign entity, but the shock of being confronted by the disavowed foundation of our own humanity'.[57] And what disavows it is capital. If the life-in-death and deadly life of the Zombie tells us something about capital, then, it is surely that under capitalism it is not *dying* that makes us zombies, it is *not-dying* that does.[58] The figure of the Zombie speaks to us about what it means when we labour for a wage, of being labour and feeling dead. Being labour and feeling dead? *Dead labour?*

In Volume 1 of *Capital*, Marx dismisses the view that capital is something distinct from labour. Instead, Marx argues that capital is nothing but accumulated labour. This is the distinction between accumulated labour and labour *per se* or, as he often puts it, accumulated labour versus 'living labour'. 'What is the growth of accumulated capital? Growth of the power of accumulated labour over living labour'. In other words, 'capital does not consist in accumulated labour serving living labour as a means for new production. It consists in living labour serving accumulated labour as a means for maintaining and multiplying the exchange value of the latter'. But if a fundamental distinction needs to be drawn between *accumulated* and *living* labour, then it makes perfect sense to treat the former – that is, capital – as dead labour. Marx had toyed with this idea in his early work where he refers to 'dead capital' or 'dead mammon', but it gets more properly thought through in his economic notebooks of the 1850s and then into the fully fledged critique of political economy, much of which focuses on the magic by which things dead are brought back to life. Inactive machinery is useless and dead without the active force of living labour: 'Iron rusts;

wood rots...Living labour must seize on these things [and] change them from merely possible into real and effective use-values'. That is, labour must 'awaken them from the dead'. The appropriation by the capitalist of the worker's productive powers is a means by which 'living labour makes instrument and material in the production process into the body of its soul and thereby resurrects them from the dead'.[59]

Yet despite being *dead* labour, capital is also a highly active social agent. Capital appears as dead labour turned into a form of life which in turn sucks the life out of labour, feasts on the blood of workers and eventually destroys them.[60] This is a fundamental part of the topsy-turvy world of capital that Marx is at pains to illustrate. 'Owing to its conversion into an automaton, the instrument of labour confronts the worker during the labour process in the shape of capital, dead labour, which dominates and soaks up living labour-power'. Hence living labour is 'subsumed under the total process of the machinery itself', becoming merely a link in the system the unity of which 'exists not in the living workers, but rather in the living (active) machinery'. Or as he puts it in *Capital*: 'the rule of the capitalist over the worker is nothing but ... the rule of things over man, of dead labour over living'.[61] Capital appears to be both dead labour and a living power.

In this sense capital appears to be an alien being and a monstrous objective power. 'By incorporating living labour into their *lifeless* objectivity, the capitalist simultaneously transforms value, i.e. past labour in its objectified and *lifeless* form, into capital ... an animated monster'.[62] Moreover, the *product* of labour also comes to appear as a living and thus alien thing.

> The product of labour appears as an *alien property*, as a mode of existence confronting living labour as independent, as *value* in its being for itself; the product of labour, objectified labour, has been endowed by living labour with a soul of its own, and establishes itself opposite living labour as an *alien power*.[63]

At the same time, the topsy-turvy world of capital has taken this one step further: not only must the worker face 'dead labour' in the form of the machinery, but the worker must become a machine devoid of all human characteristics. This is the 'alien quality of alien labour'.[64]

> Living labour therefore now appears from its own standpoint as acting within the production process in such a way that, as it realizes itself in the objective conditions, it simultaneously repulses this realization from itself as an alien reality, and hence posits itself as insubstantial, as mere penurious labour capacity.[65]

'Penurious' here is the perfect description, connoting a poverty-stricken miserable and disgruntled lack within the living creature created by the fact that capital turns living labour into lifeless objectivity, and 'man [into] a mere fragment of his own body'.[66] Thus the 'dead labour' not only determines the life of the living labourer but, worse, has the effect of turning the living labourer into a crippled monstrosity that feels like it exists as living death.

All of which is to complicate the argument somewhat, because it appears that the true horror of the Zombie is the horror of being not just *disgruntled labour* but, worse, the horror of human beings *taking on the very form of the commodity itself*, as David Cunningham and Alexandra Warwick note. It is the horror of the human being becoming part of the limitless movement of capital. 'In the zombie, value effectively "takes possession" of its own material conditions, including human beings themselves, which thus become subordinated as shambling "moments" within its own self-propulsion'.[67] In the figure of the Zombie, then, we thus find not only the figure of the worker, but in fact *capital as a whole*. We find, in other words, the social production and reproduction of human beings as completely exchangeable subject-objects. This is perhaps why Deleuze and Guattari comment in their work on capitalism and schizophrenia that the only modern myth is the myth of the Zombie, because the myth of the Zombie is first and foremost a *work myth*.[68] This is precisely why the Zombie is such a compelling figure in contemporary capitalism and why it is so central to the security imagination that underpins Emergency Planning Scenarios.

And yet Emergency Planning documents are documents of *war* as well as *work*. So, *contra* Deleuze and Guattari, we need to read the Zombie myth as *simultaneously a war myth*. Exploring this aspect of the Zombie will take us back to the security imaginary and emergency preparations via the Zombie apocalypse.

Myth II: war

When 'Zombi' starts to appear in various English-language texts through the nineteenth century, it was often with a capital 'Z' to designate a proper name, usually the name of a leader of various pre-nineteenth century slave revolts. In some accounts of the Haitian slave revolt, for example, a slave named 'Jean Zombi' is credited with leading the revolution and being the most violent of the revolutionaries.[69] This is a reminder that the Haitians are the only people to have founded a nation through a war against slavery and that of the three great revolutions of the late-eighteenth century only the Haitian insisted on the practical and unconditional application to *all* human beings of the ideas of universal human freedom and inalienable rights, thereby pitting the Haitians against the economic logic of the day.[70] These Black Jacobins founding a Black Republic opened the space for two centuries of global anticolonial revolution and form a crucial part of the Zombie myth. Following the path laid down by 'Jean Zombi', the name

'Zombie' would forever be understood as a figure willing to wage war against white colonial oppressors and so would forever be understood as a figure seeking to avenge those enslaved. 'The religious beliefs brought back from Africa constituted the bonds unifying the blacks in their war against the French armies', notes Laroche. 'They were a defensive weapon in so far as they could provide the Haitians with hope, courage and the will to fight'.[71] From the outset, the Zombie was central to such beliefs. When, over a century later, the Haitians engaged in prolonged resistance to the American pacification program, the Zombie myth continued to play a role.

This tradition of revolution and resistance is a salutary reminder of the fact that the Zombie's abasement comes with a fundamental indignation at that abasement. A reminder, that is, that as a disgruntled Worker the Zombie retains the possibility of revolution. In other words, we might think of the Zombie as not just a worker-slave but as 'a terrible composite power: slave turned rebel'.[72] This is something the ruling class knows only too well: deep within the bourgeois dream of a Worker who works faithfully and is not afraid of long hours lies the bourgeois nightmare of the disgruntled Worker who might lose faith and revolt. This is why when in his *History of Brazil* Robert Southey presents us with what appears to be the first recorded use of the term 'Zombi' in English, he is describing the 'Negroes of the Palmares, or Palm Forests' under the governorship of Caetano de Mello de Castro, who sought to escape slavery by fleeing to the forests. 'Their numbers were continually increased by slaves who fought for freedom, and men of colour who fled from justice', and as they grew in size so too did they grow in audacity and strength as other slaves joined them. They were 'full of justice', lived with 'no conspiracies or struggles for power' under an elective Chief chosen for his justice. (Note these phrases, as they will come back in Chapter 4 when we discuss the Pirate.) Southey goes on: 'Perhaps a feeling of religion contributed to this obedience; for Zombi, the title whereby he was called, is the name for the Deity, in the Angolan tongue'.[73] Eventually under siege from the Portuguese, their fortifications broke down. 'The Zombi and the most resolute of his followers retired to the summit of the rock; and preferring death to slavery, threw themselves from the precipice'.[74] The point is that in its original meaning 'Zombie' connoted a 'prototype liberation martyr-hero': nothing less than an 'early exemplar of elected ruler' and 'the chieftain of a free band of rebels who dies heroically rather than resume a life in chains'.[75] Moreover, the power of this threat of rebellion lies in the potential to rise up against the masters as a *collective* force. The Zombie so lacks individuality that it can function and threaten only as a group. In the figure of the Zombie lies the bourgeois fear of the mass. A 'lone Zombie' poses little threat and a 'lone actor Zombie' is incoherent as some kind of terror suspect. Zombies are always a mass, rabble, horde, mob, swinish multitude or, and this is a term to which we shall return later in this chapter, a crowd.

The Zombie insurrection is yet another opportunity to mobilise security (which is why the Zombie genre is shot through with the question of security)[76] so as to reconstitute political order (which is why the Zombie genre is shot through with the question of how to constitute a body politic after the Zombie uprising). This process is explicitly designed to prepare people not just for an emergency, but for an emergency defined as war. The Zombie awareness campaign is nothing less than a training in violence against the (monstrous, beastly) Other presented to us as the Enemy of all Humanity and therefore against which we must all fight. The point about a Zombie war as it might be imagined in an Emergency Planning Scenario is not just that if you can survive for several days in a Zombie outbreak then you can survive for several days in some other emergency. Nor is it that if you can survive a Zombie attack you can survive a terror attack. In other words, the point of imagining emergency in the form of a Zombie war is not just about preparations in the form of stocking up on bottled water, dried food, batteries for the flashlights and finding a way to keep the family safe. No; the point, rather, is to imagine *killing the zombies*, because *if you can kill a Zombie then you can probably kill anyone.* This is what Linnemann, Wall and Green call the normalisation of police violence: the figure of the Zombie encourages us to imagine and prepare ourselves for exercising the violence usually meted out by the capitalist state.[77] What is being planned is the continuation of the broader system of violence within which the emergency planning is to be exercised.

The appearance of the Zombie in the emergency planning documents is not only an imaginative reproduction of the idea an Enemy that does not discriminate between us and which must therefore be seen and fought as some kind of 'Enemy of All Mankind'. It is, more tellingly, the *imaginative instantiation of our own violence against that Enemy*. Don't just *bounce back* from the attack, but *fight back*. This is why the whole Zombie genre now functions in terms of the Zombie hunt, the Zombie shoot, the Zombie kill and the Zombie massacre. It is also why we are expected to think about how everyday household objects can also be objects of violence in a Zombie uprising: the baseball bat or monkey wrench that can also be used to crush a skull, the kitchen knife or screwdriver that can also be forced into the eyeball, and so on. In the light of some critical analyses of how the war power seeps into our everyday lives, this could be described as 'bringing the war back home', but the truth is the Zombie war has always been a war carried out on the domestic front: the preparation of citizens for violence in the homeland and in the name of (homeland) security is its very *raison d'être*. The Zombie reiterates the everydayness of capitalist violence in the name of security, allowing us to imagine ourselves as exercising the powers of violence usually claimed by the state and to thereby see ourselves as part and parcel of the war power. What should we do in a Zombie war? Keep calm, and kill zombies.

Figure 2.6 'Keep Calm and Kill Zombies' door, Brighton, UK, February 2015
Source: Author's photo.

Mobilized *for* security and *by* the emergency, we are to carry out violence in the name of bourgeois order against a new Adversary, one which appears to be some kind of Enemy of humanity as a whole. We are to secure bourgeois order by becoming part of its war power and defending our own so-called 'humanity' against this Enemy of All Mankind.

Yet wait: have we not already noted that they are us and we are them? What can it therefore mean to say that the emergency planning wants us to mobilize against this Adversary? What can it mean other than to suggest that preparedness for a Zombie attack is nothing less than a way for the state to get us to imagine ourselves as being able and willing to kill each other in the name of security? The contemporary figure of the Zombie is thus turning out to be the ultimate genius of contemporary capitalist violence: disgruntled workers (zombies) killing zombies (disgruntled workers). Emergency planning has taken the mobilization of security to its logical endpoint: *the subjects of security killing each other in the name of security.*

'Whose side are you on?' That's the question we are encouraged to ask and answer amidst all the Zombie material out there. And of course, we are expected to answer: it's us against the Zombies, a figure seemingly like us but also somehow an Enemy of all of us. Are you with us or with the Enemy of All Mankind? Are you with us or with the Terrorists? Are you with us or with the disgruntled Workers? Are you with us or shall we count you as part of the Universal Adversary? These are the questions through which we are expected to align ourselves with the state personnel and bourgeois ideologues who want to formulate the questions that way, the ones who want us to be prepared for the emergency, who want to train us in resilience and who want us to train ourselves in the resilience, the ones who know that at some point 'emergency planning' might mean nothing less than being prepared for mass slaughter in the name of security.

This potential slaughter underpins the idea of apocalypse and contagion in contemporary security, for as we have already seen in this chapter it would by no means be unreasonable to add 'Preparing for Apocalypse' to the Emergency Planning Scenarios discussed in Chapter 1. The apocalypse is the ultimate moment of violence, but to get to that point we must do so via the politics of contagion.

Recall the emergency planning materials cited earlier in this chapter, such as the CDC material outlining a Zombie apocalypse as infestation and how it would deal with this by lab testing, patient management, contact tracking and infection control (including isolation and quarantine). Notwithstanding my earlier comments regarding the importance of the early period in the Zombie genre, we need to register here the fact that at a certain point, somewhere around the mid-1980s and no doubt connected to the rise of AIDS but reaching its crescendo more recently in the wider context of various other viruses and the whole tenor of 'biosecurity', the Zombie came to be increasingly understood in terms of the 'outbreak' of some kind of contagious disease, virus, or plague; commentators identify Danny Boyle's *28 Days Later* (2002) as the key film signalling a shift towards the virus-oriented zombie narrative.[78] It is through the outbreak narrative that the Zombie figures as a spectacle of contagion.

Now, the vitality of the idea of contagion would mean little were it not connected in some form or other to the idea of a 'social contagion'. The word 'contagion' came into the English language in the sixteenth century and, like 'plague', is one of a family of terms through which the 'body politic' has been conceptualised and the police power mobilised. Figures of plague stalk the history of bourgeois modernity, from the rogues and vagabonds of the sixteenth and seventeenth centuries to the increasingly organised working class of the nineteenth century and then through to the Jews and Gypsies in the twentieth: all have at some point been thought of as dirty enemies contaminating and polluting the body politic.[79] Hence the 'masterless men and women' and 'rogues' that arose with the disorder associated with the breakdown of feudalism and who had not yet been 'mastered' by capital were understood to be quintessentially connected to the plague; their very condition was a contagious one. Plagues and rogues were said to coexist. 'Civic authorities considered "masterless men", a new element in a changing economic system, as harbingers of disease and as plagues themselves'.[80] The rogues *carry* the plague but they also *are* a plague. Medical plague folds into social plague; the two can never be distinguished. Indeed, the *medical* aspects are never the essential aspects. Rather, as René Girard and Michel Foucault point out, the medical aspects serve merely as a vehicle for communicating an even more terrible social threat: to security and order.[81] Plague leads to anarchy but at the same time anarchy is itself a plague. During a time of plague, the emergency situation writ large, political authority collapses. The declaration of emergency to deal with 'plague' thereby serves to legitimize the violence said to be necessary to reconstitute order out of anarchy. The declaration 'plague' always calls forth the police power: the disorder of plague to be confronted and overcome by the order of police.

It is this long history of contagious plague which underpins the outbreak narrative in contemporary emergency planning and which comes to the fore in the idea of the Zombie outbreak. Cunningham and Warwick suggest that in many ways the *urtext* of the Zombie narrative is Daniel Defoe's *Journal of the Plague Year*, published in 1722.[82] In fact, if there is any such *urtext* it is another book published by Defoe in the same year as the *Journal*, namely his *Due Preparations for the Plague*, because unlike the *Journal*, with its lists and inventories, *Due Preparations* is in many ways one of the first Emergency Planning Scenarios. As Janette Turner Hospital puts it in discussing her own novel which borrows Defoe's title, Defoe's *Due Preparations* 'was a kind of Red Alert of the kind now issued by the Department for Homeland Security: this is what you can do to protect yourself from terrorists: stay away from New York City; and if you're in the city, stay away from Grand Central Station and Yankee Stadium and the Statue of Liberty and Wall Street and airports and so on'. In *Due Preparations* the security implications of plague are laid out far more clearly than in the *Journal*: the plague threatens the security of the nation, the security of the body and the security of the soul. The only way to deal with this combined security threat is with 'due preparations': 'preparations for the body', 'preparations for the soul' and, of course, 'preparations for death'. Defoe's warning is clear: the security of the bourgeois polity depends on extensive emergency planning to deal with a contagious threat.[83]

It is the persistence of the fear of a contagious threat that connects the early modern fear of a rising class of masterless men and women in the sixteenth and seventeenth centuries to the swinish multitude of the eighteenth and nineteenth centuries and on to the Zombie multitude of the twentieth and twenty-first centuries. To extend a point just made: the rogues *carry* the plague and are thus contagious, but they also *constitute* a plague and so *their roguish condition is itself contagious*. Contagion is the enemy, but then the enemy is contagion. Where objects of contagion cannot be eliminated, they must be *sealed off* or *quarantined*; they must be *contained*.[84]

From such an origin it was easy for contagion to become one of the prime justifications of the police power. 'The attempt to control contagion found its ideal instrument not in the law ... but in an expanded police regulation', notes Andrew Aisenberg.[85] That is why the politics of contagion intensified in the 1830s and 1840s, as police powers segmented into a variety of institutions, from the 'new police' to the 'new poor laws' and taking in everything from sewers to medicine and drainage systems to street cleaning. It is also why the political control of the environment goes hand in hand with medical control, in the form of 'medical police' and especially in the exercise of this police in and over the City. This was reflected in the interest in contagion that ran through so much urban sociology and criminology as they developed in the late-nineteenth century and into the twentieth century, for the City came to be seen as a space of 'social contagion' in a way that makes major assumptions about class and race. This is also why migration of any sort is a recurring theme in the police power: contagion occurs with movement and the City is the site of movement as well as migration. It is also, we might add in the light of the previous chapter, another reason why the swinish multitude is a problem for the police power.

At the same time, contagion was also a fundamental feature of the police power in the form of the civilizing process as it turned outwards, through colonialism. From the perspective of the colonising powers, one of the primary dangers was contagious disease, as the horrors they unleashed created in turn a horror that they themselves then had to face: of contact in some form or another and thus the horror of contagion that comes with such contact, whether in the form of physical contamination or moral corruption. 'The age of globalization is the age of universal contagion', observe Michael Hardt and Antonio Negri.[86]

This need to contain contagion is why the theme reappears time and again in mainstream political thought, in particular when it considers the security mechanisms for managing rebellion and revolt. In political theory, this appears in the form of the 'contagion of example'. Hobbes, for example, when addressing the ways in which the sovereign power needs to deal with the problem of crime, notes the 'contagion of the Example'; Burke comments on 'the contagion of ill example' in revolutionary fervour; Hume notes the 'contagion of sentiments when people are inflamed on the streets as well as the 'contagion of mutiny and disobedience'; *The Federalist Papers* refer to 'insurrection' and 'insurgency' as contagion; Rousseau comments on the 'contagion of their example' when discussing criminals and social scum. This list could go on. 'Examples are contagious', notes Immanuel Kant.[87]

The problem of the 'contagion of example' in rebellion and revolution is a reminder that one meaning of 'contagion' is 'to touch together'. Although this phrase encourages the assumption that contagion takes place through physical touching – reinforced by films such as Steven Soderbergh's *Contagion*, released in the heyday of the Zombie zeitgeist (2011), which has constant flashbacks to people innocently touching one another or objects as they go about their mundane daily tasks – the more compelling point is that in its earliest usage 'contagion' referred to the circulation of ideas and attitudes. Indeed, the concept of contagion is much less a question of microbiology or epidemiology than it is a question of how ideas circulate. As its use in medical circles has declined in the last decades of the twentieth century and first decades of the twenty-first – medical dictionaries and public health handbooks now tend to use the term 'communicable diseases' rather than 'contagion' – the use of 'contagion' in non-medical contexts has expanded.[88] Sociologists ('social contagion'), psychologists ('emotional contagion', 'mental contagion'), anthropologists ('cultural contagion'), and economists ('economic contagion', 'financial contagion') all have a story to tell in their own disciplinary recycling of nineteenth century ideas about 'moral contagion' and pre-nineteenth century ideas about 'the contagion of example'. The point here, however, is that in each of these cases the narrative points to the *circulation of ideas in the crowd*. With its connotations of 'touching together', contagion connotes danger or corruption, in particular the kinds of danger or corruption that occur in 'promiscuous' social spaces when ideas can circulate among the crowd. Moreover, implicit in the concept of contagion is the belief that *revolutionary ideas are inherently contagious* (as are beliefs described as 'heretical' and which are in turn connected to ideas about 'contagious evil', 'spiritual contagion' and 'contagious sin', issues which connect to the argument in the next chapter). This is why the problem of contagion has since the origins of modernity permeated so much of what passes as 'crowd psychology' – 'contagion is particularly dangerous in crowds', Montaigne noted in 1580 – because what is at stake is the threat that revolutionary ideas will circulate 'by example' among the crowd.[89] What is therefore ultimately at stake in the politics of contagion is not the police of drains and sewers but *the police of revolutionary ideas*, and in such a police operation the problem of the crowd is crucial.

The crowd had long been held to be the 'disorganised … dregs of mankind' to which 'no right can be attributed'.[90] But by the time the proletariat arrived on the historic stage, the problem of how the crowd might be influenced and controlled needed a more thorough investigation. The founder of crowd psychology, Gustave Le Bon, comments on three ways in which a crowd can be influenced: affirmation, repetition and contagion (later adding a fourth, 'prestige'). What is interesting about these terms is that although they are Le Bon's way of thinking about the relationship between the crowd and the leader – the 'magnetic fascination' between the 'servile flock' and its 'master' – contagion turns out to have little to do with the person of the leader and everything to do with the irrationality of the crowd. 'The opinions and beliefs of crowds are specially propagated by contagion, but never by reasoning', writes Le Bon. 'Ideas sentiments, emotions, and beliefs possess in crowds a contagious power as intense as that of microbes'. Once what is called 'a current of opinion' forms 'the powerful mechanism of contagion intervenes'. This goes hand in hand with the mindlessness of the crowd or its 'hypnotised' state, according to Le Bon. 'Contagion … must be classed among those phenomena of a hypnotic order'.[91] In such a state an individual is 'no longer conscious of his acts'. In these descriptions Le Bon presents a figure somewhat akin to the Zombie: 'the disappearance of the conscious personality … [The individual] is no longer himself, but has become an automaton who has ceased to be guided by his will'. And yet at the same time Le Bon is concerned that such figures play a key role in revolution. The Zombie-like crowd is nothing less than the 'agent of revolution',[92] and although Le Bon's specific reference is to 1848 it is clear he is implying that all revolutionary movements are like this and that the socialist revolutionary movement is especially so. What is revealed is nothing less than the essence of all crowd psychology: a fear of working class mobilisation.

In his later work *The French Revolution and the Psychology of Revolution* Le Bon repeats the point that it is a particular feature of revolutionary crowds and movements to be susceptible to contagious forces, but adds that part of that susceptibility lies in the universalism espoused by revolutionaries.[93] Le Bon dates this problem from the end of the eighteenth century and the 'universal demands' that emerged in the context of the French Revolution, but adds that the impact has been felt more drastically with the demand for universal suffrage in the nineteenth century. Le Bon claims to be neutral on the issues of rights and suffrage, but he in fact attacks them precisely because of the revolutionary claim that they have 'universal' applicability. In effect, the idea of some kind of 'universal rights of man', and, even more important, the socialist and revolutionary rhetoric of universality which went with such demands, are Le Bon's targets, for they signal 'one of the most striking characteristics of our epoch of transition', namely 'the entry of the popular classes into political life'.[94] Le Bon is here playing on the fundamental assumptions in crowd psychology which underpins all conservative and reactionary political thought. It is an assumption with roots in Plato's scorn for the mass, which gets drastically intensified in the reactionary response to the rise of 'the people' in the late-nineteenth century, which reaches a crescendo in fascism,[95] and which gets repeated time and again when the bourgeois media blame riots and uprisings on the problem of contagious ideas. At its core the assumption is that the crowd is inherently irrational and fundamentally prone to violence. And yet, at the same time, part of the assumption is that the crowd might also be susceptible to an alternative violence organised by the state in order to keep the crowd in order. This is a violence to maintain law and order, peace and security, and to keep the body politic free from the contagious diseases carried by the crowd.

All of which brings us full circle to the contemporary mobilisation of security and the ways in which the crowd has once again taken centre stage in the contemporary security imaginary. Why? Because it is now increasingly the case that security is being mobilised and emergency planning constructed around one of the most fundamental problems for the police power: the crowd. The British state now operates a 'security futures initiative', led by a new organisation called 'Secure Futures', focused very specifically on the need to understand crowd behaviour and to police crowded places. Much of this is bound up with the logic of emergency, and a large part of it is founded on the work of Gustave Le Bon.[96] In the US the state has undertaken a well-funded University-led research project, under the auspices of the Minerva Programme, on the question of how to tackle mass social movements, political mobilizations and 'social contagions'. The programme references 'the 2011 Egyptian revolution, the 2011 Russian Duma elections, the 2012 Nigerian fuel subsidy crisis and the 2013 Gezi park protests in Turkey' as the basis of its research and the plan is to analyse Twitter posts and conversations on other social media during these events in order to develop an empirical model of civil unrest. Inherent in the project is the contagion narrative: the intention is to 'identify individuals mobilized in a social contagion', to note 'when they become mobilized' and thereby 'construct an "adoption curve" that tracks the number of individuals mobilized in the contagion at any given point in time'.[97] The developments concerning crowds and contagion within the security imaginary link to wider debates about how to manage the disgruntled worker within the 'networks' of contemporary capital. Popular psychology and business management now describe as 'contagious' the problems of the self which affect an individual's ability to perform as a neo-liberal subject, such as obesity and suicide. The same texts also describe as 'contagious' more positive emotional states, such as laughter and happiness. These texts thereby come together with the developing trend of trying to manage worker disgruntlement through the 'happiness agenda' noted at the end of the previous chapter. The problem for security posed by contagious crowds is thus bound up with the problem for capital posed by contagious networks.[98]

Yet as well as bringing us full circle to the contemporary mobilisation of security and problems of capital, this also takes us to the apocalyptic tone recently adopted in the politics of emergency?[99] 'The contagious body is the most characteristic modality of apocalyptic corporeality', notes Elana Gomel,[100] and compared to other narratives of monstrosity it is the figure of the zombie that is most frequently conjoined with the image of apocalypse as well as the problem of contagion. Recall the CDC material: we must prepare for a 'z-o-m-b-i-e a-p-o-c-a-l-y-p-s-e'. Much as such a claim might simply be playing on the idea of '9/11' as an apocalyptic moment, there might be a bigger story to tell.

'Apocalypse' comes from the Greek *apokalypsis*, meaning an unveiling or uncovering of truths normally hidden, and thus a kind of revelation or disclosure. The final book of the Bible in which the forthcoming apocalypse is presented, the Book of Saint John, is called Revelation (*'apocalypse'* in Greek). 'Revelation' is also the name of the Biblical Book which provides us with monster after monster: monsters with ten horns and seven heads rising from the sea, monsters made of several different animals, monsters with the ability to speak with forty-two mouths (Revelation, 13:1–11). 'All the great monstrosities, all of them are in Saint John', as Céline puts it.[101] But what about the modern monster called 'Zombie', the monster for our deeply apocalyptic times? And if the monster always calls forth the police, what does this tell us about the security politics of the Zombie apocalypse? Indeed, what is the politics of apocalypse?

There are no easy answers to these questions, no straightforward 'ideology of apocalyptic fantasy'.[102] Because the apocalyptic myth appears to be broad enough and expansive enough to act as a resource for the critique of power as well as its legitimation, it is often suggested that apocalypse can be a radically subversive concept.[103] Such a claim is often made as part of the 'secularization of Christian eschatology' thesis, which is itself a version of the Schmittian claim that all significant political concepts are secularized theological concepts.[104] Given its connotations of revolution as well as revelation – a 'new heaven, new earth' (Revelation 21:1) – 'apocalypse' has appealed to some as a powerful idea for revolutionaries to appropriate and dialectically subvert. 'Apocalypticism is by nature revolutionary', comments Jacob Taubes.[105] 'The apocalypse is part of our ideological baggage', notes Hans Magnus Enzensberger. He goes on:

You can call it a metaphor for the collapse of capitalism, which as we all know has been imminent for more than a century. We come up against it in the most varied shapes and guises: as warning finger and scientific forecast, collective fiction and sectarian rallying cry, as product of the leisure industry, as superstition, as vulgar mythology, as a riddle, a kick, a joke, a projection. It is ever present, but never 'actual': a second reality, an image that we construct for ourselves, an incessant production of our fantasy, the catastrophe in the mind … The idea of the apocalypse has accompanied utopian thought since its first beginnings, pursuing it like a shadow, like a reverse side that cannot be left behind: without catastrophe, no millennium, without apocalypse, no paradise.[106]

This is one reason why Marx's work has been described as articulating a 'passive style of apocalypticism', why Marx is said to have seen the European revolutions of the nineteenth century as the 'socioeconomic apocalypse' and why *Capital* is sometimes read as 'the revelation of last things'.[107] It is also, more generally, why the apocalyptic has had an appeal to some radicals and revolutionaries, not least as it has often been folded into related ideas about the atheist potential in the Bible or a messianic 'leap in the open air of history'.[108] On this view, the apocalyptic holds the promise of hope as well as terror, cranking up the expectation of an imminent end.[109]

There are, however, a number of reasons to be sceptical of the benefits of thinking of Marxism as a form of political apocalypticism, just as there are good reasons to doubt the 'secularization of Christian eschatology' thesis and equally good reasons to doubt the claim that all the significant political concepts are secularized theological concepts, as Hans Blumenberg argued at length.[110] For a start, the apocalyptic tends to affirm a concept of revolution as political moment rather than social process, and a political *end* moment at that, in the form of *The End*; it is interested in historical caesura rather than a shift in the mode of production and socio-economic order. This is why the genuinely apocalyptic literature is littered with reams of what Stephen O'Leary calls 'feverish calculation':

> attempts to coordinate time charts of universal history with biblical periods and contemporary historical events, deducing the age of the world and the date of its End through complex feats of addition, subtraction, and multiplication … aiming to prove the advent of the apocalypse in a particular year: 1260, 1843, 1914, 1988, 2000 … The list is seemingly endless.[111]

Such calculation and listing for predictive purposes is horribly out of place in any kind of revolutionary thought. So too is the theological or quasi-theological notion of The End as some kind of 'final' crisis of capitalism as a whole, as some kind of political event (the *political moment* of revolution), rather than a process lasting decades if not centuries and consisting of a far broader transformation of socio-economic relations (the *social process* of revolution).[112] Worse still, the ambiguous nature of the apocalyptic means that the demand for vengeance, justice and hope that is found in the apocalyptic is inescapably bound up with the fear, panic, terror and destruction.[113] This ambiguity means that although it appears to be 'equally at home at the service of radicals and reactionaries',[114] it is the reactionaries who dominate the scene (as witnessed, no less, in the aftermath of the 'apocalypse' of 11 September 2001, and with which we will begin the next chapter on the Devil). Why? Because it is the 'reactionary crackpots', as Boer dubs them, who are most willing and able to combine the language of emergency and disaster with an apocalyptic jeremiad on 'modern decadence', combining a historical pessimism with a cosmic optimism (the apocalypse-as-moral-cleansing).[115] Moreover, it is the reactionary crackpots who can best sustain the topos of evil and the mythic narrative of the intervention of power and authority to solve the problem of evil on earth (a project of defeating the Devil, no less); a topos of authority to match the topos of evil. They also have a better way of thinking about divine intervention and the notion of a redeemer – they like to 'think apocalyptically from above, from the powers that be', as Taubes puts it.[116] And we should add they usually operate in the same circles and 'think tanks' as security intellectuals.

Without wishing to denigrate the strenuous labours of those who have recently articulated a Leftist political theology, the reactionary crackpots simply do the apocalyptic far better than Marxism. Not only did Christianity consolidate the apocalyptic as a political genre but also, and more to the point, and this is the final reason to be sceptical of the narrative of apocalypse (including and especially 'Zombie apocalypse'), it did so in order to build in the minds of the people nothing less than sacred horror and a terror of sovereign power. After all, what is the ultimate 'revelation' offered by John in the Biblical book of the apocalypse? It is the same revelation that underpins the politics of security, namely that *one must live in utter fear* (1:17).

The apocalyptic is terror writ large, invoked by the ruling class and dominant groups in order to *validate the violence done to others*.[117] That is why Jacques Derrida cautions us about the apocalyptic tone of political language, despite his own wish to complicate the matter by also sometimes espousing that same tone. 'Let us imagine that there is *one* apocalyptic tone, a unity of the apocalyptic tone'. Whoever takes on the apocalyptic tone does so in order to communicate something. But what? What is revealed in the apocalypse? What is revealed is 'the truth', of course, and it is revealed in order 'to signify to you that it reveals the truth to you'.[118] Derrida has in mind those who claim access to the truth, and the fact is that in the current conjuncture those who lay claim to the apocalyptic tone, and the truth supposedly being revealed therein, are the theological and reactionary conductors of state power. The 'truth' revealed is rooted in the Bible narrative of the apocalypse as the story of fear:

> A proclivity to think and feel in polarities of 'good' versus 'evil'; to identify with the good and to purge the evil from oneself and one's world once and for all, demanding undivided unity before 'the enemy'; to feel that the good is getting victimized by the evil, which is diabolically overpowering; to expect some cataclysmic showdown in which, despite tremendous collateral damage (the destruction of the world as we know it), good must triumph in the near future with the help of some transcendent power and live forever in a fundamentally new world.[119]

The violent antagonism that ensues under the label 'apocalypse' is where the concept of emergency takes hold, which is precisely why emergency planning has come to the fore alongside and as part of the increasingly apocalyptic nature of political discourse. At the moment of the (Zombie) apocalypse, everything that *can* get played out under the logic of emergency *will* get played out and *must* get played out. The apocalyptic tone recently adopted in the politics of security and emergency, reinforced by the more general theological tone which we shall discuss at length in the following chapter, is the very tone which opens the space for the exercise of the violence embedded in the state's police power: for the state to kill with impunity for reasons of security but also, as we have seen, for the state to encourage us to kill for the very same reasons. To imagine the Zombie apocalypse, then, is to imagine the mobilization of security against an Enemy of All Mankind, to imagine the victory of the war power and to imagine the reassertion of order by the police power.

This is how the 'yet-to-come' nature of both the apocalypse and emergency planning converge. 'Apocalypse has become an event that is happening and not happening', as Susan Sontag put it in her analysis of AIDS. And as she should have added: *is always happening*, in the sense that we must constantly prepare for it. Apocalypse has become a long-running serial: 'not "Apocalypse Now" but "Apocalypse From Now On"'.[120] We are to live with the apocalypse, to expect the apocalypse, to prepare for the apocalypse and to mobilise for the apocalypse, just as we are to live with the emergency, expect the emergency, prepare for the emergency and mobilise for the emergency: not 'Emergency Now', but 'Emergency From Now On'. The emergency/apocalypse becomes a mode for the perpetual mobilisation of security, police powers put in place and then kept in place in permanent preparation for an emergency that never ends.

The Zombie is the figure that has come to occupy the centre ground of the apocalyptic tone in contemporary security and, as such, it is unsurprising that the Zombie is the figure that occupies so much of the time and energy of emergency planning. Presented to us as a very contemporary Enemy of All Mankind, we are expected to think of the Zombie as a Universal Adversary in search of our apocalyptic end, in a way that facilitates our acceptance of the unparalleled violence that the apocalypse both performs and permits. What we are to learn from the emergency planning, then, is that the Zombie must die or be somehow contained: subject to the war power and the police power. Perhaps we have a new definition of security: the containment of the living dead of capital. The problem we face is thus not the Zombie war but the insistence that we take sides in this war in order to kill all zombies; not the Zombie apocalypse but what is offered to us should we survive this apocalypse, which turns out to be the very powers with which we are expected to side in the Zombie war: the war power, the police power, and the reconstitution of capitalist order.

Chapter 3

'The ringleader of Rebellion': on the Devil

…it followeth, me thinks, very necessarily, that that which is thus said concerning Hell Fire, is spoken metaphorically; and that therefore there is a proper sense to bee enquired after … both of the *Place* of *Hell*, and the Nature of *Hellish Torments*, and *Tormenters*.

And first for the Tormenters, wee have their nature, and properties, exactly and properly delivered by the names of, *The Enemy*, or *Satan*; *The Accuser*, or *Diabolus*; *The Destroyer*, or *Abaddon*. Which significant names, Satan, Devill, Abaddon, set not forth to us any Individuall person, as proper names use to doe; but onely an office, or quality.

(Thomas Hobbes, *Leviathan*, 1651)

If I had plenty of time at my disposal and enough energy … I would write a vast, serious and well-documented opus several volumes long, entitled *The Metamorphoses of the Devil.*

(Henri Lefebvre, *Introduction to Modernity*, 1962)

'Today our Nation saw evil', commented George W. Bush on 11 September, 2001. Whatever term was used to describe the attackers, from 'terrorists' to 'killers', 'enemies' to 'criminals', 'murderers' to 'outlaws', the overarching theme was the wider metaphysical narrative of 'good versus evil'.[1] Any Adversary that would resort to such a form of attack must by definition be irredeemably evil. 'Evil is real, and it must be opposed', commented Bush in his State of the Union Address in 2002.[2] 'We are in a conflict between good and evil, and America will call evil by its name' he said six months later. 'By confronting evil and lawless regimes, we do not create a problem; we reveal a problem'.[3] This idea of 'flat evil', of acts for which 'the only motivation is evil', which emerge from a 'cult of evil', conducted by 'evil ones' and 'evildoers', and therefore the question of 'how we can best conduct a war against evil', was to be one of the key ideological tropes of the war on terror. The same trope would in turn feed into the *National Security Strategy*, 2002, which sought to 'rid the world of evil' and combat the 'evil designs of tyrants'.[4] In the 2002 State of the Union Address Bush also used a phrase which was to very quickly become widely used to describe the enemy: 'axis of evil'. In telling the story of how that Address came to be written, David Frum, the speechwriter who helped write it (and who with Richard Perle would also write a book called *An End to Evil*), claims that the first drafts described an 'axis of hatred', using the phrase 'axis' in order to reference the historical fight against the 'axis' powers of WWII. But in a series of edits Bush incorporated the theological language that he wanted to use. 'He reached right into the Psalms for that word' says Frum, and the 'axis of hatred' became the 'axis of evil'.[5] Bush was clearly angling to be the 'President of good and evil', comments Peter Singer, who also calculates that in the two years following the attacks of 11 September, 2001, Bush would use the term 'evil' over a thousand times – 914 times as a noun and 182 times in adjectival form.[6]

'The categories of good and evil are no longer viable objects of thought', notes Adam Phillips.[7] Yet the categories have nonetheless remained part of the political vocabulary and indeed have flourished in the twenty-first century, in the same way that other categories which one would have hoped would by now have disappeared, such as 'contagion' discussed in the previous chapter. Indeed, the category 'evil' has flourished even among critical theorists. Such theorists usually start with Kant – 'the point of departure' for any analysis of evil 'can only be Kantian'[8] notes one recent commentator – but will often work its way through Nietzsche to Arendt, taking in Levinas and Freud, usually concentrating on issues such as the Holocaust though now adding '9/11' to the list of issues addressed. But to understand the role of 'evil' we need a discussion that is a little more diverse, especially if we want to use it to make sense of the idea of the Universal Adversary. For much as the idea of evil might in this context be attributed to Bush's own desire to conduct the 'war on terror' on the grounds of some kind of political theology in search of 'Infinite Justice',[9] and whatever we might note about the political leaders before him who referred to the 'evil empire' against which America must fight, there are more general issues at stake. Such issues become even more pressing when we recall the extent to which Bush and other Western leaders made great claims about not wishing to 'demonize' Islam, and continue to do so, and yet nevertheless slip easily into the discourse of 'evil perpetrators' of terror on the one hand and 'innocent victims' on the other.

It is pertinent to note that despite being a formally secular state, the United States has long been the land of religiosity *par excellence*, as Marx and a whole host of other writers noted in the nineteenth century. 'Religion, which among the Americans never directly takes part in the government of society, must be considered as the first of their political institutions', noted Alexis de Tocqueville in 1835, and nothing much has changed. As a consequence, Tocqueville added, 'Christianity rules without obstacles, with the consent of all'.[10] As well as underpinning the apocalyptic imagination we noted in the previous chapter, this culturally entrenched belief system underpins the imagined political community that is America: the national myth is of a 'redeemer nation' founded like a Biblical 'city on a hill', a 'chosen people' with 'manifest destiny'. The long-standing convention that has American Presidents closing their speeches with 'God Bless America' registers and confirms this culturally entrenched belief system, reconciling the formally secular state with the belief system in question. (Yet even allowing for this convention, Bush took it one step further: 'May God *continue* to bless America'.)[11] The Presidential injunction rehearses a belief widely shared in the US: that as much as 'God watches over the affairs of men',[12] he would appear to watch over the affairs of American men more than any others. This is why 'American values' were regarded as so important to the war: 'the liberty we prize is not America's gift to the world [but] God's gift to humanity'.[13] Secretary of State Condoleezza Rice picked up the theme: 'The United States and Israel share much in common', commented Rice at the Israel Public Affairs Committee's Annual Policy Conference in 2005. 'We both affirm the innate freedom and dignity of every human life, not as prizes that people confer to one another, but as divine gifts of the Almighty'.[14] Security and theology go hand in hand: by delivering liberty and security to the world, America is doing nothing less than God's work. 'This work continues, the story goes on', Bush commented in his Inaugural Address in 2001, adding the rhetorical flourish that 'an angel still rides in the whirlwind and directs this storm'.[15]

In this storm looms another figure: the Devil. Surveys have shown time and again that between 60% and 73% of Americans believe in the existence of the Devil,[16] a much higher figure than found in comparable Western states. 'Satan will not go away', notes W. Scott Poole, of American political discourse. Quite the opposite: 'The Devil plays a more significant role in our public vocabulary today than at any time since the seventeenth century'. Or as Robert Munchembled puts it: 'at the end of the twentieth century, American society was deeply imbued with a fear of the devil'.[17] Any nation that sees itself as blessed by God and as carrying out a divine mission is especially prone to demonize its enemies, and one finds that the state that regards itself as possessing a manifest destiny has a long tradition of suspecting that those who oppose 'the American way' must be in league with the Devil.[18] Groups that have been identified as working in league with the Devil include indigenous peoples, communists, socialists, anarchists, trade unionists, blacks, Jews and homosexuals, but individuals have also often been singled out as similarly aligned, including George III, Napoleon, Hitler, Mussolini, Stalin and every other Soviet leader, Moshe Dayan, Anwar el-Sadat, Moammar Qadhafi, King Juan Carlos, Sun Myung Moon, and, of course, Saddam Hussein and Osama Bin Laden.[19] Hence in retelling the story of the comments made about the 'evil ones' by Bush in the first days after the attack, David Frum notes that 'in a country where almost two-thirds of the population believes in the existence of the devil, Bush was identifying Osama bin Laden and his gang as literally satanic'.[20]

Literally satanic? The sound of the falling towers was 'like the roar of the devil', Bush commented.[21] It was a view that permeated the higher echelons of the regime. 'On a warm September morning, America encountered the darker demons of our new world', claimed Condoleezza Rice.[22] General William Boykin, the man specifically charged with the job of capturing Bin Laden, gave a sermon in Oregon. He commented that the enemy was not just Bin Laden himself: 'the enemy is a guy named Satan'. 'Terrorists in general', he said, came from 'the principalities of darkness' and were in essence 'demonic'.[23] Lieutenant-Colonel Gareth Brandl, fighting in Iraq, commented that 'the marines that I have had wounded over the past five months have been attacked by a faceless enemy …But the enemy has got a face. He's called Satan. He lives in Falluja. And we're going to destroy him'.[24] Novelists followed suit: parading his patriotism by declaring that 'the United States is God's most extreme and heartfelt experiment', Normal Mailer concluded that the 'best explanation' for 9/11 must therefore be that 'the Devil won a great battle that day'. Until a better explanation can be given, Mailer insists that we have to believe that 'this was the Devil's big day'. 'Yes – Satan was the pilot who guided those planes into that ungodly denouement'.[25]

Towards the end of his 1969 lectures on the idea of Satan in the seventeenth century, Christopher Hill comments that by the early nineteenth century 'antichrist disappeared into the nonconformist underworld, ultimately into the world of cranks'.[26] Hill had obviously not foreseen that far from ending up in the 'underworld' the cranks who believe in the Antichrist might end up holding the reins of global power, often alongside the same reactionary crackpots we met in the previous chapter. For judging by comments from Bush and his military leaders (and maybe even right down to the torturers themselves, who reportedly ordered prisoners to 'thank Jesus' that they were still left alive[27]) it would appear that the political theology of security underpinning the 'war on terror' was lifted straight out of the textbook of Christian demonology. Indeed, one gets the general theme from some of the imagery from the immediate days after 9/11. 'Images of Tuesday's terrorist attacks have been captured in thousands of photographs', reported the website Urban Legends.

> Some of the pictures are horrific, some poignant, and some gut-wrenching, but viewers have written in to newspapers and television stations, saying that that they see an even more haunting image in the smoke billowing from the World Trade Center. Viewers said that in two specific instances, in a photo taken by an Associated Press photographer, and in a video by CNN, they can clearly identify the eyes, nose, mouth and horns of a devil in the black and gray smoke.[28]

The same CNN images were seen time and again, and were the spring-board for the appearance of countless photographs of 'Satan in the Smoke' (Figures 3.1 and 3.2).

Figure 3.1 'Satan In the Smoke'
Source: © Mark D. Phillips/markdphillips.com[29]

Figure 3.2 'Devil Face in Smoke of 9/11'
Source: © ChristianMedia/ChristianMedia.US

The internet is also replete with video footage of the same kinds of images.[30]

'Disneyland for Demons'. This was how the events were described by the organisation called Christian Media:

> You may have heard of the pictures taken of the World Trade Center while it was burning, in which the smoke formed the face of Satan. Some of these photos can be seen on videos of the blast. I have included an animation from another website that shows the same demon face. Then the second set of photos are yellow and red and the shape indicates that it is from exploding/burning jet fuel. You can also see lots of debris falling from the result of the impact and explosions...
>
> People may ask themselves, why would there be faces in the smoke, and also, why so many? I believe I know the answer to that question.
>
> Demons can feel and experience things like we can. Consider that picture of the demon ... that has its head sticking up like it is on some kind of rollercoaster ride. An act of hatred and violence is a thrill ride for a demon, they not only participate, in so far as influencing some-one to commit acts of violence, they get a thrill during the act. Demons knew what was going to happen in New York and they gathered there to jump in at the point of the impact, like a human jumping onto a moving train to have a thrill.

Most acts of violence are not as huge as this one, or last as long, or kill this many people, so this was Disneyland for demons. There was the planes impacting and exploding and people jumping, and then the buildings falling down and killing over 2,000 people in the process. This was a dream come true for demons.[31]

A few years after noting that religion is in fact the most fundamental of American political institutions, Alexis de Tocqueville added that 'religious madness is very common there', and on the basis of what we have said so far in this chapter we might be inclined to agree with him.[32] But as Marx points out, religion needs to be understood and criticised in terms of material conditions, however irrational some of its ideas appear to be. To understand what is going on with all this talk of the Devil, then, we need to start with the political invention of the Devil, grasp the idea that the Devil was invented as the Enemy of All Mankind, and situate this invention in the wider context of the material trends and conflicts concerning classes, peoples and states.[33] We need to therefore consider the Devil and contemporary capitalism and, at the same time, the role the Devil plays in the mobilisation of security; a kind of political theology of security organised around the figure of the Devil. Following through on such considerations might help us understand what is at stake in the concept of the Universal Adversary. Perhaps the Universal Adversary is a new articulation of one of the oldest figures of enmity, the very first Enemy of All Mankind?

War on evil I: the political invention of the Devil

The Devil was a fairly unobtrusive presence during the first Christian millennium, notes Munchembled. Anything that now goes by the name 'Satanism' was far from coherent. One reason for this is because the Bible contains many different versions and stories about Satan and the Devil, as Henry Ansgar Kelly has shown in great detail.[34] But at some point the figure of the Devil as we now know it started being (re-)invented in such a way that suited the rising powers in Europe. This was 'a movement from the top down', notes Robert Munchembled, and it was to transform the history of Europe and then America.[35]

In the Old Testament, the 'satan' is one of God's angels. Far from being 'evil' or even an opponent of God, the 'satan' is a member of the heavenly council and one of God's obedient servants: an 'angel' in the form of a messenger (the word 'angel' translates the Hebrew term for 'messenger' into the Greek 'angelos') whose characteristics are so close to God as to be identical with him.[36] Part of the role of this messenger is to act as a kind of adversary: in the Old Testament, 'satan' derives from the Hebrew 'har-Shatan', meaning 'the Adversary', though this was translated into Greek as diabolos, meaning 'Devil'. 'Devil', derives from the Greek diabolos like the

German *Teufel* and Spanish *diabolo*, and has connotations of 'slanderer', 'perjurer' or 'adversary'; translated literally, *diabolos* means 'one who throws something across one's path', and according to some writers 'Devil' first emerged in the translation of the Old Testament into Greek in the third and second centuries B.C.E. to render the Hebrew *satan*, 'adversary', 'obstacle' or 'opponent'. The later 'anti-Christ' stems from the Greek 'anti-Christos' meaning adversary of Christ.[37]

In other words, the early meaning of terms such as 'Satan' and 'Devil' lies in their adversarial role. Yet the picture is complicated because what was to eventually develop within Christian Europe as 'the Adversary' involved a huge development from the Old Testament to the New Testament and then to the consolidation of Christianity within the wider European state system.

In the Old Testament, God is responsible for the entire cosmos and thus forms 'light and darkness, good and evil' (Isaiah 45:7). Any 'satanic' messenger is by no means malevolent, and the adversarial role of such messengers is often to protect a person. In Numbers, for example, Balaam decides to go precisely where God had told him not to. 'God's anger was kindled because he went; and the angel of the Lord took his stand in the way as his *satan*' [or 'adversary', in some translations] (Numbers 22:22). Even when the satan appears malevolent, it is with God's permission. In the Book of Job, for example, when Job is confronted by the satan, the latter's role is to act as an adversary in the form of challenges for Job. Such challenges involve finding ways to destroy Job's family and possessions and to smote Job with running sores from head to toe. This is done not only with God's permission but more or less under God's command; the satan is an angel in alliance with God and operating as God's servant. In the Book of Job, notes Norman Habel, '*Satan* is not a proper name but a title meaning "the adversary". Here Satan is not equivalent to the devil of later Christian theology, but functions like a prosecuting attorney in a court of law'.[38] As Jeffrey Russell says, 'the Old Testament God is powerfully benevolent, but he had a shadow side, and that shadow is part of the background of the Hebrew Satan'.[39] What appears there is, in effect, a monotheistic religion with a dualistic God: the Hebrew God must be omnipotent, yet must also be somehow 'responsible' for the evil spirit, the key task of which is to be an adversarial figure with the function of accusing and opposing.

This adversarial role is precisely what gets developed and transformed in the New Testament and then the first Christian millennium, albeit inflected and tweaked through the Essenes, the Gnostic tradition, and Zoroastrianism. It is important to note that the main gospels of the New Testament were written by followers of Jesus who had lived through the Jewish rebellion against Rome of 66 C.E. and the subsequent 'Jewish war'. This is the 'social history of Satan' mapped out by Elaine Pagels and others, which points to the political invention of the Devil as we know it. As Pagels puts it, 'we cannot fully understand the New Testament gospels until we recognize that they are, in this sense, wartime literature'.[40] As she goes on to show, dissidents began to increasingly invoke the *satan* to characterize their opponents, in the process transforming this angel into a far grander and far more malevolent figure. This involved simultaneously suppressing paganism and offering a Christian twist to a variety of myths and traditions found among the pagans, the Gnostics and the Manicheans.[41] According to Munchembled, Christianity was successful in achieving this 'because it adopted one of the most important narrative models of the Near East, that is, the cosmic myth of the primordial combat between the gods, in which it was the human condition that was at stake'. Munchembled continues:

> This version may be summarized as follows: a god rebelling against Yahweh made earth an extension of his empire in order to reign there by the power of sin and of death. 'God of this world', as he was called by St Paul, he was opposed by the son of the Creator, Christ, in the most mysterious episode in Christian history, the Crucifixion, in which both defeat and victory combined. The function of Christ in this battle, which would end only at the end of time, was to be the potential liberator of humanity, in the face of Satan, his chief opponent.[42]

These ideas about opposition and harm get increasingly affirmed to the point where they give rise to God and Satan in complete opposition: one 'cannot drink of the cup of the Lord and the cup of demons', as Paul's First Letter to the Corinthians has it (1 Corinthians 10:21). There then appeared what Kelly calls 'the most significant retro-fitting in the history of Satan', namely 'a thoroughgoing re-interpretation of the Satan of the New Testament, identified with the various satanic figures of the Old Testament, as a *rebel against God*'.[43]

Out of this emerged a fully developed demonology focused on the figure of Satan. 'The satan' becomes less and less one of God's faithful servants and more and more what he becomes for Christianity by the end of the first millennium: God's rival, God's antagonist, God's Adversary. What was created by the development of Christianity in the West was a set of claims and assumptions about not just *a* satan of the kind who tests and persecutes Job in the Old Testament, but *Satan*; not just *a* devil but *the Devil*; not just an enemy, but a *Demonic Enemy*; not just *an* adversary but a *Universal Adversary* with which there can be nothing but absolute enmity. The 'adversarial' nature of Satan transforms in the New Testament into a struggle between God and the rebel Angel who has become a fundamentally evil enemy, now simply called 'Satan' or, increasingly, 'the Devil'. As liar and sinner, in his association with flesh, death and darkness (the 'Prince of Darkness'), and with his hatred of God and humanity, the Devil came to be held responsible for the downfall of the human race.

In effect, the Devil was understood as having a vital role in the history of mankind, as nothing less than the Universal Adversary of Christian power (the Universal Church and the Universal Holy Roman Empire). This is why a text such as Daniel Defoe's *History of the Devil* is replete with comments on the universal character of the Devil's adversarial nature: standing for 'universal degeneration', seeking the 'universal destruction of Mankind', encouraging 'universal crime', and seeking to institute a new 'universal monarchy'.[44] More importantly, it is also why one of the epithets that came to be used to describe the Devil was *hostis humani generis* or the Enemy of All Mankind. The Devil is 'the Enemy of Mankind', claimed the 1484 Papal bull, *Summis Desiderantes Affectibus*. The Devil and his army 'are wicked, lying, false, enemies of the human race', Jean Bodin put it a century later. 'There are Devils and Witches, the Scripture asserts, and experience confirms, that they are Common Enemies of Mankind', leading colonist Increase Mather put it yet another century later. Or as the official exorcism ritual of the seventeenth-century Church articulated it: 'Hear then and obey, Satan, attacker of the faith, *enemy of the human race*'.[45]

The theological identification of the Devil with the Enemy of All Mankind is crucial, notes Dan Edelstein, because it implies that the Enemy is so diabolical that it threatens each and every soul.[46] The struggle between God and the Devil is one in which human beings are expected to take sides, not least because the struggle is one which has grand theological, political and historical implications. It is, to put it bluntly, a cosmic war and universal struggle. As C. S. Lewis observes, at the heart of Christianity is the belief that the universe is at war, a civil war formed out of rebellion, and humans are living in rebel territory.[47] At the heart of Christianity is a 'martial exhortation'.[48] This is why the talk is always of 'Satan, God's enemy', or 'God's and man's mortal and sworn enemy', or 'Satan, our enemy', or 'Christ and Satan are enemies', and why we are told that 'the day when the Lord will deliver us from the hand of all our Enemies' is the day when he delivers us 'from the hand of Satan'.[49] 'The devil was God's enemy in the hearts of men', Robinson Crusoe explains to the savage Friday in Defoe's novel.[50] This is a war with the whole world as its battleground but which also takes place in the hearts and minds of human beings; a war which therefore permeates all human institutions. It is a war over the nature of Universal order. Such a war interprets social forces and human relations in supernatural terms, a technique of power through which the fundamental enmity between God and the Devil demonizes the Enemy: if God and the Devil are enemies and I am a true believer in God, then my enemies must be in league with the Devil. The Enemy, in other words, is in league with and constitutes part of the Universal Adversary.[51] The war between God/Christ and the Devil/Satan is at the heart of the struggle for power at a crucial time in the history of the West and comes to occupy a central role in the Christian-European psyche and culture.

Central to that role is the political theology of heresy. Norman Cohn suggests that up to the eleventh century there were no heretical sects in the territories of the Christian west:

> But from then onwards they began to develop along the trade routes from the Balkans and to proliferate in the developing urban civilizations of northern Italy, France, and the Rhine valley; finding their adherents first among the nobles and the clergy, and then among the merchants and artisans. The authorities, both ecclesiastical and secular, reacted sharply to these signs of organized dissent.

In the context of this struggle over heresy, groups of human beings were increasingly castigated as Devil-worshippers.[52] This problem of heresy reached its crescendo in the twelfth century, especially between the Third and Fourth Lateran Councils in 1179 and 1215. The Inquisition, founded after the Albigensian Crusade against the 'heretical' Cathars (1209–29), intensified the search for heretics and a century later Pope John XII issued three anti-Satanic bulls between 1318 and 1326 justifying the persecution of the Templars. At the same time, during the thirteenth century the apparatus for the persecution of Jews and lepers – the latter inherently associated with heresy – was fully worked out. A century later this expanded to include a search for witches, figures who were thought to have voluntarily entered into Satan's service and become pawns in his strategy, to which we shall turn below. By the sixteenth century religious conflict saw both Protestantism and Catholicism enlist the Devil in their causes, though both also accused the other of Devil-worship: the Inquisition incriminated Protestant heretics while Protestants denounced the Pope as the Antichrist and castigated the Catholic Church as the Church of the Devil and the Synagogue of Satan. The term 'Synagogue of Satan' was taken from the book of Revelation (2: 9) and also used by both Protestants and Catholics to describe Jewish places of worship.[53]

From the twelfth to the sixteenth century, then, a two-fold myth was invented and slowly disseminated. First, a myth of a terrible power reigning over an immense demonic army; and second, the idea that within the sinner lies some kind of evil beast inextricably linked to the power in question.[54] (The representation of the Devil as a beast and even as The Beast is a reminder of the ways in which workers, Indians, Africans, Arabs, criminals and paupers were all also castigated for their beastly lawlessness and untameable qualities, as we noted in previous chapters.) At the heart of this two-fold myth is the war between God and the Devil, Good and Evil, Sovereign and Beast.

This Manichean world view found its way to America through two routes and two versions of Christianity. On the one hand, Protestant sects took from the main Protestant thinkers the view that Christ and Satan are involved in a cosmic war for mastery over the world: Luther held that 'the Devil and God are two enemies' and the imagery of the warfare between them saturated Calvin's writings, as Max Weber and others have shown. Protestant sects combined this world view with elements of the apocalyptic tradition, which flourished under the colonial power exercised by the Puritans. On the other hand, the Protestant sects were joined in America by explorers from Catholic states who brought with them a profound belief in the Devil, the practices of the Inquisition and the well-established mechanisms for attacking heretics.[55] Hence 'when New England ministers addressed their congregations in sermons and treatises, one of their objectives was to educate layfolk in the constant threat posed by the Devil ... In so doing, the clergy drew on a demonological tradition common to Protestants and Catholics alike'.[56]

Finding the Devil among indigenous peoples was therefore one of the central 'discoveries' made by colonising states, Protestant and Catholic alike. As Anthony Barker puts it:

> Devil-worship, and diabolic interventions, were perhaps the most widely reported aspect of the newly encountered non-European societies in the early seventeenth century. From the Lapps to the Samoyeds, to the Hottentots and Indonesians, from the American Indians to the Chinese and Japanese, there was no society, north, south, east west, which was not labelled [as being] under diabolical influence.[57]

For the colonisers, the Indians were not only monstrous, pagan cannibals, they were also in league with the Devil. Just as more and more thinkers were beginning to discuss the idea of a 'universal humanity' (in the form of a universal human nature, morality, law, or a combination of all of these and more) which might include the Indians, so at the very same time ways were found to discuss the Indians' fundamental *inhumanity*. The accusation of 'Devil-worshipping' was one such way, easily and quickly used as a direct mechanism for the subjugation of indigenous peoples.[58] In *The Wonders of the Invisible World* (1692), for example, leading Puritan colonist Cotton Mather makes various 'observations' concerning 'the Nature, the Number, and the Operations of the Devils'. The main focus of the book is the figure of the Witch (Mather had written the book in response to Governor Phips's request for a report on the Salem Witch trials), but here we can note that for Mather the colonisers had come to a country in which the Devil was already everywhere:

> What cause have we to bless God, for our preservation from the *Devils wrath*, in this which may too reasonably be called the *Devils World*! While we are in *this present evil world*, We are continually surrounded

with swarms of those Devils, who make this *present world*, become so *evil*. What a wonder of Mercy is it, that no *Devil* could ever yet make a prey of us! ... We are poor, Travellers in a World, which is as well the Devils *Field*, as the Devils *Gaol*; a World in every Nook whereof, the Devil is encamped, with *Bands of Robbers*.[59]

Ten years later, in *Magnalia Christi Americana* (1702), intended as a history of New England 'under the aspect of Eternity', Mather claims that the Devil had 'peopled America by sending Indians into it'.

Though we know not *when* nor *how* those Indians first became inhabitants of this mighty continent, yet we may guess that probably the devil decoyed those miserable savages hither, in hopes that the gospel of the Lord Jesus Christ would never come here to destroy or disturb his *absolute empire* over them.[60]

The Enemy thus took the form of demons in the shape of armed Indians as well as the colonizing forces of other states.

Such an Enemy was perfect for defining the Christian community and allowed the colonisers to treat the Indian wars as one phase in the much greater universal war between Satan and Christ.[61] More tellingly, this Enemy appeared as a kind of antihuman part of a humanity increasingly seen as universal. As an irredeemably Satanic other, the Indians could be understood as a *human* and yet *evil Enemy of Humanity*, and the Indian wars as part of nothing less than a war against the Enemy of All Mankind.

The Devil therefore shaped the American religious and popular imagination from the outset, including the revolutionary ideology that emerged in the eighteenth century and then well beyond that too, right up to the events of 11 September, 2001, and beyond. The Devil is 'America's silent partner and the key to its secret history', notes W. Scott Poole. 'At almost every crucial turning point in American history, at every moment of transformation in American social and cultural life, Satan has embodied, structured, and legitimized, America's self-identity',[62] to the extent that more or less every war fought by America thereafter would have a familiar hue: a crusade against the Devil and his agents. As well as Native Americans being massacred for fighting on the side of Satan, women would be slaughtered as having carnal knowledge of the Devil, pirates would be executed for acting out the 'Devil's anarchy', communism would have to be fought as 'Satan in action' (as *Time* magazine once put it),[63] and, eventually, terrorism would be seen as the new incarnation of this very old evil. Once the Devil had been invented there was no end to the enemies that could be described as in league with him; no end to the mobilisation of security in the name of God and the Good. The Enemy was everywhere; the Adversary was Universal.

Once he was invented in this form, the Devil could be found anywhere – literally *anywhere*: 'a French judge warned people about demonically possessed apples in 1602'[64] – but especially within the political community and in the form of anything seen as different or understood as threatening. The consequence of an 'everywhere war' fought in the bodies and souls of anything was the elevation of the Devil to the status of the leader of a vast army with power and influence at every level of human experience.[65] So vast was this army that it could include the 'invisible crowd'[66] of the dead: early modern thought gave serious consideration to the number of devils that might exist among the dead; the Devil could enter corpses and reanimate them enough to come back and wander among the living (hence when the Zombie enters western consciousness it is often in connection with the Devil);[67] and the rising of the dead was deeply connected to the apocalypse but was also, more than anything, evidence that the Devil was at work.[68] But as well as a war over the dead, the war took the form of a battle over living bodies and souls. The Devil was the source of mankind's 'inner demons', and so the pursuit of the Adversary and his accomplices would increasingly turn inward, in the form of the police of morality. The security guards of the realm always like to double up as policemen of the soul, and it is around the figure of the Devil that the police of morals, the consolidation of state power and the technologies of the self could come together so that temptation and desire of all kinds (sexual, ethical, political) could be managed.[69] In the name of bourgeois security and liberal order, desires have to be proper, temptations thwarted, consciences clean, pleasures pure and behaviour saintly. Each of our souls becomes a little church within which the Devil seeks to exercise his power, notes Michel Foucault. Each of our souls is thus reconstructed as a battlefield, adds Silvia Federici.[70] Each of our souls becomes the terrain on which security wars get played out.

Such wars constitute the heart of what historians have called a 'persecutory imagination' and 'persecuting society'.[71] The crucial point to note about this persecution is that it not only took on a secular form but actually needed secular foundations in order to be successful. And yet at the same time it is also the case that the consolidation of the modern state organised around the logic of security thrived on the persecution that became possible with the invention of the Devil. It was easy enough in the early stages of absolute monarchical authority for the royal power to use the fiction of the Devil 'to cow its enemies and to justify its extortions', notes Messadié. But the Devil was also a useful fiction used against the subjects, for the idea of the Devil encouraged the people to see the state as the very hallmark of security and sovereignty.[72] To put it another way: the viability of the state and its security measures could be dramatically enhanced if the state claimed responsibility for co-ordinating the war on the Devil as the Enemy of All Mankind as well as the Enemy of God. The supposed threat of evil and the fear of the Devil among us thus became a crucial weapon in the consolidation of sovereignty and the reform of Christian states and societies: the Devil could become an instrument of political power as much as anything else.

In this way the Devil came to play a central role in the structures of security through which the modern state and capital would operate. First, through the advance of political, judicial and administrative centralisation; second, through the formalisation of juridical power and the enhancement of this power through new methods of punishment and repression, most notably torture but eventually also including the prison; third, through the attempt to discipline as well as punish, and thus through the growing efforts of the state to police society; fourth, through the increasing political control over the church or, where the issue was not 'control', a growing rapport with the church over matters previously dealt with by the ecclesiastical authorities. All of this cohered with the development of doctrines such as reason of state.[73] The political invention of the Devil meant that the state and its security measures could be offered as the main line of defence against the Devil and everything for which the Devil was said to stand. If the Enemies of God could be condemned as Enemies of State then it took little effort to condemn the Enemies of State as equally Enemies of God; *Protego ergo Obligo* had an important theological twist: Protection from Satan, therefore Obedience.

The demonology that was developed and refined through the fifteenth and sixteenth centuries therefore went hand in hand with the new science of power and the new logic of security that emerged at the same time, crystallizing around the figure of a Universal Adversary of mankind. We can explore this a little further through the figure that has been described as the most 'remarkable example of how the concept of "evil" has been deployed in Western culture',[74] namely the Witch. In doing so we can also open the space for an exploration of the witch-hunt as a political technology of security.

War on evil II: the witch-hunt

What is a witch-hunt? The question has no easy answer. On the one hand, 'witch-hunt' is a seventeenth-century term referring to the hunting of vast numbers of women who were regarded as working for the Devil and thus seen as a threat to social order, who were then captured, often tortured, always prosecuted and usually executed. On the other hand, 'witch-hunt' is a term that became popular in debates about security in the twentieth century, first with reference to the hunt for communists but then broadened out to describe the hunt for any individuals or groups who might be the Enemy within. The witch-hunt in both its historical and contemporary instantiations (and the rest of this chapter shall deliberately oscillate between these two instantiations) thus raises fundamental questions about supposed enemies of security; as we shall also see, such enemies turn out to be enemies of capital.

In 1484 Pope Innocent VIII issued a Papal bull, *Summis Desiderantes Affectibus*. The bull held that 'many persons of both sexes, unmindful of their own salvation and straying from the Catholic Faith, have abandoned themselves to devils, incubi and succubi'. These same persons were said to have been 'committing and perpetrating the foulest abominations and filthiest excesses to the deadly peril of their own souls', bringing about 'terrible and piteous pains and sore diseases, both internal and external; they hinder men from performing the sexual act and women from conceiving, whence husbands cannot know their wives nor wives receive their husbands; over and above this, they blasphemously renounce that Faith which is theirs by the Sacrament of Baptism'. How has this happened? It has come about 'at the instigation of the Enemy of Mankind'.

The Papal bull was written partly by two Professors of Theology, Heinrich Kramer and Jacob Sprenger, who two years later published *Malleus Maleficarum* [*Hammer of the Witches*], which in turn reproduces and extends the arguments in the bull. This book is frequently described as the definitive book of the early witch-hunt, and with its roots in the Papal bull and its authors being Professors of Theology it is easy to think of the book in terms of the common misunderstanding of the witch-hunt: that the persecution of witches is a sign of a pre-Enlightened, superstitious and religious world long gone. Yet far from being the product of religious frenzy, the hunt for witches was a politically organised and legally ordained campaign of terror against an Adversary regarded as fundamentally demonic. Even an early and deeply theological text such as *Malleus Maleficarum* hints at this by positing the witch as threat to *law* as well as God and Church and moving from the question of whether witches really do exist to arguing for a legal framework in which they can be tried and punished. The move is an important one because it helped set the stage for the intensification of witch-hunting a hundred years later under the auspices of the early modern state. Most of the trials and executions of witches were conducted by secular not religious courts, but what would also emerge from the episode of the witch-hunt is the willingness on the part of the state to mobilise citizen-subjects around the belief that those whom one distrusts or fears could somehow be the agents of an alternative so profoundly threatening that the only option is a universal war to defeat them. The point of the original Witch was that she – and the fact that the vast majority of persecutions were of 'the Devil in the shape of a woman' or 'the handmaidens of the Devil'[75] is a reminder that the police power is an inherently patriarchal power and security is a remarkably masculinist concept – functioned as *internal* Enemy who could to all intents and purposes look like a member of the community. What followed was the mass production and punishment of a form of deviancy known as 'witchcraft', a process organised by and through the state at the very moment that the state was being grounded on the logic of security. Let us explore this a little through the work of one of the first significant theorists of absolute state power, Jean Bodin, and in the process try to develop some of the points made in the previous section.

Bodin is often regarded as 'the undisputed intellectual master of the later sixteenth century', 'one of the most energetic minds of his age'.[76] Such a reputation rests heavily on the political theory of sovereignty he presents in *The Six Books of the Republic* (1576), often taken to be the first attempt at systematically outlining a theory of the state as an 'absolute and perpetual power'.[77] To illustrate how absolute this power needs to be we can briefly note the argument Bodin makes concerning treason in Book II. Bodin claims that someone is guilty of treason not only if they kill the prince, but also if they attempt to kill him by taking up arms against him, or if they counsel someone else to do so, or even if they simply wish to do so. This applies even to those suffering under tyrannical forms of rule, and applies to those thinking about killing magistrates or public officials and not just the prince himself.

> It would be a waste of time to meet point by point the trivial arguments of those who maintain the opposite view. One does not argue with the man who doubts if there is a God, one merely subjects him to the merited penalties of the law. They should be treated in the same way who have called in question a principle so obvious, and have maintained in print that the subject can justly take up arms against a tyrannical prince, and compass his death by any means in their power.

For Bodin, then, 'the subject is never justified in any circumstances in attempting anything against his sovereign prince, however evil and tyrannical he may be'.[78] What this means in turn is that insurrection or rebellion of the people is never justified, but also that 'factions and parties are dangerous' because they form the basis of treason and sedition.[79] The *Six Books* is thus a fairly comprehensive justification of the absolute power of the sovereign and the absolute obedience of the subject.

Four years after the publication of the *Six Books*, Bodin published *On the Demon-Mania of Witches* (1580), which we have already cited earlier for its definition of the Devil as the Enemy of All Mankind. The book was very quickly translated into Latin and Italian and ran to several editions in French. Now, the *Six Books* and the *Demon-Mania* are often treated entirely separately in the contemporary academy. On the one hand, when Bodin is taught as a figure in the history of political thought it is usually as a key bridge between Machiavelli and Hobbes, helping to pave the way for an argument about the state as an absolute authority; treated in this way, his later book on witches is often ignored or dismissed as 'strange and repulsive'.[80] On the other hand, he is often regarded as an important figure in the history of witch-hunting, with the book on witches seen as a significant step up from the *Malleus Maleficarum*; treated in this way, his earlier book on the state is often ignored as merely political theory and of no relevance to the witch-hunt. In fact, as Stuart Clark argues, 'the Bodin who sought to establish the first principles of absolute sovereignty is in fact on common ground with the Bodin who urged the juridical destruction of witches'.[81] The *Six Books* is in many ways a thoroughly religious work, not least in its claims about the Prince being made in the image of God, the great sovereign God and the majesty of kings and princes. Likewise, the *Demon-Mania* is in many ways a thoroughly political work, not least in its demand for state power to be exercised against the Witch. Bodin's two books therefore need to be read together, not least for what they tell us about demonology and the politics of the witch-hunt more generally. For the Witch in Bodin's 'demonology' occupies the same space as those who challenge order and security in his 'political theory'. The Witch and the rebel constitute one kind of enemy and thus one kind of threat to security. And because witches are 'wicked, lying, false, enemies of the human race',[82] the enemies of order and security come to be understood in the same way. We therefore need to read the *Six Books* and the *Demon-Mania* together, not just to see how the former is religious just as the latter is political, but because reading them together opens up the space to explore the centrality of political demonology to one of the first fundamental statements of political theory in the West. In so doing we can unravel the ways in which the witch-hunt comes to be acted out as part of the spectacle of security and the ways in which this might connect back to the contemporary debate with which this chapter began: a political theology of security organised around the figure of the Devil.

In the *Demon-Mania* the central issue is the crimes committed by witches. These are the same crimes as those committed against the combined power of divine and natural law on which Bodin places so much weight in the *Six Books*. At the same time, he had also argued in the *Six Books* that it is religion which preserves the state by securing the obedience of subjects, not least by inculcating a 'reverence for the magistrates'. This points to one of the key issues in the *Demon-Mania*: the intense enmity between the Witch and the Magistrate, which is itself a micro version of the intense enmity between Satan and the Godly sovereign: 'Satan holds nothing in higher recommendation than to entice Princes'. Hence the magistracy envisaged as the key agency in the war against demons in the *Demon-Mania* is the same magistracy envisaged as the key agency in the war against disorder in the *Six Books*. For Bodin, the Witch's power could be disarmed by confronting them with the Godly power of the public authority in the form of the magistrate. Witchcraft thereby gets aligned with crimes such as treason, which we have already noted is for Bodin a heinous crime and which we should also note was considered a crime for which emergency measures and brutal treatment were needed, a point to which I return below. For Bodin, the Witch's 'treason' is a crime against both human law and divine law. It is therefore not just the conjunction of religion and politics that is at stake, but also, and more importantly, the politics of law and order.[83] This, it turns out, is why law and the lawyer are central to *both* the *Demon-Mania* and the *Six Books*. Bodin was himself a jurist and time and again he falls back on law as the solution to the problems he presents in the two books: French law, Roman law, natural law and even sometimes foreign law.

The *Demon-Mania* needs to be read not in terms of what it says concerning the Witch as such, but in terms of the mechanisms of power 'to secure the safety of the good' that the talk of witches helps set into action.

> If ever there was a way to appease the anger of God, to obtain his bless-ing, to dismay some by the punishment of others, to preserve some from the infection of others, to reduce the number of the wicked, to secure the safety of the good, and to punish the most despicable wickedness that the human mind can imagine, it is to chastise witches with the utmost rigour.[84]

That the Witch is not the issue is precisely why so many historical accounts of witch-hunting end up suggesting that witch-hunts create the very thing they are supposed to be hunting. In other words, what Bodin has to say about the figure of the Witch itself is in many ways neither interesting nor novel. What is interesting and novel is what he has to say concerning the juridical powers to be mobilised and used against this Adversary. For exam-ple, when in the Preface of the *Demon-Mania* Bodin outlines the case of Jeanne Harvillier, 'reputed to be a very great witch' and the case which prompted him to write the book, he has little interest in her guilt, which turns out to be more or less irrelevant. Rather, what is important is the *form of punishment*. The central issue concerns the extent to which the state can and should carry out the harshest punishment of all. Bodin's aim is to refute the arguments of those at this particular trial who had been 'lenient and more inclined to pity', and yet, at the same time, he is also concerned with attacking the wider judicial laxness he sees in the way the courts were dealing with witchcraft in general.[85]

More than simply a sixteenth-century update of the *Malleus Maleficarum*, Bodin's argument was in fact a major contribution to a political theory of demons and a handbook for how to mobilise the state and its law against an Adversary with seemingly universal and demonic powers. The key point about the Witch for Bodin, but also for most other thinkers of the time, is that the Witch is an 'enemy of the human race'.[86] The Witch is in league with the Universal Adversary of Christian power. The hunt for and punish-ment of the Witch – in effect, a *war on witches* – is thus a fundamental exercise of the sovereign power. But the Witch stands for the Enemy in general, which is precisely how and why the term 'witch-hunt' would eventually emerge to describe the search for the Enemy within. We might say that Bodin's world-view as a whole – that is, his view of sovereignty as well as his view of witches, his view of divine order as well as his view of satanic power and, in effect, the world-view of early modern state theory – is more or less untenable without the hunt for a demonic Enemy within: a hunt for dangerous human subjects who covenant with the forces of evil in their desire to undermine the state and who must therefore be treated as the Enemy of All Mankind. Such a war reinforces the power of the state itself in the eyes of the people. 'It is, therefore, a very salutary thing for the whole body of a state diligently to search out and severely punish witches. Otherwise there is a danger that the people will stone both magistrates and witches'.[87] The state thus *asserts its power as a state* by waging a war on an enemy defined as the Enemy of All Mankind.

Moreover, the Enemy is defined as such because it engages in a *crime of the most exceptional nature*. 'There are no crimes which are nearly so vile as this one, or which deserve more serious penalties'. Against such an Adversary, Bodin articulates a view that will be familiar to anyone who has sought to understand the police wars carried out by the state in the name of security: 'one must, rather, adopt an entirely different and exceptional approach'. 'One must not be limited to the normal procedures ... It is certain in terms of law where there is a danger, necessity or any inordinate situation that one must not be bound by legal strictures'. But note that Bodin is astute enough to say that this does not take them outside the law. 'On the contrary', he says, 'this is *proceeding soundly according to law*'. In other words, the law *permits* the use of emergency powers to deal with a certain kind of Adversary. 'The trial of so despicable a crime as this must be handled in an extraordinary way and differently from other crimes', but the trial nonetheless retains the power of law.[88] Law permits whatever needs to be done in the emergency.[89] This opens the space for Bodin to argue that the magistrates can use any methods necessary to prove the witch's guilt: special courts, anonymous denunciations, offering legal immunities to those who denounce others while renouncing Satan themselves, interrogation of the suspects for long periods and without any breaks (so that Satan is not given an opportunity to 'dissuade them from telling the truth' but also to stop them committing suicide), and, most famously, the use of torture, which can be conducted outside the normal courts if necessary and which must be ferocious; 'one must not submit witches to mild torments'.[90] One further method Bodin regards as acceptable is lying to the suspect and we might pause for a moment to consider this in a little more detail.

Lying had long been a practice associated with the Devil. The Devil is 'the father of lies', St. Augustine claimed in the fifth century of the Christian era, and he was articulating a view which all Christians considered true.[91] By the sixteenth and then into seventeenth centuries, however, this truth began to unravel. 'Protestants in Catholic lands and Catholics in Protestant lands had to ask themselves if it was acceptable to lie, conceal, or dissimulate their true beliefs in order to avoid jail, torture, and death', notes Dallas Denery. 'The question of deception was seemingly everywhere during these centuries, in conduct manuals and ethical treatises, in plays and novels, touched on directly or implicitly, at length or in passing'. Now, on the one hand, and harping back to what appeared to be the universal truth as explained in Augustine's claim, this debate was closely tied to the idea of the Devil. 'The proliferation of treatises on the Devil and Antichrist throughout the sixteenth and well into the seventeenth century testified to his ubiquity and the deafening cacophony of his lies', Denery notes.[92] On the other hand, the fact that the question of lying had arisen so powerfully was tied to the fact that this was the period when new secular theories were being developed to account for and legitimise the new state system that was emerging. Diplomats in this system were increasingly having to think about how and when lying might be needed but also, and more generally, lying became part and parcel of the principle of reason of state.

As I have argued at length elsewhere, according to the principle of reason of state one should not expect to engage in politics on the basis of moral or Christian principles concerning good conduct and morality. 'Political power cannot be wielded according to the dictates of good conscience', as Francesco Guicciardini puts it. Courses of action that would be condemned as immoral if conducted by individuals – so immoral, in fact, as to be the work of the Devil – could be sanctioned when they were undertaken by the sovereign power. Hence Guicciardini's comment that 'when I talked of murdering or keeping the Pisans imprisoned, I didn't perhaps talk as a Christian: I talked according to the reason and practice of states'. In asserting the superiority of reason of state over morality the doctrine appeared to undermine the very foundations of Christian values, as witnessed in Guicciardini's claim that he was not talking as a Christian, in Machiavelli's suggestion that the prince 'cannot practice all those things for which men are considered good, being often forced, in order to keep his position, to act contrary to ... religion', and in Trajano Bocalini's suggestion that reason of state is 'a law useful for Commonwealths, but absolutely contrary to the laws of both God and Man'.[93] And yet despite what appears to be an anti-Christian dimension to reason of state, Christian thinkers were themselves gradually convinced by the force of the doctrine. Initial Christian outrage at reason of state was little more than a 'holy pretence', as George Mosse puts it and as others have confirmed,[94] just as the later liberal outrage was little more than a liberal pretence. In other words, practices which had long been associated with evil were becoming increasingly accepted as necessary by the very religion which had been so keen to declare them to be work of the Devil. One such practice was lying.

Essentially, those articulating the doctrine of reason of state accepted lying as a necessary feature of statecraft. To call it 'lying' however, was a little too straightforward, and so the term widely used to capture the practice was 'dissimulation'. 'Dissimulation is one of the most striking characteristics of our age', Montaigne would observe in 1580. Although Montaigne's comment is in part a reflection on individual behaviour, dissimulation as a whole had become such a striking characteristic by virtue of its political role. The 'fox-like' cunning needed to maintain political power, as explained by Machiavelli in *The Prince* – a book some thought was 'written by the finger of Satan' – was worked into what was, in effect, a rationalisation and justification for political dissimulation. As Machiavelli puts it in Chapter 18 of *The Prince*, the good statesman 'must be a great simulator and dissimulator'. The comment is a key moment in the development of political theory, as thinker after thinker would repeat the point. 'Dissimulation is a great aid', notes Botero in *The Reason of State* (1589), to give just one example. Deception became part and parcel of the new statecraft and reason of state became a doctrine of legitimate dissimulation. The new theories of political power that were being developed and which would stay in place for centuries to come, were, in effect, theories of dissimulation.[95]

The implications of this are important, but before we spell them out let us also note that part and parcel of political dissimulation was secrecy. '*An habit of secrecy is both politic and moral*', Francis Bacon noted in an essay called 'Of Simulation and Dissimulation', and he goes on to add that dissimulation is part of the cover (the 'skirt' or 'train') of secrecy. All the writers before him who sought to articulate a version of reason of state make the same point: for Guicciardini, secrecy is a necessary feature of government; for Botero, 'no quality is more necessary to those who conduct important negotiations in peace or war than the ability to observe secrecy'; for Bocalini, 'secrecy is no less necessary for the well-ordering of States, than good council'.[96] Jon Snyder has shown that 'the discourse on dissimulation … participates in the growing specialization of political discourse in early modernity, with secrecy and dissembling serving as interchangeable code words for it'. Moreover, dissimulation itself had to remain as secret as the secrets it was intended to preserve. As Snyder comments, 'reason-of-state theorists … tended to see "political" dissimulation as a legitimate technique of information-control for princes to practice in the interest of state security'.[97]

What then are the implications of these points for the general issues in this chapter? In assuming that dissimulation and secrecy are acceptable practices when the security of state is said to be under threat, the *new statecraft was coming to imitate the very Enemy it thought of itself as fighting*. The security of the state came to be regarded as of such fundamental importance that anything that could be done to preserve it became acceptable, including tactics hitherto assumed to be the work of the Devil. In the name of security, the state was adopting the tactics of its Adversary. Despite all its talk of being on the side of God and the Good, the state can be a remarkably devilish creature when it wants to be.

So, to return to Bodin, when Bodin insists that lying to a suspected Witch is acceptable he is revealing nothing less than one of the truths of modern statecraft: that for reasons of security the state can and must employ *any* measure against its Adversary, including those measures for which the Adversary has itself been labelled 'evil'. And if we stay with Bodin just a little longer, we can note that his argument also extends to punishment itself which, as we noted, is the problem with which Bodin begins the *Demon-Mania*. For Bodin, 'there is no penalty cruel enough to punish the evils of witches', including stoning and burning. More tellingly, the stoning and the burning can be carried out even when the evidence against the Witch is non-existent or weak, so long as the 'presumption' of the witch's guilt is strong.[98]

> This is why one who is charged and accused of being a witch must never be simply let off and acquitted, unless the calumny of the accuser or informer is clearer than the sun. Since the proof of such wickedness is so hidden and so difficult, no one would ever be accused or punished out of a million witches if parties were governed, as in an ordinary trial, by a lack of proof.[99]

This is the very argument made time and again when it comes to security: persons can be detained without trial, tortured and executed, and the state can and should exercise its powers of dissimulation through the whole process, because security demands nothing less.

Bodin is also aware that such procedures have additional benefits, in the form of 'striking fear and terror into others'.[100] It is the performance of power that is at stake: the spectacle of security and the spectacle of the security wars conducted against the Enemy. Hence in the case of dissimulation, the dissimulation is never a straightforward lie or denial. It is useful for the state if the people know something of what is happening, for the lesson in obedience it brings. It is equally useful for the people to know that torture or something like torture is taking place, so that they learn what might be done to them if they themselves become a security threat; the role of torture in modern power is less about achieving a confession and much more the performance of torture itself, which is why so many spaces of torture are understood as part of the *theatre* of operations and often given names such as the 'production room' (in the Philippines), the 'cinema room' (in South Vietnam) and the 'blue lit stage' (in Chile).[101] The striking of fear into subjects takes place through the performance of power and the spectacle of security operations. This is why Hobbes, who in contrast to Bodin did not believe in witches or demons, nonetheless also thought that they should be persecuted and punished anyway, for the lesson such punishment can bring: 'As for Witches, I think not that their witchcraft is any reall power; but yet that they are justly punished, for the false beliefe they have, that they can do such mischiefe, joyned with their purpose to do it if they can'. Such punishment coincides with Hobbes's claim that innocent people who are not subjects of the sovereign may be punished too for the benefit of the common good: 'the Infliction of what evill soever, on an Innocent man, that is not a Subject, if it be for the benefit of the Commonwealth ... is no breach of the Law of Nature'.[102] The real target, in other words, for both Bodin and Hobbes, is not the Witch and never will be. For Bodin, witchcraft exists and should be persecuted and punished; for Hobbes, witchcraft does not exist but should be persecuted and punished. The real target in both cases is the population as a whole and the fear that can be generated among them. Why? Because 'fear keeps them mindful of their duty'. And, given the discussion of contagion in the previous chapter, fear helps 'preserve them from being infected and harmed by the wicked, as plague victims and lepers infect the healthy'.[103] The whole argument is thereby connected to Bodin's wider claims concerning the political rationality of enmity in the *Six Books* (claims which are later reiterated by Hobbes and with which this book began). 'The best way of preserving a state, and guaranteeing it against sedition, rebellion, and civil war is to keep the subjects in amity with one another', he notes, adding that the best way to do this is 'to find an enemy against whom they can make common cause'. Thus the sole end of war is not peace, but keeping the subjects in their place by giving them a common Enemy. The end of war is the obedience and fear of the subjects, for it is obedience and fear which sustains the 'well-ordered Commonwealth'.[104] Here we encounter the political function of security's sister term, 'order'.

'A commonwealth may be defined as the rightly ordered government of a number of families', is the opening definition of the *Six Books*, and Bodin goes on to elaborate the point time and again by pointing to the need for a 'well-ordered commonwealth' and 'rightly ordered government'.[105] Such claims suggest that we need to understand the statecraft surrounding the Witch in terms of the mobilisation of security in the fabrication of order. We can follow and develop this analysis by pointing to a very similar set of ideas in the *Daemonologie* of King James VI and I.

Published in 1597, going through two further editions in 1603, and quickly translated into Latin, Dutch and French, James's demonology stems from his desire to articulate a vision of monarchy and stately order rather than religious belief as such. Following Bodin, James restates the claim that the battle against witchcraft, as part of the grander war against Satan, could be fought by bringing the Witch face to face with God's power on earth in the shape of king, the magistrate, or some other authority of state. Neither original nor profound, the importance of the *Daemonologie* lies in its restatement of the power of kingship but also, and more broadly, a cosmology of order managed by the public authority.[106] In the sixteenth and seventeenth centuries 'order' was part and parcel of the 'great chain of being' (it was 'Order' rather than simply 'order'). In this chain there was understood to be a correspondence between God and the monarch. The latter's position as 'head of state' meant that the cosmology of order was understood through the analogy of the body. Part of the power of the 'body politic' as an idea lies in the fact that threats to the body can be understood through the language of contagion, as we saw in the previous chapter, but the wider point to make is that a community imagined in terms of the body appeals because it connotes *order*.[107] The conceptual world of the educated and privileged, of witch-hunters and demonologists such as Jean Bodin and King James, 'was dominated by the principle of order'.[108]

The power of such claims, arguments and assumptions about order relies heavily on the imagination of disorder, with disorder implying the dissolution of all authority. As Christina Larner puts it, 'witchcraft was imagined as the summation of all possible forms of disorder'.[109] Now, this concept of order signified the emergence of a secular sovereign state. The move 'from divine cosmos to sovereign state' relied on an increasingly secular idea of order. Society moved from being understood as 'a transcendentally articulated reflection of something predefined, external, and beyond itself which orders existence hierarchically' to being 'a nominal entity ordered by the sovereign state which is its own articulated representative'.[110] Despite this 'secularization', the idea that God was the source and strength of order – if not social order, then certainly *universal* order, which many regarded as the ultimate foundation of social order anyway – remained important. The implication of this was that God's Adversary is the embodiment of (universal) disorder and thus the creature responsible for all (social) disorder on earth. Defeat the Devil and one defeats disorder. Conversely: maintain order and one defeats the Devil. To identify the Devil as the universal Enemy was thus one of the presuppositions of the ideology of order as well as the politics of security.

A society organised around the concepts of order and security is a society under a perpetual police power. Such a society will invent witches in order to hunt them, will engage in witch-hunts in order to mobilise the forces of security, and will wage a war on witches in order to mobilise the war power. As such, we are now in a position to identify the whole *raison d'être* of the witch-hunt in all of its instantiations: it is necessary '*so that the good can live in security*'.[111]

The very vagueness of terms such as 'Witch', 'Devil', 'Satan' and 'Antichrist', along with the vagueness of threats such as 'witchcraft', 'evil', 'treason' and 'terrorism', generates security advantages. This is why the coming of the 'Age of Reason', scientific rationalism and Enlightenment sees not the elimination of witch-hunts but, rather, their multiplication and intensification under the liberal refinement of the apparatuses of security. 'The bonfires are still smoking with the witches burned alive at the time of the scientific revolution', notes Bruno Latour.[112] We might say that security is still being mobilised against the same creatures. Security mobilised, but also capital defended. Why capital defended?

Feudal property had been understood as part of the body of the monarch, but the new forms of property that were emerging rested on claims of personal ownership to the exclusion of all others, in the form of *private* property. This development created a sense of disorder centred on the relations between the new 'classes' that were then emerging. The problem of protecting the new 'private' property released from the body of the monarch was deeply connected to the question of the nature and condition of the newly emergent class of wage-labour. Outside the traditional feudal forms of power and law, such 'masterless men and women' were 'without subjection to Lawes, and a coercive Power to tye their hands'.[113] In their very condition they appeared to be fundamentally disorderly and thus needed to be *ordered*, in both senses of the term: ordered in the sense of being organised and ordered in the sense of being commanded. Organised and commanded into the new property regime. This is precisely why one answer to the question posed time and again by those studying the history of the witch-hunts of the sixteenth and seventeenth centuries, namely 'why did so many educated and privileged believe in witches?', is that the conceptual world of the educated and privileged, of men like Jean Bodin and King James, was not only dominated by the principle of order but that this 'order' was increasingly understood as under threat from the rising numbers of masterless poor. This is also why so many historians have concluded that for the most part the witch-hunt was driven not by the irrational fears of the masses but was a systematic ruling class campaign of terror. 'Witch-hunting, to put it directly, was a ruling class activity', notes Jon Oplinger, summing up the scholarship on the question.[114] The witch-hunt, then, raises questions concerning the state's role in the development and defence of capital. Which is a way of saying that the witch-hunt needs to be seen as part of the history of the proletariat.

'The witch-hunt rarely appears in the history of the proletariat', comments Federici,[115] an oversight which her work has done a great deal to overcome. Historians of Europe have pointed to the fact that 'there are multiple connections between the rise of trials for witchcraft and the social crisis that began in Europe in the second half of the sixteenth century and culminated in the well-known "crisis of the seventeenth century", a lengthy phase of decline or stagnation'.

> Two different developments coincided decisively at this time. On the one hand, a population plagued by frequent subsistence crises felt the need to persecute witches, understood as sorcerers (men or women)

who raised storms, damaged crops and brought disease on people and livestock. The rise in accusations of witchcraft corresponded to relevant agrarian crises... On the other hand, radical changes in the mentality of the upper classes also inclined them to perceive the deterioration in living conditions as a sign of God's wrath and as proof of demonic activity, either as the result of greater sinfulness or in the context of eschatological interpretations.[116]

Such historians have pointed to the connections between crisis and the witch-hunt: 'taking the long view, the equation of crisis and witchcraft becomes ... striking', notes Henry Kamen.[117] But Federici makes a more compelling point: as well as the connection between the witch-hunt and general crisis, she suggests that it is also:

> significant that the witch-hunt occurred simultaneously with the colonization of the populations of the New World, the English enclosures, the beginning of the slave trade, the enactment of the 'bloody laws' against vagabonds and beggars, and [that] it climaxed in that interregnum between the end of feudalism and the capitalist 'take off' when the peasantry in Europe reached the peak of its power but, in time, also consummated its historical defeat.[118]

The witch-hunt, in other words, was part and parcel of the process of primitive accumulation. Far from being 'the last spark of a dying feudal world', the witch-hunt was 'one of the most important events in the development of capitalist society and the formation of the modern proletariat',[119] which is precisely why witch-hunting is a permanent feature of the reproduction of capital.[120] The evidence for this claim is overwhelming.

We could point, for example, to the fact that the women who were persecuted were usually poor and on public assistance: 'witch-hunting' was 'woman-hunting' but was also very much a hunting of women in the lower classes. We could point to the fact that the 'magic' said to be carried out by the witches seemed to also imply a refusal of work, by virtue of being an attempt to obtain some means of subsistence without going through the hardship of labour; in Britain, for example, fortune-telling, palmistry and other such 'magical' powers were often punished under vagrancy laws, and often still are (for example under the Vagrancy Act of 1824, which is still in operation). We could point to the fact that the attack on witchcraft was an attack on the body: a permanent police power put in place for the capitalist disciplining of the body, to empty the body of any 'magical' or 'occult' or 'devilish' forces and thereby help constitute those bodies as bodies of wage labour, enacting in the process a permanent police power to outlaw any sexual activity that threatened procreation and to carry out a war against any 'rebel body'.[121] We could point to the fact that the pact between

the Witch and the Devil went by the name of *conjuration*. The full title of
the key 1604 English law on witchcraft, for example, passed in the light of
King James VI and I's *Daemonologie*, was 'An Act against Conjuration,
Witchcraft and Dealing with Evil and Wicked Spirits'. 'Conjuration' is a
term stemming from the late-fourteenth century which took up from the
Latin *coniurationem*, meaning a 'swearing together' or 'conspiracy', but also
connoting a 'calling upon something supernatural' or 'conjuring', from
the Old French *conjuracion* meaning spell or incantation, and the point is
that it was a term used by lawyers and the ruling class to describe the oaths
made between workers in their resistance to the new institutions of power
being developed.[122] Finally, we could point to the fact that in the New World
the witch-hunt was a deliberate strategy used in the colonies to enclose
bodies and land, destroy collective resistance and instil terror in the population.[123] All these points remind us of one thing: the witch-hunt and the
class war coincide. Which brings us back to the Devil.

'What is the relationship between the image of the devil and capitalist
development?', asks Michael Taussig.[124] Taussig suggests that belief in the
Devil intensifies during historical periods of radical transformation. Using
the beliefs found among Colombian and Bolivian labourers Taussig shows
that periods in which their work was being commodified and new money
relations were taking root under colonial rule were also periods which
witnessed a rise in Devil-beliefs. The new monetary relations and commodification of social life seemed to the labourers to be simply diabolical
compared with their more traditional social forms. In this context, the
poor turned to the concept of the Devil to try and make sense of their
experience. Now, Taussig suggests that the Devil became 'a stunningly apt
symbol of the alienation experienced by peasants as they enter the ranks of
the proletariat',[125] whereas we have already noted that witch-hunting in
Europe and colonial North America was a ruling class activity. But Taussig's
more general point is that 'the fetishization of evil in the form of the devil
is born from the structure of caste and class oppression that was created by
European conquest',[126] and here we can build on his argument, because the
Devil was seen to be central to the whole problem of disorder which was
plaguing the emerging world of capital.

In the context of a world increasingly dominated by assumptions about
bourgeois property and propriety, 'order' was the order of accumulation
and such accumulation required the creation of a class of wage labourers.
The biggest threat to the creation of such a class was the problem of disorderliness and unruliness. For the ruling class, at the heart of disorderliness
and unruliness lay the problem of idle workers. As I have shown at greater
length elsewhere, idleness was central to the early class war as the nascent
bourgeois class became obsessed with eradicating idleness as part of its
wider war on waste and its obsession with 'improvement'. To leave people
idle is to leave them to 'waste' in the same way that land might be 'wasted';

to leave people idle is to fail to improve them and to use their labour to improve the earth. To leave people idle is to allow them time to organise and mobilise politically, not least against the whole ideology of wage labour and capital.[127] And what figure do we find at the heart of this problem of idleness? The Devil. Witness the number of sayings connecting the Devil and idleness: 'idle hands are the Devil's workshop', 'idleness is the Devil's handmaiden', 'the Devil makes work for idle hands', 'idle hands are the Devil's tools'. For the ruling class, lurking in the soul and body of the idle worker is the Devil. Given that the systematic colonisation of the world by capital is assumed by the ruling class to be God's will, it is easy to equally assume that the idle, disorderly, recalcitrant and disgruntled Worker – in effect, the unruly subject – is in league with the Devil.

The fundamental problem of how to constitute a capitalist order out of such workers is, for the ruling class, *the* fundamental problem of the class war. It is a problem that straddles law, politics, theology, and police science. It is a problem which will, eventually, underpin the whole logic of criminality and psychiatry when those 'sciences' emerge. It is thus a problem which connects the idle and disgruntled Worker with the criminal and the deviant, a problem traversing delinquency and idleness, deviance and disorderliness, social conflict and political rebellion. As Foucault points out, all of these differences and conflicts could and eventually would be assimilated, so that political infractions run hand in hand with common crimes and social conflict hand in hand with concepts of delinquency and deviance, in order to be better able to discredit them all together and as a whole. And thus, gradually, out of all these minor rebellious figures and major adversaries of the social order being created, 'an image was constructed of an *enemy of society*', one '*who could be the revolutionary*'.[128] Revolutionary? Well, if not revolutionary then certainly, in the *lingua franca* of the contemporary security imaginary, 'radicalised'. In one fell swoop the rebel, the revolutionary, the radicalised and a whole host of related others – the seditious, the treasonous, the treacherous, the conspiratorial, the insurrectionary, the unruly, the mutinous, the resistant – could be regarded as being on the side of the Devil.

The act often said to be the first moment of human disobedience is intimated at in the third chapter of Genesis and is usually blamed on the Devil. From thereon disobedience and rebellion would forever be associated with the work of the Devil. The Devil, as 'God's great Enemy' must by definition be 'the ringleader of Rebellion', thought Samuel Willard.[129] 'If thou be a man, and murmurest against God, thou art a Devil, if thou be a Subject and murmur against thy King, thou art a Rebel', thought Nicholas Breton.[130] One Christian sermon popular in England took the form of a 'Homily Against Disobedience and Wilful Rebellion'. The second part of this sermon held that:

What be they who do rebel against a most natural and loving prince?
... What be they, who are so evil subjects, that they will rebel against
their gracious prince? ... Surely no mortal man can express with words,
nor conceive in mind, the horrible and most dreadful damnation that
such be worthy of, who, disdaining to be the quiet and happy subjects
of their good prince, are most worthy to be [the] miserable captives
and vile slaves of that infernal tyrant Satan.[131]

The third part of the sermon talks of rebels as friends of the Devil and uses
this connection to demand political obedience:

Let us, as the children of obedience, fear the dreadful execution of
God, and live in quiet obedience ... For as heaven is the place of good
obedient subjects, and hell the prison and dungeon of rebels against
God and their prince; so is that realm happy where most obedience of
subjects doth appear, being the very figure of heaven: and contrariwise,
where most rebellions and rebels be, there is the express similitude of
hell, and the rebels themselves are the very figures of fiends and devils,
and their captain the ungracious pattern of Lucifer and Satan, the
prince of darkness; of whose rebellion as they be followers, so shall they
of his damnation in hell undoubtedly be partakers, and as undoubtedly
children of peace, the inheritors of heaven with God the Father, God
the Son, and God the Holy.[132]

The point is not just a theological commonplace to be repeated to those
attending church in order to steer them away from rebellion. Rather, it is a
reiteration of the fundamental belief that just as the Devil is rebellious, so
rebellion – and by implication any challenge to authority – is fundamentally evil. Hence to return briefly to the Witch, the point was that the
fundamental *sin* of witchcraft was the *disobedience* and *rebellion* implicit in
the witch's actions. All the Witch's sins, from blaspheming and abusing the
Sabbath to kissing the Devil's arse, from making oaths with the Devil to
burning their own children, from surrendering to sexual passions to
having the Devil's children, from incest to cannibalism, from bestiality to
the keeping of pigs (the figure of the Witch seemingly connecting the
beastly to The Beast),[133] from murder to causing famine, all these sins and
many more are part of and even subsumed under the greatest crime and
sin of all: rebellion. 'Rebellion is as the sin of witchcraft', the Bible tells us
(1 Samuel, 15:23), and the point was repeated by clergyman after clergyman and statesman after statesman.[134] It is part of the Devil's power and
desire to tempt man to rebellion and disobedience, treason and dissent,
and to thereby render the universe disorderly.[135] (This is precisely why
rebellion against the established order in literature such as Rabelais's
Gargantua and Pantagruel and Miton's *Paradise Lost* adapts the character of

the Devil and the trope of devilishness.) Slaves who rebelled were said to have done so at the command of Satan and white colonial rulers saw in their non-white colonial subjects an inherent evil and thus potential for devilish rebellion. Rebel leaders were understood to be intermediaries for Satan, representing 'an underworld allied with Satan'.[136] The Devil, on this view, is a revolutionary.

'There is a satanic quality to … Revolution', Joseph de Maistre would comment in 1797.[137] He was referring specifically to the revolution in France, but his point has been generalised by reactionaries and conservatives and gets repeated by them time and again when they search for the Devil – and, perhaps unsurprisingly, find him – in not just every revolution but also in every rebellion and every threat to security and order. The Devil, then, is the *Lord of Misrule,* and as the Lord of Misrule is easily implicated in everything that security finds dangerous or suspicious, which is, in effect, anything that threatens the social consensus.

All of which is to say that the political invention of the Devil helped prepare the ground for *absolute obedience.* Obedience becomes the desired state and desired by the state. This is the key to what Foucault calls the 'pastoral power' that develops over fifteen centuries of the Christian era: the 'pastoral government of the world meant that the world was subject to a system of obedience'.[138] What does this obedience produce? asks Foucault. The answer is not difficult: 'obedience produces obedience'. It reproduces itself as obedience. That is, 'one obeys in order to become obedient, in order to produce a state of obedience so permanent and definitive that it subsists even where there is not exactly anyone that one has to obey and even before anyone has formulated an order'.[139] Obedience thereby becomes a way of being, a permanent condition, and essential to the subject and to the subjection of the subject. The training in obedience is a training of and for political order. Obedience becomes one of the fundamental principles of reason of state, demanded by the state for security reasons but also because it is on obedience that capital will thrive.

Thus when a figure such as Martin Luther comments that the Devil and God are two enemies, as we noted above, the comment needs to be situated in the context of his claim that public authority exists solely by God's command and that *rebellion is a crime against all authority.*[140] Luther makes this claim with reference to Romans 13, and the person to grasp some of the political implications was one of the targets of Luther's comment, Thomas Müntzer, the revolutionary who in his final confession under torture insisted that 'all property should be held in common' and that 'any prince, count or lord who did not want to do this … should be beheaded or hanged' (an opinion which led to him being labelled 'the Satan of Allstedt' by Luther). 'The key to the knowledge of God', Müntzer says, 'is that people are so ruled that they learn to fear God alone, Romans 13'.[141] Why Romans 13? Here is what it says:

Let every person be subject to the governing authorities. For there is no authority except from God, and those that exist have been instituted by God. Therefore he who resists the authorities resists what God has appointed, and those who resist will incur judgment. For rulers are not a terror to good conduct, but to bad.

(Romans 13:2)

Christians are to learn that secular authority is 'an authority which God has sanctioned by the surest edicts', as Calvin puts it.[142] Secular authority is 'authorised' by God and so anyone who disobeys the secular authority is disobeying an authority 'instituted by God'. Any such creature must by definition be on the side of God's Adversary. This is the political secret of Christianity and the reason why Christians must make the endless struggle against disobedience part of their life's mission.[143]

A society that believes that witches exist is a society under perpetual police power, we noted above. The same can be said of a society that believes that the Devil is at work against it. This is one reason why police forces are themselves obsessed with things 'Satanic': the mobilisation of security against the Witch has as its corollary a police preoccupation with Satanism, satanic crime, and occult forces.[144] And once that belief becomes widespread then it will be suspected that the Devil and his agents are anywhere and everywhere: in workplaces, in the home, in the streets, in schools, colleges and Universities, or even in a hideout somewhere in Fallujah. And such a belief will assume that any disobedience, unruliness or rebellion by those who live or work in such places is a sign that security is under threat. A society that believes that the Devil is at work and that wants to hunt the Devil's agents will be a society under universal suspicion. 'If you see something, say something', as the security state's latest slogan has it. That friend or colleague or family member or lover or resident of Fallujah could be an Enemy of All Mankind. In league with the Devil. Or maybe the Pirate. The Pirate? Why the Pirate?

There had long been an association made between the Pirate and the Devil: the Devil was understood as the Pirate's patron; key pirates such as Blackbeard were understood to be either working with the Devil or the Devil incarnate, while others took on names with Satanic connotations such as Diaboleto ('Little Devil'); the 'Jolly Roger' flag associated with piracy is sometimes said to stem from 'Old Roger' which was the nickname for the Devil, reinforced by the image of death on the flag; piracy in general was known as the 'Devil's Anarchy' and as offering people a 'Demonic independence'; and pirates were considered the 'anti-Christians' of Christian Europe (and their regular conversion to Islam reinforced this view). Rebellious and disobedient, anarchical and criminal, anti-Christian and flying a flag with the image of death, it was easy to see the Pirate as an ally of the Devil. But one further reason the link between the Pirate and the

Devil was made is because pirates were thought of as operating a little like the way we are told the contemporary terrorist operates: with no motive other than malice or hatred, to the extent that no compromise or understanding could be possible with such an Adversary. This pure hatred and lack of understanding meant that the Pirate, like the Devil, has been known for centuries as *hostis humani generis*, the Enemy of All Mankind. And remarkably, though perhaps unsurprisingly, one finds that the Pirate is a central figure in contemporary pronouncements about both security and capital. To the Pirate we must therefore turn.

Chapter 4

'An offence against the universal law of society': on the Pirate

Suffer pirates, and the commerce of the world must cease.
(Henry Newton, Comment in the trial of Joseph Dawson, 1696)

The crime of piracy ... is an offence against the universal law of society.
(William Blackstone, *Commentaries on the Laws of England*, 1769)

Terrorism will be viewed in the same light as ... piracy.
(*The National Security Strategy of the United States of America*, 2002)

Johnny Depp has a lot to answer for. If there is one figure that might be said to compete with the Zombie as representing the early twenty-first century zeitgeist, it is the Pirate. Pirates are now one of the most popular children's characters, more than a few sports teams openly identify themselves as pirates (Orlando Pirates in football, Portland Pirates in hockey, the Cornish Pirates in rugby, and many more), there is an annual 'International Talk Like a Pirate Day', radical groups are setting themselves up as Pirate Parties, and cinemas are full with films of swashbuckling and adoringly roguish pirates with whom the audience are clearly meant to identify or fall in love. I doubt that all of these are down to Johnny Depp, but they do all capture some aspect or other of the romantic myth of the pirate as a nomadic and brave figure exercising a liberty and alternative form of existence beyond the normal strictures of bourgeois civilisation. We will have much to say about such things in this chapter, but before we do we must note that there is yet another way in which pirates have come to the fore.

In 2002 the US released a *National Security Strategy* (*NSS 2002*) in the light of the attacks on the World Trade Centre and to underpin the 'war on terror' that was by then underway. One of the claims made in the document is that in the emerging security strategy 'terrorism will be viewed in the same light as slavery, piracy, or genocide'.[1] It doesn't take much reflection to see that this is an odd series of connections: terrorism-slavery-piracy-genocide. The link that those framing the document clearly hope we will all make is to forget the handsome swashbuckling hero and desire for a nomadic liberty and simply agree with what is presented as part of the logic of security: that terrorism must be universally condemned in the same way that certain other kinds of acts are universally condemned. After all, what right-minded person now advocates genocide? What kind of person defends slavery? Yet although the issue appears straightforward in the case of slavery and genocide, it is far from clear in the case of piracy. It is rare for children and adults to identify with slave-traders or the architects of genocide and if they do they tend to keep fairly quiet about it. I know of no 'International Talk Like a Genocidal Maniac Day'. So for the *NSS 2002* to suggest a continuum between piracy and terrorism, a suggestion regularly repeated by other states,[2] begs an obvious question: what is it about piracy such that the security state has to regard it in this way?

Asking such a question puts us up against a quite formidable body of work, as security intellectuals fall over themselves in the rush to peddle the same line that 'piracy is terrorism' and 'terrorism is piracy'.[3] More or less as soon as the attacks on the World Trade Centre took place there were plenty of people making a link with piracy: 'Two centuries ago the fledgling United States prosecuted a similar war against terrorism. Only, we didn't call it "terrorism", but piracy'.[4] The point has been repeated by historians who sought to draw a link between some of America's historical struggles against some forms of piracy as an early form of the 'war on terror',[5] by IR scholars,[6] and by commentators and journalists.[7] But more than anything, it is international lawyers who have been most willing to consider how and why the war on terror could be understood through and possibly even justified in terms of the much longer war on piracy.[8]

So what is it about piracy that resonates in the security imagination? Why must security be mobilised against piracy? Perhaps a more telling question could be: why must security be mobilised against a figure with whom so many people express a romantic identification? Might there be something in the figure of the Pirate that the security state recognises as somehow fundamentally adversarial to the whole logic of security? In the fourth volume of his *Commentaries on the Laws of England* (1769), Sir William Blackstone notes that piracy was once a crime dealt with by the admiralty courts but has now passed into the normal courts because of the nature of the offense:

> The crime of *piracy*, or robbery and depredation upon the high seas, is an offence against the universal law of society; a pirate being, according to Sir Edward Coke, *hostis humani generis*. As therefore he has renounced all the benefits of society and government, and has reduced himself afresh to the savage state of nature, by declaring war against all mankind, all mankind must declare war against him.[9]

Piracy on this view is a crime that requires a war to defeat it: a *war on a crime*. But not just any crime. Rather, a crime so universally condemned that the pirate could be labelled the 'Enemy of All Mankind'. Exploring piracy might therefore help us understand what might be at stake in the category of the Universal Adversary and, at the same time, what might be at stake in contemporary capitalist accumulation.

As if I: 'styled by us as piratical'

It is a truism to note that part of the construction of the state's territorial form required an understanding of what could count as the legitimate use of violence. To do this the distinction between the 'legitimate' use of force ('privateering') and 'illegitimate' use of force ('piracy') had to be made coherent and acceptable. But the problem was that in the fifteenth and sixteenth centuries privateering and piracy were so closely allied as to be indistinguishable, to the extent that 'the conduct of privateers and pirates was about the same'.[10] The *conduct* was more or less the same, but the difference was that privateers operated under license: the privateers had legal permission to act as they did; privateering was, in effect, legalised piracy. The first privateers 'licenses' issued by Henry III in 1243, for example, stated that the king had 'granted and given license to Adam Robernolt and William le Sauvage, and their companions whom they take with them, to annoy our enemies by sea or by land, wheresoever they are able, *so that they share with us half of all their gain*'.[11] Francis Drake operated under the 'letters of marque and reprisal' issued by the British crown with orders to engage in acts of violence against Spanish and Portuguese ships to seize their goods; he returned from one voyage in 1572–3 with enough gold and silver to support the state and all its expenses for 7 years.[12] So highly regarded were such acts of violent theft on a global scale that Drake was later knighted by Queen Elizabeth, who is said to have addressed him as 'my dear pirate', and appointed him Admiral in the Royal Navy. Drake is just one example of how 'in Elizabeth's reign piracy had become a relatively respectable occupation',[13] and the same applies to other states. In France, for example, privateering meant *faire la course* and anyone undertaking such work was a *corsair*, operating entirely honourably under a *lettre de marque*.

Such figures are examples of how state-building and commercial expansion went hand in hand as the modern state in its early formation exercised violence alongside and often in conjunction with a range of 'non-state' or 'semi-state' organizations. Plundering was considered an entirely legitimate practice (just as 'raiding' and 'trading' also appeared to be two ways of describing very similar operations). Or at least, the acts were an entirely legitimate practice to those states which issued the letters of marque and the licenses to privateers. The development of commercial capital was, in effect, so intimately bound up with piracy and plunder that it is no exaggeration to say that capital was born of a certain kind of piracy or even that capital *was* a kind of piracy.[14]

So obvious was this connection between capital and piracy that in 1707 Daniel Defoe commented that if piracy was eradicated the financial centres of the world would collapse: 'It would make a sad Chasm on the *Exchange* of *London*, if all the Pyrates should be taken away from the Merchants there, whether we be understood to speak of your Litteral or Allegorical Pyrates'.[15] Defoe suggests that several types of action which might be called 'literal piracy' were discernible: officially sanctioned piracy, commercial piracy, and marauding, though they were far from being mutually exclusive and pirates often moved from one to the other. But note Defoe's term 'allegorical piracy'. The term is a hint as to how powerful the category would become, as we shall see. That such confusion and overlap could exist was due to the fact that the central issue was the violence of appropriation, and such violence was the official policy of more or less all 'imperialist pirate states', as Bukharin dubbed them. A kind of 'juridical nomad' who traversed the porous spaces between the lawful privateer and the pariah entrepreneur, between the law and the outlaw, the Pirate's desire was so close to that of the empire-builders that it was more or less identical. As Amedeo Policante suggests, the genealogy of piracy is the genealogy of an imperial concept. The words '*peril*' and 'em*pire*' have the same Greek root as the word '*pirate*', and Alfred Rubin argues that 'it is the disregard of the legal powers of others to determine property and personal rights that is common to both "piracy" and "imperialism"'. Any historical analysis of piracy reveals just how culpable imperial states were in perpetuating it and, conversely, just how central piracy was in building those states. As a number of commentators have noted, given the nature of colonial plunder it must have felt to the non-European world it felt that *all* Europeans came to their shores as pirates.[16] 'War, trade, and piracy, as three in one, allow no separation', as Mephistopheles puts it in Goethe's *Faust* (Act V, Scene III).

The picture now is very different. Once capital became mature enough to devise new modes of violence it could denounce piracy, and when it matured further still in the nineteenth century it could denounce privateering (by which point privateering had anyway become insignificant). Piracy would then be treated as an act of violence divorced from the authority of any state and thereby presented to us as a crime. Indeed, it came to be presented not just as a crime, but an act so *heinous* – a term to which we shall return – that the Pirate would come to be persecuted as the Enemy of All Mankind. To reach this state of affairs a campaign against piracy was required which ran from roughly 1660 to 1750. Carl Schmitt has the key date as the Treaty of Utrecht in 1713 and radical historians tend to focus on the 1720s as the crucial turning point, but either way it is clear that between roughly the mid-seventeenth through to the mid-eighteenth century pirates went from being knighted and made Admirals in the Navy to being hanged *en masse* in public executions. 'A whole new period of the *jus publicum Europaeum* began in 1713 with the Treaty of Utrecht' notes Schmitt, as 'state control over the pirate ships of its own subjects became stronger, while the old style freebooters sank to the level of criminal pirates'.[17] As the ruling class increasingly realised that a regular and stable trading system politically managed by the state suited its imperial and commercial interests much better than the more ad hoc and irregularly organised piracy and privateering, a campaign was launched to transform the ways in which commercial violence was exercised: 'non-state' violence had to move from being an exploitable resource to one in which it was a practice to be eliminated.[18] From being a key player in the systematic colonisation of the world by capital, the Pirate came to be regarded as one of the key agents of its disruption.

To distinguish between legitimate and illegitimate plunder required a new set of norms on which to base the distinction:

> No clear norm could develop, much less be universalized, until the state system produced a clear definition of what constituted piracy. *And this was impossible so long as states continued to regard individual violence as an exploitable resource.* Simply put, piracy could not be expunged until it was defined, and it could not be defined until it was distinguished from state-sponsored or -sanctioned individual violence.[19]

In effect, states had to distance themselves from the fact that the rise of both state and capital was heavily dependent on piratical acts. The witty rejoinder offered to Alexander the Great by a captured pirate when the latter was asked what business he had in infesting the sea in the way he did – 'because I do it with a tiny craft, I'm called a pirate: because you have a mighty navy, you're called an emperor' – had to become reality.[20]

The detailed history of this process is beyond the scope of this chapter, though we will have reason to pick up some of the key moments and issues, but the impetus would appear to have been a crisis of imperial trade. Defoe begins the *General History of Pyrates* by noting that 'As the Pyrates in the *West-Indies* have been so formidable and numerous, that they have interrupted the Trade of *Europe* into those parts; and our *English* Merchants, in Particular, have suffered more by their Depredations, than by the united Force of *France* and *Spain*, in the late War'. These 'Desperadoes', notes Defoe, are nothing less than 'the Terror of the trading Part of the World'.[21] Eradicating what the trading states regarded as terror required that those same states define themselves as the sole legitimate organization in the exercise of plunder. 'Piracy' came to represent the exercise of a violence that had no legal sanction and thus a form of 'crime' on a massive scale. From being an ally of the ruling class the Pirate came to be regarded as an *enemy* of that same class by virtue of the kind of *crime* it was said to be committing. 'The classification of some action or condition as illegal is patently a quite deliberate outcome of legal imagination and endeavour' notes Fleur Johns,[22] and nowhere is this clearer than in the way that the Pirate was imagined and fought against as nothing less than the Enemy of All Mankind.

Piracy thus passed through a number of historical stages. As Peter Linebaugh and Marcus Rediker have argued:

> There was a long-term tendency for the control of piracy to devolve from the top of society down to the bottom, from the highest func-tionaries of the state (in the late sixteenth century), to the big merchants (in the early to middle seventeenth century), to smaller, usually colonial merchants (in the late seventeenth century), and finally to the common men of the deep (in the early eighteenth century). When this devolution reached rock bottom, when seamen – as pirates – organized a social world apart from the dictates of mercan-tile and imperial authority and used it to attack merchants' property (as they had begun to do in the 1690s), then those who controlled the maritime state resorted to massive violence, both military (the navy) and penal (the gallows), to eradicate piracy.[23]

This violence to suppress piracy is part and parcel of what has often been described as the monopolization of legitimate violence by the state, but the point to grasp is that this was simultaneously the regulation of imperial plunder, though no longer seen as plunder. This regulation took the form of what Foucault calls the juridification of oceanic space and what Schmitt hails as the extension of law to the space of the free sea. The war on piracy is therefore coterminous with the legal constitution of the world market and the construction of the sea as a space of security: a foundational moment in the history of modern global integration and a constitutive moment in the transition to an ordered system of capital accumulation.[24] Thus despite being *born* of a certain kind of piracy, the *maturation* of capi-tal depended in part on a war to eradicate that very thing. Hence the range of comments and slogans produced by state officials and colonial gover-nors: 'suffer pirates, and the commerce of the world must cease', or 'Pirates Expelled, Commerce Restored', as the Governor of the Bahamas declared on taking power in 1717.[25] From that point, piracy was constituted as both a *security problem* and a *threat to capital,* and the history of bourgeois moder-nity as nothing less than a *war on piracy*.

The figure of the Pirate thus raises some fundamental questions about capital, violence and legal order. As we well know, the nexus capital-violence-order is at the heart of the question of 'security', which is why we are dealing with it here. But *why* are fundamental questions raised about capital, violence, law and security, given that when the courts and the lawyers have tried to define piracy the best they could come up with is that it is little more than 'robbery at sea'? We have seen Blackstone following Coke in defining the crime of piracy as a form of robbery on the high seas and we can likewise point to other cases: in the Old Bailey in 1696 Sir Charles Hedges held that 'piracy is only a sea-term for robbery'; in a trial at Charlestown in 1718 Judge Nicholas Trott declared that 'piracy is a robbery committed upon the sea'; in his *Dictionary of the English Language* (1755) Samuel Johnson defines 'pirate' as 'a sea-robber'; in *United States* v. *Smith* in 1820 the Supreme Court held that the 'true definition' of piracy is 'robbery upon the sea'; in the major piece of research conducted by the Harvard Law School Research in International Law, which produced an internationally renowned Draft Convention on Piracy in 1932, Sir Leoline Jenkins is cited to the effect that 'a robbery, when it is committed upon the sea, is what we call piracy'.[26] But if it is simply robbery at sea, why does piracy come with such a dramatic epithet, 'Enemy of All Mankind', in a way that appears to grant special status to the Pirate? The short answer is one implied by comments we have already made: that far from being an Enemy of All Mankind, the Pirate was in fact the Enemy of Empire. Fleshing this answer out will involve a long and sometimes circuitous route, because to get there we need to understand that the attempt to eradicate piracy and legitimize the violence of states and corporations had the effect of radicalising the nature of piracy itself. And fleshing the answer out will also take us back to the concept of the Universal Adversary.

The radicalisation in question supplies the basis of the approach to piracy which reads it as an anti-capitalist practice and form of social rebellion. In other words, to understand the Pirate as the Enemy of All Mankind and thus the contemporary trope of piracy within the discourse of universal enmity, we have to appreciate piracy in terms of the long history of proletarianization and the struggle for democratic organizational formations. Here lies one of the political points drawn out by a number of historians, including Christopher Hill, Peter Linebaugh, Marcus Rediker, Erin Mackie and Stephen Snelders, who have highlighted the anti-colonial and thus anti-capitalist nature of the figure of the Pirate. In so doing their work has drawn out the 'social' aspects of piracy and the political purposes to which these social aspects were put. 'There is much talk about fighting capitalism', it is suggested, but 'pirates show to do it'.[27] We might then argue that what they have done is spell out the fundamentally adversarial nature of piracy and why it is that the trope of piracy is so prevalent in the contemporary mobilisation of security and defence of capital.

In *The History of the Pyrates*, Defoe reports the comments of Captain Roberts about the 'honest service' performed by some workers at sea: '*In an honest service, says he, there is thin Commons, low Wages, and hard Labour*'.[28] Working for (low) wages on ships was in fact one of the earliest forms of proletarian labour, not least because being pressed into service on ships was one of the punishments in the vagrancy laws. The work was hard, deeply unpleasant, heavily disciplined and poorly paid. It was a life lived among the 'ranks of the damned', as Fernand Braudel puts it. 'Was it possible to escape from this hell?', Braudel asks. 'Occasionally yes, but never unaided, never without accepting some kind of close reliance on other men. One had to swim to the shore of social organization, of whatever kind, or build an alternative society from scratch, a counter-society with its own laws'. One such form of social organisation and counter-society was the world of piracy.[29] In contrast to the 'thin Commons, low Wages, and hard Labour' of 'honest service' described by Captain Roberts, piracy offered a radical alternative: '*Plenty and Satiety, Pleasure and Ease, Liberty and Power*'.[30]

The chapter on Captain Roberts in *The History of the Pyrates*[31] reports a time when Roberts and crew 'formed a set of Articles, to be signed and sworn to, for the better Conservation of their Society'. The first of these Articles holds that '*Every Man has a Vote in Affairs of Moment; has equal Title to the fresh Provisions, or strong Liquors, at any Time seized, and may use them at Pleasure*'. Such Articles were commonplace for pirate ships. One of the Articles would almost always concern the election of the Captains – the voting performed by people who otherwise had no right to vote anywhere in the world – and other Articles would hold Captains answerable to their crews. 'They only permit him to be Captain, on Condition, that they may be Captain over him', notes Defoe of Roberts. Hence when it came to choosing a supposed 'Captain' of the ship, the crew held 'that it was not of any great Signification who was dignify'd with Title; for really and in Truth, all good Governments had (like theirs) the supream Power lodged with the Community ... *We are the Original of this Claim* (says he) *and should a Captain be so sawcy as to exceed the Prescription at any time*, why down with Him!'[32]

This egalitarian and democratic spirit permeated other Articles. The social order of the pirate ship was 'conceived and deliberately constructed by the pirates themselves', Rediker notes. Rediker has also calculated that in the first quarter of the eighteenth century over 70 percent of active pirates came from two extended pirate groups, and that it was through this network that the social organization of the pirate ship took on a political significance with a 'rough, improvised, but effective egalitarianism that placed authority in the collective hands of the crew'. Decisions on policy were taken democratically by the ship's 'council' as the highest authority on board and disciplinary measures were agreed by the crew, all of which contrasted sharply with the despotism of naval captains and the rule of the lash. The emphasis was on majority rule, often meaning that the minority were asked or forced to leave in order to retain a consensus among the remaining crew. Law and laws as such did not exist on board ship or in the pirate settlements and hierarchy was constantly undermined by the

democratic spirit which sought to give the men a voice in their affairs.[33]
'When the authorities came into contact with the pirates', notes Ritchie,
'they were often shocked by their democratic tendencies'.[34]

When pirates did seek to make a permanent settlement they carried
these principles with them, which is why pirate activities on land in the
form of pirate communities should be considered just as significant as their
activities at sea, as the 'temporary autonomous zone' of the ship got trans-
ferred into the 'temporary autonomous zone' of the 'pirate utopia'.[35] As
piracy took on a more and more radical form through the seventeenth and
into the early eighteenth centuries, a number of 'pirate utopias' came into
being, including settlements at Hispaniola, Libertatia (or 'Libertalia' as it
is sometimes rendered) in Madagascar, Ranter's Bay in Madagascar, and
Nassau in the Bahamas. The stories told of 'permanent' settlements such as
Libertatia include an equal division of booty and cattle, money being held
in a common treasury (on the principle that money can be of no use in a
system where everything is held in common), hedges being forbidden, and
governments democratically elected. It was nothing less than a 'radically
revolutionary society in the context of eighteenth-century society, harking
back to the radical traditions of the English Revolution and looking
forward to the great revolutions at the end of the century'. Yet even then it
was 'still not radically libertarian enough for some of the pirates'.[36] One
pirate community on Madagascar elected by lot a man to be governor for
three months, after which he was ineligible to be chosen again until everyone else had had their turn. One community was led by Captain Bellamy
who, in a speech reported by Defoe, said that the ruling class vilify pirates
when there is only one difference: 'they rob the Poor under the Cover of
Law [while] we plunder the Rich under the Protection of our own
Courage'. The pirate community, he claimed, was notable for refusing to
'submit to be governed by Laws which rich Men have made for their own
Security'.[37]

For these reasons piracy has been described as instituting a 'culture of
masterless men'[38] – and, we might add, 'masterless women', but also
perhaps, 'masterless women dressed as men'[39] – operating an anarchic code
removed from traditional authority, beyond disciplinary labour, driven by
egalitarian and democratic impulses and underpinned by liberal social
relations (including an entrenched toleration for homosexuality).[40] 'By the
1720s', note Linebaugh and Rediker, 'thousands of pirates had ... self-
consciously built an autonomous, democratic, egalitarian social order of
their own, a subversive alternative to the prevailing ways of the merchant,
naval, and privateering ship and a counterculture to the civilization of
Atlantic capitalism with its expropriation and exploitation, terror and slavery'.[41] Even more significant is that pirates exercised a preference for
'shares' rather than 'wages' in a way that made them appear to be trying to
abolish the wage. 'They are very happy, well paid and they live in amity with

each other', wrote the Viceroy of New Spain to the Queen in 1669. 'The prizes that they make are shared with much brotherhood and friendship'.[42] In other words, pirates considered themselves risk-sharing partners rather than wage labourers; hence the name of famous pirates such as Captain Kidd was often coupled with that of Robin Hood, and some pirate crews claimed to be 'Robin Hood's men'.

All told, the disdain for the kinds of regimes of power and property that existed in the states from where they once hailed meant that piracy appeared to offer a counterculture in direct opposition to the prevailing powers of state, church, property and colony. In differentiating the codes and values of piracy from the will of the sovereign and the expectations of capital, piracy 'crossed all established limits of order'.[43] On this basis, it would appear that the Pirate's status as the Enemy of all Mankind stems from the Pirate's antipathy to capital accumulation and bourgeois law and order. If it really is the case that 'pirates supply popular literature with its demonology',[44] then the demon in question looks remarkably like a radicalised worker, and piracy not just a simple robbery at sea but a much wider protest against the kind of labour and social order that private property made necessary.

The social organization of piracy appeared to be part of a radical and rebellious tradition linking medieval peasants, seventeenth-century radicals such as the Ranters, Levellers and Diggers, slave rebellions in the colonies (in 1715 the ruling Council of the Virginia colony connected the 'ravage of pyrates' with the 'insurrection of Negroes'), and the uprisings of indentured white servants and wage labourers through the eighteenth century. Seen in this light, the Pirate appeared as a figure in the international class struggle and piracy as a structure of outlaw power and labour militancy that formed the basis for successfully undermining merchant property and international commerce.[45] Libertarian democrat and proletarian radical, espousing an ideology of autonomy, equality and community, and constructing communities that were havens for outlaw identities: in effect, an Enemy of both security and capital and thus also of the security of capital. Such an adversarial form resonated for the revolutionary international thereafter: not for nothing did the Paris Commune of 1871 issue a daily paper called *Le Pirate*; not for nothing did part of the youth resistance to Nazism call itself the *Edelweiss Pirates*; and not for nothing have *Pirate Parties* begun to emerge on the Left.

The Pirate looked so radical, so adversarial, so driven by an enmity for the world of bourgeois security and capital accumulation that 'in truth', comments Rediker, 'pirates were terrorists of a sort'.[46] Terrorists? Of a sort? What sort? The sort that might be described as the Enemy of All Mankind? The sort that might therefore be described as some kind of Universal Adversary? We haven't got there yet with this argument, but let us move towards it. And let us do so by returning to the question raised earlier: why is something that appears to be simply an act of robbery at sea understood as so much more than simply robbery at sea?

To answer such a question we have to grasp two key issues. The first one, which we have already noted, is the Pirate's wider political significance in the process of primitive accumulation and the constitution of wage-slavery. For to declare the Pirate the *Enemy of All Mankind* is to simultaneously say something about the fear of the *proletarian form* which underpins this supposed enemy. If the Pirate could be seen as 'a monkey wrench thrown into the colonisation process',[47] the monkey wrench appeared to be somehow intimately connected to the organised, radical and mobile working class being brought into existence by capital itself but which had the potential to be a weapon against capital itself. Even if piracy was not quite the obstacle to capitalist accumulation and commercial expansion that many have claimed, it certainly felt like it was to the rising merchant class when that class imagined the nature of this adversary and feared its advance. This takes us to the second issue, which is that so powerful was this ruling class fear that it began to use the category 'pirate' or 'piracy' for *anything* that it regarded as standing in the way of accumulation.

Rubin points out that the word 'piracy' entered modern English 'to cover almost any interference with property rights, whether licensed or not, and was applied as a pejorative with political implications but no clear legal meaning'. In its Latin form 'piracy' was used by lawyers concerned with public order to describe an unauthorized action related to property.[48] This continued to be the case whenever European powers confronted obstacles to accumulation. Hence a century after the piracy's supposed 'golden age' and thus well past the moment when piracy could be realistically regarded as a threat to global accumulation, one finds 'piracy', 'pirate states', 'pirate coasts', 'land pirates' and 'piratical peoples' being used as labels by European imperialist states to justify their so-called 'police actions' in the colonisation of more and more parts of the world. Rather than recognising some nations and peoples as sovereign entities and bona fide members of the international system of states, the concept of piracy was mobilised so that the communities in question could be castigated as failing to meet the 'standard of civilisation' and thus be denounced as the Enemy of all Mankind.[49] During its imperial expansion in the nineteenth century, for example, Britain found itself needing legal labels to justify military action against those interfering with British shipping but which for various legal and diplomatic reasons it did not wish to call 'war'. Rubin takes up the point:

> Such military action could then be seen either as an option of policy unfettered by the usual legal restraints on the decision to go to war in municipal law and international law, or as a mere enforcement action by a 'policeman' of the international order, or even by a 'policeman' of

the British legal order as it was extended to all seas for the purposes of securing universal 'rights' to commerce.[50]

It is significant that the terminology of piracy is still widely used in this way, mobilising security, legitimising the exercise of the police power, obfuscating the real nature of what is being suppressed and treating all objections to these things as irrelevant.

The second issue, then, is that well after the 'golden age of piracy', the terms 'pirate', 'piracy' and 'piratical' came to be used as key ideological tools in the hands of the ruling class against its enemies. This is a reflection of the fact that 'pirate', 'piracy' and 'piratical' are remarkably mobile and singularly productive categories.[51] As Viscount Palmerston observed in 1838, the label 'piracy' was politically useful as an 'infamous designation'. In the same year that Palmerston made his observation the British naval officer Sherard Osborn made the following comment on the subject of Mohamed Saad's fleet: Saad's fleet, he said, 'was styled by us as a piratical one'.[52] In the context of nineteenth century imperialism, the idea was to *civilise* these states and spaces – that is, to police them – and so *styling them* as 'piratical' enabled the exercise of the police power to move them from the supposedly *lawless* state of piracy to the *legal order* of bourgeois civilisation. The phrase '*styled* by us as piratical' reveals the extent to which 'piracy' and 'piratical' could so easily be used as labels for any obstacle to accumulation or opponent of colonial power. To *style* them 'piratical' was to automatically *criminalise* them and to thereby legitimise the violence against them. And where things could not be styled as piracy, they could be styled as 'quasi-piracy', a term that came into play in the nineteenth century to help 'widen the concept of piracy'[53] and thereby apply it in such a way that helped mobilise maritime police powers.

Regardless of whether these were acts formally understood as 'war' or 'police', an issue to which we shall shortly turn, the point is that the label 'piracy', much like 'terrorist', came to have no meaning other than that imposed on it by the state for ideological purposes. The ability and authority to name, define, label and categorise – the ability to *style things in a certain way* – is a key function of state power, and being able to impose the terms used in an argument, and repeating those terms time and again until they become 'common sense', is a fundamental feature of political rule. The ability to 'style things piratical' invests certain forms of action and modes of being as a dangerous Other. It has the immediate effect of rendering non-state forms of violence as illegal, non-capitalist forms of production as illegitimate and non-wage forms of subsistence as dangerous and disorderly.

One gets a sense of the importance of being able to style things *as if* they are piratical from the various moments in which the ruling class have enquired about what exactly the phrase really means. In the 1693 trial of John Golding and several others accused of piracy, known as the Golding case and commented on by Matthew Tindall in his *Essay Concerning the Laws of Nations and the Rights of Sovereigns* (1694), a text widely cited in trials thereafter, Tindall cites one of the legal experts in the case, Sir Thomas Pinfold. Pinfold's basic defence was that all his clients had done was to commit the simple crime of robbery. Tindall notes:

> Then, Sir T. P. [Thomas Pinfold] said, it was impossible they [the defendants] should be Pirates, for a Pirate was *hostis humani generis*, but they were not Enemies to all Mankind, therefore they could not be Pirates. Upon which all smiled, and one of the Lords asked him, Whether there ever was any such thing as a Pirate, if none could be a Pirate but he that was actually in War with all Mankind.

Pinfold had confronted the court with the obvious question: how could the defendants be pirates if they were not at war with all mankind? All that the lawyers, judges and officials could offer was a knowing smile and then point out that it would be hard to find any such person who was actually at war with mankind. In response, notes Tindall, Pinfold repeated a point he had made before: '*hostis humani generis*, is neither a Definition, nor so much as a description of a Pirate, but *a rhetorical Invective to show the Odiousness of that Crime*'.[54] So much can the term 'piracy' be styled by those in power as a piece of 'rhetorical invective' that it is, in effect, a *legal fiction*, one which means nothing other than that the Pirate must be treated *as if* he were the Enemy of All Mankind.[55] This treatment of the Pirate *as if* he were the Enemy of All Mankind has probably been taken for granted by those in power since at least the seventeenth century. Contra Foucault's comment that in an age in which utopian spaces disappear, the police come to take the place of pirates,[56] it is much more the case that 'piracy' comes to operate as a category of police power.

All told, it is no surprise that the figure of the Pirate – or rather and more generally, anything that looked like it could be *styled as* 'piratical' or treated *as if* a pirate – became the target of a permanent and international police hunt, as the ruling class and state functionaries interpellated piracy as a crime against everything for which that class and those functionaries stood: private property and corporate accumulation, law and order, peace and security, bourgeois individualism and class power, colonial force and imperial might, Church and Crown, the state and the state system as whole. Piracy, as one colonial lawyer put it, is a

> crime so odious and horrid ... that those who hath treated on that Subject have been at a loss for Words and Terms to stamp a sufficient Ignominy upon it: some calling them Sea-Wolfs; others Beasts of Prey, and Enemies of Mankind, with whom neither Faith nor Treaty is to be kept.

The comment was from Richard Allein, Attorney General of South Carolina in 1718, and he went on to point out that beasts of prey kill to satisfy their hunger and have no concept of good and evil. 'Pirates prey upon all Mankind, their own Species and Fellow-Creatures, without Distinction of Nations or Religions'.[57] So complete was the Pirate's villainy and adversarial nature that the Pirate had to be treated *as if* the enmity was universal.

The universal nature of the crime meant that the Pirate was regarded as worthy of excommunication according to the Bishops[58] and guilty of treason according to lawyers,[59] which is precisely why when Blackstone declares piracy to be a 'species of treason' he also describes the pirate the Enemy of All Mankind, in a passage we noted above and about which we can now say a little more.

Here is the passage from Blackstone again:

> The crime of *piracy*, or robbery and depredation upon the high seas, is an offence against the universal law of society; a pirate being, according to Sir Edward Coke, *hostis humani generis*. As therefore he has renounced all the benefits of society and government, and has reduced himself afresh to the savage state of nature, by declaring war against all mankind, all mankind must declare war against him.

Coke appears to have imported the phrase *hostis humani generis* from Roman law, with Cicero often cited as the main source of the phrase, though as Rubin points out the phrase Cicero uses is *communis hostis omnium*. Either way, by the time Blackstone was writing the position was clear: the pirate is the 'Common Enemy of All', the 'Enemy of the Human Species' or the 'Enemy of All Mankind' (*hostis omnium*; *communis hostis omnium*; *hostis humani generis*).

Now, we noted at the end of the previous chapter that the phrase *hostis humani generis* was one of the terms used to describe the Devil, but the origins of the idea of the Pirate as 'Enemy of All' must also be traced back to the attempt by the Romans to impose their imperial power across the seas. The Greeks (who 'were, as is known, great pirates'[60]) had previously failed to do so, but the Romans sought to do so in order to control the seas and maritime commerce. To this end piracy was identified by the Romans as a practice to be eradicated and this required a rethinking of some parts of Roman law by writers such as Cicero. Rubin shows that when the Romans used the term 'pirates' they did so not simply to connote 'robbery at sea' but to castigate what they saw as a fundamental impropriety: a way of life that was antithetical to the new commercial and political order being imposed by the Romans themselves. Far from simply a crime committed at sea, piracy was regarded as an act of enmity against the imperial order. What was 'piratical' was a form of political community which the Romans could regard only as an enemy form against which it had to be at war. Moreover, the elaboration of the concept of the 'pirate' occurred during the consolidation of Rome as an imperial power with a self-proclaimed responsibility for imposing 'peace and security' at sea as well as on land. The more Rome considered itself as a form of power responsible for such peace and security, the more it thought of itself as possessing the right and the power to impose a universal law (the *ius gentium*), and so the more inclined it was to brand as the Enemy of All Mankind those accused of violating the *ius gentium*.[61]

The problem, however, was that by virtue of their nature pirates could not qualify as a real and proper enemy. Roman law is replete with comments along the lines that 'enemies are those upon whom the Roman people have publicly declared war, or who themselves have declared war against the Roman people; others are called robbers or brigands' (Ulpian), and 'those are enemies who declare war against us, or against whom we declare war; others are robbers or brigands' (Pomponius).[62] But there could be no formal declaration of war against pirates nor any kind of peace agreement at the end of any such war. Working through the Roman documents, Rubin suggests that the implication of such passages is that the Roman conception of 'piracy' involved a distinction between robbers, who were simply criminals at law, and 'piratical' communities, with the latter being understood as a form of political society pursuing an economic course at odds with Roman commercial interests. These were communities with which the Romans clearly thought they could and should be at war, but against whom war could not easily be declared other than as a war for the imperial peace in general; or, put another way, a war against the piratical formations which appear antithetical to that imperial peace and security. The imperial violence in question thus took the form of the persecution of outlaw groups: a *persecutio piratarum* which constituted a kind of *war* as a form of *police power*.

In one sense, then, when jurists such as Blackstone started using the language of the 'Enemy of All' to describe the Pirate, they were playing a little on the status of the Pirate in Roman law. Yet they were also making moves towards a modern conception of *universal jurisdiction*: the right and power to impose a certain kind of 'peace and security' over spaces which appeared to be under no territorial jurisdiction. This was especially pressing since, as Schmitt points out, the emerging new world and its radically modern conception of the space of the globe meant that it was confronted with *free space* beyond territorial jurisdiction.[63] If, as Foucault puts it and as we have already noted, the history of piracy and the way in which it was used, encouraged, combated and suppressed needs to be read in terms of the elaboration of a number of legal principles for the constitution of a secure worldwide market,[64] then nowhere is this clearer than in the legal principle of universal jurisdiction. This is one reason why the idea of universal jurisdiction emerged with the very birth of international law and has remained in place through international law's history. From its inception international law has been founded on the idea that there exists a universal community of the kind we noted in the previous chapter – Vitoria, Suarez, Grotius, Vattel and many others based their arguments on claims about universal human nature, morality and law. The idea of 'universal' jurisdiction played on such claims but was also designed to deal with a very specific issue: the policing of the high seas beyond the territorial control of any state. The implication was that any state has the ability to punish any offenders committing crimes on the high seas, regardless of the offender's relation to that particular state. The 'universality' underlying universal jurisdiction allows for the exercise of an international police power over offenders wherever they occur and regardless of nationality. Thus the idea of universal jurisdiction was intended to ensure the high seas as a space of 'peace and security' and 'law and order' despite those spaces being outside territorial power and beyond sovereign jurisdiction. But as well as intending to *secure space*, universal jurisdiction was, as part of the system of international law, also intended to *secure international trade* and thereby help *constitute the market as a universal norm*.

Now, it is often said that international law permits states to exercise universal jurisdiction over pirates, but the more telling point is that the concept of universal jurisdiction was understood to apply *specifically to piracy*. Piracy is therefore often treated as the first international crime.[65] So central is the idea of piracy to the concept of universal jurisdiction that at key moments in the twentieth century when universal jurisdiction has taken centre stage, such as during Nazi war crimes tribunals, the Eichmann trial and the Yugoslavian war crimes tribunal, the lawyers in question have all invoked the piracy analogy. The crimes were treated *as if* they came under the same universal jurisdiction with which piracy was treated.

The standard definition of universal jurisdiction appears in Article 105 of the United Nations Convention on the Law of the Sea (UNCLOS, 1982), which repeats article 19 of the 1958 Convention on the High Seas, as follows:

> On the high seas, or in any other place outside the jurisdiction of any State, *every State may seize a pirate ship or aircraft*, or a ship or aircraft taken by piracy and under the control of pirates, and arrest the persons and seize the property on board. The courts of the State which carried out the seizure may decide upon the penalties to be imposed, and may also determine the action to be taken with regard to the ships, aircraft or property, subject to the rights of third parties acting in good faith.

The universal jurisdiction is said to stem from the fact that the crime happens on the high sea, putting it into the category of 'international crime'. The question of how the modern state system might punish international crime is one that troubled international law from its inception, but the fact that many things could be *styled* piratical helped.

> The first breakthrough occurred when international law accepted the concepts that pirates are the 'enemies of mankind' and that piracy is 'an offense against the law of nations'… Once this concept of an international crime was developed in one area, it was soon applied by analogy to other fields.[66]

Yet this alone is hardly enough to render the crime subject to universal jurisdiction. Rather, the crime took on such a status by virtue of the belief that some crimes are universal in nature, which generated in turn the belief that the perpetrators of such crimes are subject to universal antipathy to the extent that they can be regarded as a kind of Enemy of All Mankind. In other words, one of the rationales usually given for subjecting piracy to universal jurisdiction is that pirates are *hostis humani generis*. To put it bluntly, the conjoint development of the concept of piracy and universal jurisdiction is 'the fundamental conceptual basis on which the whole structure of modern international criminal law has been built'.[67]

The figure of the Pirate has therefore often been treated as a 'subject' of international law since the inception of the modern law of nations. Yet as Schmitt points out, despite this the Pirate is more often than not *denied* the status of a subject of international law because only states, as the *bona fide* subjects of international law, are considered capable of infractions of that law.[68] The international order has always sought to treat the Pirate as a problem for that order, yet cannot quite interpellate the Pirate fully in terms of the law through which that order is said to be constituted. The solution to this problem lay in the idea that individuals could be recognised as legal personalities in international criminal law, but this only begs the question of why international criminal law needs to treat the Pirate as the Enemy of All Mankind. This problem arises on the basis that the Pirate is *hostis humani generis*, but the Pirate is only *hostis humani generis* by virtue of being described as such by the international order. This begs an obvious question, first asked by Edwin Dickinson many years ago: 'Is the jurisdiction [over pirates] universal because they are *hostes humani generis*, or are they said to be *hostes humani generis* because the jurisdiction is universal?'[69] A comment from Justice Story in the US Supreme Court in 1844 (in *United States* v. *Brig Malek Adhel*) is interesting in this regard. Dealing with some acts of violence which had been called piracy, the case turned on the term 'piracy' as it appeared in an earlier statute.

> Where the act uses the word 'piratical', it does so in a general sense; importing that the aggression is unauthorized by the law of nations, hostile in its character, wanton and criminal in its commission, and

utterly without sanction from any public authority or sovereign power. In short, it means that the act belongs to the class of offences which pirates are in the habit of perpetuating, whether they do it for purposes of plunder, or for purposes of hatred, revenge, or wanton abuse of power. A pirate is deemed, and properly deemed, *hostis humani generis.* But why is he so deemed? Because he commits hostilities upon the subjects and property of *any or all* nations, without any regard to duty or right, or any pretence of public authority... The law looks to it as an act of hostility, and being committed by a vessel not commissioned and engaged in lawful warfare, it treats it as the act of a pirate, and of one who is emphatically *hostis humani generis.*[70]

The 'jurisdiction' is thus less a question of territorial sovereignty and much more to do with something in the alleged offense, construed of as a wanton act of aggression committed out of pure hatred and detached from any sovereign power. This is what has become known as the supposed *heinousness* of the crime of piracy, as we noted earlier and about which we can now say a little more.

The Princeton Principles on Universal Jurisdiction put it in the following way: 'National courts can exercise universal jurisdiction to prosecute and punish, and thereby deter, *heinous acts* recognized as serious crimes under international law'.[71] The issue concerns the supposed heinousness when compared with the other crimes that are regarded as heinous enough to warrant universal jurisdiction, such as torture, war crimes, genocide and slave-trading. Indeed, when in 1838 Palmerston wanted to use the term 'piracy' as an 'infamous designation' it was meant to apply to the slave trade: he thought he could give the slave trade a bad name by 'branding' it 'with the name of piracy' (and the Quintuple Treaty for the Suppression of the African Slave Trade, agreed in 1841 between England, France, Prussia, Austria and Russia, held to the exact same line). Likewise, when Eichmann went on trial in Jerusalem 1961 accused of crimes against the Jewish people, crimes against humanity and war crimes, the court claimed its competence for the trial in the name of universal jurisdiction, which it said 'was applicable because crimes against humanity are similar to the old crime of piracy, and he who commits them has become, like the pirate in traditional international law, *hostis humani generis*'.[72] So heinous were Eichmann's crimes that prosecuting him solely as an engineer of mass murder on the scale committed by the Nazis was somehow not enough, and so he had to suffer the indignity of being treated *as if* his crimes were similar to piracy. (To get a sense of the importance of the heinousness attached to piracy we might observe that although people are generally taught that in England capital punishment was abolished in 1965, the death sentence was in fact abolished for *all* crimes only in 1998, with the passing of the Crime and Disorder Act, which removed the death penalty as a punishment for 'piracy with violence' (as well as for treason); the supposed *heinousness* of murder during an act of piracy, which is what was meant by 'piracy with violence', was thought to make it somehow worse than murder during non-piratical acts.)

What we have then, is the situation in which just *one act* of robbery on the high seas, which has shown to be sufficient grounds for a charge of piracy to be brought, is treated as heinous a crime as genocide or slave-trading. How can this be? Wilhelm Grewe suggests that what is revealed in such moves is the political function of international law, and he is of course right.[73] But what is also revealed is the political function of the category 'piracy'. For the answer to the question would seem to lie in piracy's history: in the fact that it was denounced as a heinous act because of its supposed effects on international commerce and imperial violence. Piracy's heinousness would appear to lie in it being a challenge to global accumulation, to the extent that the Pirate had to be treated as a figure of *hate*. 'heinous' was taken from the Old French *hainos* meaning hateful as well as unpleasant and odious, and then from the Modern French *haineux* with its implications of hatred. For the ruling class piracy was by definition an act so abominable it had to be treated *as if* it was an act of pure hatred, *as if* it was hated by all and thus *as if* it was a crime of universal nature, and this remains the case now.

In one sense, then, a combination of its heinousness and the fact that it is generally assumed to be a crime conducted on the seas means that piracy appears to be a crime of international dimensions and thus a crime against the law of nations (and therefore a crime against the system of states *per se*), making it far more than simply 'robbery at sea' and much more a crime requiring some kind of 'universal jurisdiction', just like those other crimes to which universal jurisdiction is said to apply: genocide, torture, slave-trading and now terrorism. In another sense, however, it is possible to suggest that, as Rubin puts it, 'universal jurisdiction' was at best a rule of international law only for a limited period and under specific political circumstances, while at worst it was a British attempt to force the international legal order into accepting rules forbidding 'piracy' and trying to make all nations apply such rules on the high seas. It is for this reason that many people have for a long time argued that despite having been a key issue in international law since the 1720s and maybe even longer, 'it is possible to assert with some confidence that there is no international law of "piracy" at all'.[74] The Draft Convention on Piracy produced by the Harvard Law School Research in International Law found that 'there is no authoritative definition' of piracy, and others have more recently made the same point.[75] The problem is that it is widely held that the defining characteristic of piracy is, as the Harvard Law team put it, 'an act of violence ... by persons not acting under any proper authority'. But if pirate acts are seen as distinct from any state then it is difficult to make them come under international law, which deals precisely with relations between states. It is for this reason that many find problematic the idea of the Pirate being an *Enemy* of All Mankind, since 'enemy' appears the wrong term. Daniel Defoe cites in his *General History of the Pyrates* the Civil and Statute Law of the time: 'A *Pyrate is* Hostis humanis generis, *a common Enemy, with whom neither Faith nor Oath is to be kept'*, but adds that

> Though *Pyrates are called common Enemies, yet they are properly not to be term'd so. He is only to be honor'd with that Name, says Cicero, who hath a Commonwealth, a Court, a Treasury, Consent and Concord of Citizens, and some Way, if Occasion be, of Peace and League.*[76]

Distinct from the Enemy who might be a formally equal opponent – publicly recognised as a formally equal opponent and thus publicly recognised as a *just* Enemy – this other Enemy was thought to deserve no such recognition (indeed could be given no such recognition) and could thus be denied the rights pertaining to an equal. Moreover, the fact that in the eyes of many commentators what defined an act as piracy was that it was performed for private gain rather than political ends, thereby rendering it 'unpolitical', meant that action against pirates have been required to look 'unpolitical' in character as well, as Schmitt noted.[77] Which is precisely why the action against piracy had to be cast as a police operation.

Hence even though the UNCLOS contains a definition, in Article 101, calling piracy 'illegal acts of violence … committed for private ends', more than enough scholars have suggested that this merely reiterates that piracy is simply a crime and therefore resolves nothing. So using the term 'crime' when it comes to thinking about piracy is also not very helpful for those who want to argue that piracy is a problem in international law. Moreover, whatever the range of international treaties and codes may say, the *crime* of piracy was always handled within the national framework. As Rubin points out, 'the only legal definitions of "piracy" exist in municipal law and are applicable only in municipal tribunals bound to apply that law' and which 'do not represent any universal "law of nations"'.[78] The claim by the framers of the 1932 Draft Convention on Piracy was made on the grounds that the issue with piracy is not one of universal jurisdiction, but rather *extraordinary* jurisdiction: piracy is the grounds for an 'extraordinary jurisdiction' on the part of every state to seize and punish persons for offences committed outside territorial jurisdiction.[79] The framers were alert to the fact that those who wish to claim that piracy is a crime under international law do so because they wish to draw an analogy with genocide, torture, slave trading (and we can now add terrorism). But they also knew that to claim piracy was somehow a crime under international law is not tenable, a fact that has since been shown time and again by critically minded scholars. At great length and after detailed analysis of the history of legal debate about piracy as it developed over two thousand years, Rubin claims that:

it is possible that there never has been any such law except in the autointerpretive projections of some states from time to time seeking either to expand their jurisdiction to safeguard their own trade or establish imperial interests, or in the theories of those who prefer to call their personal moral insights 'law' *as if* universally applicable and not requiring a legislative decision by a 'legislator' empowered within a legal order.[80]

Note once more: *as if* universally applicable. Rubin offers a compelling case to show that the persistence over two millennia of some concept of 'piracy' and some idea that it falls under a 'universal jurisdiction' creates a presumption that there is some fundamental international law forbidding piracy, a view reinforced by the fact that the activities in question occur at sea, when in fact there really is no internationally agreed offence or crime of piracy and thus no international law of 'piracy'.[81]

Hence the classical meaning of piracy which could never be shaken off is one that has had to treat piracy *as if* it is a violation of international law; the existence of numerous treaties and codes encourage this view. As others have pointed out, this is why attaching the word *hostis* ('enemies') was important, since it implied an enemy against whom war was being waged, as opposed to *latrones* ('brigands') or *praedones* ('robbers'). The phrase *hostis humani generis* could be taken to mean that pirates are not criminals in law at all (that is, not simply engaged in 'robbery at sea'), but are *political communities at war* – that is, an Enemy and, moreover, an enemy of not just this or that state but of all states and the state system as a whole.[82] 'This sort of Criminals are engag'd in a perpetual War with every Individual', commented John Valentine in 1723 during his prosecution of 36 pirates.[83] Piracy is in essence an act of antagonism which appears general enough to be treated *as if* universal. We have to see how the Pirate was defined as some kind of *universal Enemy* to understand whether and to what degree such a status also holds for those more modern figures who go by the name 'Pirate', including 'criminals against humanity', 'enemies of the human race', 'unlawful combatants' and now 'the Universal Adversary'.

The idea of a 'war on piracy', then, makes sense only if we forego the 'classical' or 'Clausewitzian' understanding of war so common to strategic studies and IR and read it instead as a police war, on a par with a 'war on drugs', 'war on crime' or, as we shall increasingly see, a 'war on terror'. Like these other wars, the war on piracy makes things possible, creates subjects and targets and even subjects as targets, and thus enables security to be mobilised in myriad ways in the formation of order. To see the war on piracy as a police mechanism helps make sense of the continual iteration of statements such as Blackstone's with which we began this chapter, that the *crime* of piracy demands that all mankind must declare *war* against the Pirate, or the statement of John Valentine just cited, that the sort of *criminal* that is the Pirate means they are engaged in a perpetual *war* with all. This *styles* piracy *as if* it were both a 'universal war against all' and a 'crime against humanity'. A war and a crime, and thus also a kind of 'war-crime'. The power of the category 'piracy', then, in part lies in being styled in such a way that it collapses any distinction between the criminal and political.[84] Or to put that another way, the operation against piracy requires all the powers of war and police combined.

In his discussion of piracy and the law of nations Daniel Heller-Roazen notes four distinctive traits associated with the term 'piracy'. First, the piratical action takes place in a territory judged 'exceptional' with respect to ordinary jurisdiction; second, it involves an agent who displays an antagonism that cannot be defined as that of one individual with another or of one political association with another; third, the action dubbed 'piratical' collapses the distinction between criminal and political categories; and fourth, by collapsing the distinction between the criminal and the political, the piratical action involves a transformation in the concept of war. He goes on to make the following connection: 'the "enemy of all" can be located wherever all four elements of the paradigm may be found. Today [2009], it would surely not be difficult to identify examples'. His allusion is obvious, and much earlier in the book he made a similar allusion by asking an obvious question: 'What precisely links the "enemy of all" of the age of Cicero ... to the so-called "terrorists" of our times?'.[85] Well, what does link them? What is at stake when we find it said in the *NSS 2002*, cited at the beginning of this chapter, that terrorism will be viewed in the same light as piracy?

In an interview conducted in July 2005, John Yoo, who had been Deputy Assistant Attorney General during the first two years of the 'war on terror', was asked about the application of the Geneva conventions to people who might be 'enemy combatants' or 'prisoners of war'. The issue of how and when the Geneva conventions applied was a central issue in the early years of the war on terror and has remained very much so for critically minded scholars. Yoo replied by pointing out that this was the key question they faced when launching the war:

> I had to answer right from the beginning: Is it war or not? And then, should they be treated the same as a nation or not? Because I think some people think, well, crime is just one sort of sphere with its own rules, and war is just one sphere and its own rules, and everybody in war gets treated the same. But that's not actually the case. War has different rules for a nation and different rules for people who choose to fight kind of like pirates who are outside the control of a nation.[86]

In other words, from the outset the security strategy underpinning the 'war on terror' would mean treating terrorists *as if* ('kind of like') they are pirates. In another interview conducted around the same time he made the same point:

> Why is it so hard for people to understand that there is a category of behavior not covered by the legal system? ... What were pirates? They weren't fighting on behalf of any nation. What were slave traders? Historically, there were people so bad that they were not given protection of the laws. There were no specific provisions for their trial, or imprisonment. If you were an illegal combatant, you didn't deserve the protection of the laws of war.

The point, he added, was that the 'simple binary classification of civilian or soldier isn't accurate'.[87] The terrorist needed to be treated less like an Enemy soldier and more like the Pirate of old.

We might likewise note the 2007 Memorandum on Maritime Security (Piracy) Policy. Annex B of the document, a 'Policy for the Repression of Piracy and other Criminal Acts of Violence at Sea', runs as follows: 'Piracy is any illegal act of violence, detention, or depredation committed for private ends by the crew, or the passengers, of a private ship and directed against a ship, aircraft, persons, or property on the high seas or in any other place outside the jurisdiction of any state'. Note the simple definition: piracy is a criminal act on the high seas. From this it makes the next obvious move, based on the long history of international law: 'Piracy is a universal crime, and all states are obligated to cooperate to the fullest possible extent in the repression of piracy'. From that, there is only one more connection to make: 'Piracy threatens U.S. national security interests ... undermines economic security, and contributes to the destabilization of weak or failed state governance'.[88] From robbery at sea to a national security threat, in two simple moves. Such claims have not gone away with the change of Presidency: the CIA under President Obama has included countering piracy as part of its security mandate.[89]

The point should by now be obvious, but let me spell it out. The logic of security now holds that terrorism exhibits a set of characteristics traditionally associated with piracy: acting outside the authority of any existing state; denationalised and highly mobile; a crime so heinous it must be seen *as if* it is an act of war against all of us; committing supposedly indiscriminate acts of violence on persons not formally engaged in a state of war; secretly or semi-secretly working beyond or even against the international system of state power.[90] This contemporary version of the 'piracy analogy' means that the 'war on terror' resembles the *persecutio piratarum* of the early modern wars of accumulation. As Policante notes:

> Since the beginning of the global 'War on Terror', the spectre of the pirate as *hostis humani generis* has been evoked in order to justify the

practice of 'targeted killings' of suspected terrorists throughout the world. Moreover, it has also served the aim of justifying the right to ignore the Geneva Convention in exceptional spaces like Guantanamo and Abu Ghraib.[91]

The concept of The Terrorist today performs a similar role to the one that has been historically played by the concept of The Pirate. It is an empty signifier that can be applied to anyone who challenges the power of the state and capital, anyone who resists the violence being conducted in the name of 'peace and security' and anyone who looks to be a threat to 'law and order'. As such, it is of no surprise that the figure of the terrorist is offered to us *as if* they are the new Enemy of All Mankind, to be treated *as if* the Terrorist is as bad as the Pirates. To be treated, that is, *as if* they are an Adversary whose enmity is Universal.

As if II: 'the commerce of the world must cease'

'Terrorism will be viewed in the same light as slavery, piracy, or genocide', we noted the *NSS 2002* claim at the beginning of this chapter, and we have explored some of the historical roots of this claim and its links with contemporary security. Yet there is another meaning of 'piracy' at work here, one that enables us to bring contemporary capitalist accumulation into the frame of the ongoing war on piracy, thereby revealing the centrality of capital to the contemporary concept of the Pirate as the Enemy of All Mankind and so bringing this book to a close.

In 1993 a US Judge made the following observation:

> Saddam Hussein wants to keep advertisers from using his picture in unflattering contexts. Clint Eastwood doesn't want tabloids to write about him. Rudolf Valentino's heirs want to control his film biography. The Girl Scouts don't want their image soiled by association with certain activities. George Lucas wants to keep Strategic Defense Initiative fans from calling it 'Star Wars'. Pepsico doesn't want singers to use the word 'Pepsi' in their songs. Guy Lombardo wants an exclusive property right to ads that show big bands playing on New Year's Eve. Uri Geller thinks he should be paid for ads showing psychics bending metal through telekinesis. Paul Prudhomme, that household name, thinks the same about ads featuring corpulent bearded chefs. And scads of copyright holders see purple when their creations are made fun of. Something very dangerous is going on here.[92]

What was going on, the Judge noted, was that the accusation of 'piracy' was being used to defend products, images, ideas, persons and just about anything else.

The judge was registering the fact that capital was increasingly being talked about in terms of 'knowledge', 'ideas' and 'intangible assets', and the defence of capital increasingly conducted through a defence of such 'intellectual property'. The 'displacement of human physical effort by ideas', as Alan Greenspan put it in 1996 whilst Chairman of the Federal Reserve, has been widely held to constitute a significant shift in accumulation in the latter decades of the twentieth century and then into the twenty-first.

> The world of 1948 was vastly different from the world of [today] … The quintessential model of industrial might in those days was the array of vast, smoke-encased integrated steel mills in the Pittsburgh district and on the shores of Lake Michigan. Output was things, big physical things. Virtually unimaginable a half century ago was the extent to which concepts and ideas would substitute for physical resources and human brawn in the production of goods and services.[93]

Greenspan's claim is now commonplace, though often it is not so much a direct substitution of physical goods with 'ideas' but, rather, that the profit produced through physical goods is now heavily dependent on 'intellectual property'. It is estimated, for example, that the cost of manufacturing a pair of Nike shoes is 4 percent of its retail price, while the rest consists of the patenting, trademark and branding.[94] A 2011 report by a Washington-based think tank specialising in economics and security estimated the total value of US intellectual capital at between $8.1 trillion and $9.2 trillion, the equivalent of 55 percent to 62.5 percent of US GDP.[95] Thus, as Michael Perelman has noted, the shift to a so-called 'weightless economy' is a shift in which intellectual property and intellectual property rights have become central to capital accumulation and class power.[96] Those who want to defend the intellectual property regime like to talk about protecting the creative process in general and the struggling musician or author in particular: 'patents and copyrights are … a man's right to the product of his mind', noted Ayn Rand in one of the most systematic defences of capitalism ever written, co-authored with Greenspan.[97] Yet this concern for the struggling creative individual masks the fact that the bulk of what is said to be 'intellectual property' is owned largely by corporations.[98]

The creation of the World Trade Organization (WTO) in 1995 was a key step in the consolidation of an intellectual property accumulation regime, essentially applying the General Agreement on Tariffs and Trade's (GATT) mission of liberalizing the trade in goods to the trade in intellectual property. The process was continued with TRIPS (Trade-Related aspects of Intellectual Property Rights), which operates in tandem with GATT as a mechanism for 'yoking copyright to trade', as Peter Baldwin puts it, thereby making intellectual property and the trade in goods and commodities practically inseparable. In effect, poorer countries are now obliged to adopt the intellectual property laws of wealthier nations as a condition of being part of the international trading system and WTO.[99] Operating under the auspices of the WTO but pushed through by major corporations within the multi-national information industries and their lobbying group the Intellectual Property Committee, TRIPS enacts an ideology of intellectual property rights which presupposes that ideas and genetic material are commodities like any other, to be marketed as such and managed by monopolies through patent and copyright law. Much like the underlying assumptions inherent in the concept of 'intellectual property', TRIPS encourages the idea that anything and everything might count as intellectual property, right down to some of the most banal ideas ever: 'Patent 5498162 A' passed by the US Patent Office covers the 'methods for demonstrating techniques for lifting objects, and more particularly, to a method for demonstrating a lifting technique which reduces the likelihood of back injury'. In other words, knowledge of the best way to lift an object is somehow a form of 'intellectual property'. TRIPS also, and again like the debate about intellectual property in general, moves back and forth between the question of products under copyright and the patenting of certain products as medicine.

The term 'intellectual property' thus serves to privilege the global capitalist appropriation and commodification of the commons – appropriation that plays on the idea of creativity by being described as an act of 'authorship' as well as 'ownership' and which in turn encourages the view that it is capital that is the world's creative power – and simultaneously seeks to delegitimize any attempt to re-appropriate those resources.[100] In so doing it has enabled resources once used by peoples on a collective basis to be appropriated as property and either patented or copyrighted in the name of accumulation: just as the Indian *neem* plant has been patented for oral hygiene use or the West African *karité* butter has been appropriated by the cosmetics industry, so Disney appropriates and copyrights *Snow White* and *Cinderella* from the many stories once told by European peasants. For this process to work the legal status of the resources have to be changed from being the common property of indigenous communities to being the private property of corporations; the intellectual commons becomes intellectual property. This process has therefore unsurprisingly been called the 'new enclosures' or the 'second enclosure movement', although we might also describe it as a new moment in the permanent process of primitive accumulation. Just as the 'old' or 'first' enclosures was crucial to primitive accumulation, so the 'new' or 'second' enclosures reminds us of the fundamental role that intellectual property currently plays in realising capital's constant demand: Let there be Accumulation!

All told, contemporary capitalism takes the idea of a 'marketplace of ideas' literally and not just metaphorically; the capitalist tradition of using the power of the state to help the ruling class loot the commons and establish a 'marketplace' for both goods and labour has been extended to knowledge and information.[101] Given that, in effect, the class war has become a war over intellectual property, it is no surprise that the defence of capital takes place through the struggle over intellectual property. Central to this war is the term 'piracy'. Since the idea was first mooted that 'intellectual property' needs to be legally protected and regulated, the protection in question has amounted to nothing less than a 'war on piracy', a war fought by the conjoined forces of capital and the state.

The first major steps in this direction occurred in the days when music was produced on vinyl LPs and could be easily copied onto blank cassette tapes. The music industry sought to stamp out the process with a major campaign claiming that 'home taping is killing music' and pointing out that taping an LP and giving the tape to a friend was a criminal act. The symbolism and language used, however, was not simply one of crime and destroying creativity but, rather, of treating the crime *as if* it was piracy. To this end the industry appropriated the pirate flag (Figure 4.1).

The idea stuck. Debates about 'piracy' are therefore now central to questions of culture, medicine and biotechnology, to the point where it is now commonplace to speak of 'pirated' music, film, games and other forms of cultural property, 'pirated' trademarks, images and brandings, and 'pirated' drugs and medicines. Despite the fact that there exists a variety of terms to describe theft of what is regarded as intellectual property, including 'counterfeit', 'bootleg' and 'knock-offs', 'piracy' has become the term preferred by corporations and the state, for three reasons. First, because

Figure 4.1 Copyright pirate

the weight of its historical baggage gives it a rhetorical power evoking a threat far greater than these other terms.[102] Second, because the label 'piracy' more explicitly connects the problem to issues in global trade and international trade disputes, thereby allowing the war on piracy to be declared an international problem requiring an international police power. And third, as we shall see towards the end of this chapter, the label 'piracy' also conveniently connects this threat to accumulation with the threat to security.

It is remarkable just how frequently capital's representatives now seek to catalogue and publicise the supposed 'losses' from piracy. The Organisation for Economic Co-operation and Development (OECD), for example, launched a project in 2005 to assess the impact and magnitude of pirated intellectual property:

> International trade in counterfeit and pirated products could have been up to USD 200 billion in 2005. This total does not include domes-tically produced and consumed counterfeit and pirated products and the significant volume of pirated digital products being distributed via the Internet. If these items were added, the total magnitude of coun-terfeiting and piracy worldwide could well be several hundred billion dollars more.[103]

That was in 2007. Two years later the OECD raised that figure to $250 billion.[104] A year later the Business Alliance against Counterfeiting and Piracy (BASCAP) estimated a global trade in counterfeit and pirated prod-ucts as much higher, at somewhere between $455 and $650 billion, and predicted that it would rise to $1,770 billion by 2015.[105] The fact that these figures are almost entirely fictitious (the losses 'could be' as high as x, are 'estimated' to be as high as y) is a reminder that we are dealing here with a powerful form of rhetoric which underpins debates about the political economy of capital in such a way as to connect the supposed losses from 'piracy' in the 'creative' or 'digital' industries to the supposed losses in other industries such as biotechnologies. And the problem is said to be piracy. Hence, to take just one well-known example, a company such as Monsanto runs a 'Seed Piracy Hotline' and each year is involved in a number of 'seed piracy' cases against farmers who save seed from one harvest to re-harvest the following year. This ancient agricultural practice is now subject to what the farmers call the 'seed police', namely the company's inspectors and lawyers, because Monsanto regard the practice as piracy.[106] We are once more on the terrain of the police versus the pirates, though the struggle looks very different to the wars on the high seas in the seventeenth century. But is it?

'Twenty-first-century pirates ... are not that different from the seven-teenth-century sea pirates', note Durand and Vergne, and the point is especially true if it connects piracy to capital.[107] For as we have seen, the history of piracy and the history of capitalism go hand in hand, and this remains the case as regards intellectual property. For a start, if piracy means using the concepts and ideas of others without their permission, then the history of every form of creative industry is part of the history of piracy. In the case of film, for example, following the patents granted to Thomas Edison, based on the East Coast, a large number of 'independent' film-makers fled to the West Coast. As Lawrence Lessig tells it:

> California was remote enough from Edison's reach that film-makers there could pirate his inventions without fear of the law. And the leaders of Hollywood film-making, Fox most prominently, did just that. Of course, California grew quickly, and the effective enforcement of federal law eventually spread west. But because patents grant the patent holder a truly 'limited' monopoly (just seventeen years at that time), by the time enough federal marshals appeared, the patents had expired. A new industry had been born, in part from the piracy of Edison's creative property.[108]

In other words, the Hollywood film industry was built by what were, in effect, fleeing pirates, and the same point can be made about the whole range of cultural industries. 'Every important sector of "big media" today – film, records, radio, and cable TV – was born of a kind of piracy so defined'. More generally, '*every* industry affected by copyright today is the product and beneficiary of a certain kind of piracy'.[109] Just as we noted above that capital was born of a certain kind of piracy and only later sought to denounce as 'piratical' acts which it had once exploited, so we might also note that now in another important stage of capitalist development the accusation of 'piracy' is equally bandied about in order to distance a new industry at the heart of capital from its own acts of appropriation.

At the same time, we have also noted that the point of the word 'piracy' as it entered modern law was that it was a word used to cover an interference with property rights. 'Findings of "piracy" ... presuppose rights in the entity expropriated'.[110] This is the very reason the term has been used in debates about intellectual property: a patent, copyright or trademark is granted by the state to prevent third parties from using the patented, copyrighted or trademarked product for commercial purposes. The history of capitalism teaches us that capital always generates possibilities for its own corruption and parasitism, a so-called shadow or marginal or informal or black economy existing beyond the law (or at least at its edges), producing a profit but not for corporations and providing no revenue for the state.[111] That this is named after the historic Enemy of All Mankind needs comment.

The cry of 'piracy!' is a capitalist expression of fear,[112] and whenever capital articulates a new fear new forms of police power are usually created. In the case of the media industry, for example, as well as GATT, TRIPS, the WTO and the BASCAP, there also exists the Association of American Publishers (AAP), the Business Software Alliance (BSA), the Entertainment Software Association (ESA), the Independent Film and Television Alliance (IFTA), the International AntiCounterfeiting Coalition (IACC), the International Federation of the Phonographic Industry (IFPI), the International Intellectual Property Alliance (IIPA), the Motion Picture Association of America (MPAA), the National Music Publishers' Association (NMPA), the Recording Industry Association of America (RIAA) and many others. All these organisations claim that piracy is both morally reprehensible (that is, *heinous*) and is now a greater threat than ever due to the rise of digital reproduction. It is said to be morally reprehensible for the obvious reason that it undercuts the profit margins in the sphere of media property, cultural production, ownership of the image, and the 'star properties' of celebrities,[113] but what is interesting is that the argument is often made purely on the basis of the *potential* harm: *as if* the actions will lead to something else. Jennifer Litman has pointed out that using the term 'piracy' in this way describes the kinds of activities in which people have long engaged: the 'pirates' in question are doing the things that unlicensed users have always done, namely making copies of things for personal use and for sharing with friends. What has changed, however, is the epithet applied to them:

> If we untangle the claim that technology has turned Johnny Teenager into a Pirate, what turns out to be fuelling it is the idea that *if* Johnny Teenager were to decide to share his unauthorized copy with 2 million of his closest friends, the *effect* on a record company would be pretty similar to the effect of some counterfeit CD factory's creating two million CDs and selling them cheap.

What the record companies have done, argues Litman, is they have persuaded a lot of people in power that any behaviour that has the same *effect* as piracy must *be* piracy and must therefore be subject to the same moral condemnation.

> Worse, any behavior that *could potentially cause the same effect* as piracy, even if it doesn't, must also be piracy. Because an unauthorized digital copy of something *could* be uploaded to the Internet, where it could be downloaded by two million people, even making the digital copy is piracy. Because an unauthorized digital copy of something could be used in a way that could cause all that damage, making a tool that makes it *possible* to make an unauthorized digital copy, even if nobody ever actually makes one, is itself piracy, regardless of the reasons one might have for making this tool.[114]

Thus the whole intellectual property regime acts *as if* any infringement will undermine accumulation as a whole. 'According to The New York Times, 43 million Americans downloaded music in May 2002. According to the RIAA, the behaviour of those 43 million Americans was a felony'.[115] Those figures are now almost certainly higher, given how little most people seem to care about copyright law. 'Farcical' as this is,[116] in that it implies the citizens of modern capitalist states constitute a 'fake nation',[117] there is a more important point, which is that citizens are criminalised by undertaking what most regard as a fairly mundane and perfectly legitimate activity.

A fake nation, however, is nothing less than a *pirate nation* and a *nation of pirates is by definition a security problem*. Why? Because people are not just being criminalised, but are doing so in such a way as to make them part of a terror network. 'Pirates were terrorists of a sort', we noted Rediker commenting on the original pirates. Might the same point now also be made about the pirates of intellectual property? If so, might this then connect the contemporary defence of capital to the mobilisation of security?

There is a widespread belief in the security state that the profits generated from pirated music, films and games funnel back to organizations labelled 'terrorist'. The link between piracy in intellectual property and terrorism gained legitimacy in 1995, when New York's Joint Terrorism Taskforce claimed that profits from counterfeit T-shirt sales helped fund the 1993 bombing of the World Trade Centre. But during the 'war on terror' a wide range of organizations have naturalized the relationship between pirated intellectual property and terrorism, to the point at which the claim with which we began the chapter – that piracy is terrorism and vice versa – is said to apply to the piracy of intellectual property as well, only this time with the intellectual property lawyers rather than the international lawyers having their say.[118] Organisation after organisation now line up to tell us that piracy in intellectual property is integrally linked to terrorism. For example, the IFPI holds that 'the clandestine nature of terrorist organisations requires large sums of money to maintain operatives in the field' and that 'evidence and intelligence is available to prove that these groups are involved in the fabrication, distribution and sale of counterfeit music and other intellectual property'.[119] The IACC likewise claims that

terrorist organizations are attracted to counterfeiting and piracy because it is a lucrative business, but also because it allows terrorists to remain relatively anonymous. Counterfeiting and piracy rings often operate as cash enterprises, they lease manufacturing equipment from third parties and generally do not maintain reliable paperwork or business records. Upon suspicion of detection, terrorist counterfeiters can move merchandise, hide assets and equipment, switch manufacturing locations, destroy evidence, or simply disappear without leaving a paper trail. And, most importantly, any profits made in this type of underground market are obviously difficult to trace.[120]

The 'evidence' provided by such organisations is sketchy at best – certainly as sketchy as the calculated losses cited above – and often relies on absurd insinuations, such as 'CD-R's containing pirate music compilations recovered by investigators in Paraguay contained inlay cards depicting images of the exploding Twin Towers of the World Trade Center along with representations of Osama Bin Laden'.[121] And yet the claims have become part of the 'common sense' of terrorism studies, on the basis of which the United Nations Office on Drugs and Crime now runs a Counter Piracy Programme (CPP). The CPP is said to be at the forefront of efforts to establish a 'piracy prosecution model' in which piracy is subject to the international police power; the *persecutio piratarum* has come full circle.

Let us elaborate on the place of piracy of intellectual property in the full spectrum of security management with brief details of five very different kinds of events from just one year. The year is 2003 and the choice is not entirely random: it was the same year in which the culture industry in the US launched a major crackdown on piracy by issuing law suits against its own users.[122]

First: in September 2003 Interpol extended its list of organizations seen as security threats and suspected of using profits from pirated material. Chechen separatists and Northern Irish paramilitaries were added to a list which already included Al Qaeda, Hezbollah, Hamas, FARC, Albanian and Basque separatists, anti-Arroyo agitators in the Philippines, and the Cosa Nostra. The claim made was that profits from pirated films and games funnel back to organizations which supposedly threaten our security.[123]

Second: a conference on 'Security Measures for Music' – the title being somewhat revealing of our times: even music is now a security issue – held by the Indian Music Industry in Chennai. The conference was informed by a former police commissioner that music pirates in Europe, the US and Pakistan have strong links with terrorist organisations, and that rooting out music piracy was a means of countering terrorism. For example, it was claimed that pirated films sold in Canada help fund the LTTE and that pirated games sold in the UK help fund Al Qaeda.[124]

Third: the US Department of Transportation explained in its *Transit Security Newsletter* why the Terrorist-Pirate is such a threat:

> They run what looks like legitimate businesses, travel to 'business meetings' in Frankfurt, Amsterdam, and New York, and pay fictional 'employees' with money that feeds and houses terrorist cells. They run computer manufacturing plants and noodle shops, sell 'designer clothes' and 'bargain basement' CDs ... The end game, however, is ... to blow up a building, to hijack a jet, to release a plague, and to kill thousands of innocent civilians.[125]

Fourth: in July 2003 the House Committee on International Relations held a hearing entitled, *Intellectual Property Crimes: Are Proceeds from Counterfeited Goods Funding Terrorism?* At the hearing, the Secretary General of Interpol, Mr. Ronald K. Noble claimed that 'Intellectual property crime is becoming the preferred method of funding for a number of terrorist groups'. The comment was repeated in a later Hearing before the Committee on Homeland Security and Governmental Affairs, at which Department of Homeland Security Under Secretary Hutchinson said that 'Terrorist organizations worldwide are looking for a variety of illegal activities to fund their efforts. They have looked at contraband and counterfeiting and piracy, all as means of illegal activity to fund their organizations'. The Hearing went on to note that 'the challenge to our domestic security will have exponentially increased'.[126]

Fifth: in Iraq in 2003 just a few months after the hunt and capture of Saddam Hussein the US announced the revision of Iraq's patent law. For generations, farmers in Iraq operated in an essentially unregulated, informal seed supply system, whereby farm-saved seed and the free innovation with and exchange of planting materials among farming communities was standard agricultural practice. Yet the Coalition Provisional Authority established after the invasion of Iraq changed the law (with Order 81), making it illegal for Iraqi farmers to re-use seeds harvested from new varieties registered under the law. The parallel with Monsanto's policy noted above should be clear. As the GRAIN organization noted in an opinion piece on the *war* being waged against Iraqi farmers, 'the purpose of the law is to facilitate the establishment of a new seed market in Iraq, where transnational corporations can sell their seeds, genetically modified or not, which farmers would have to purchase afresh every single cropping season'. In other words, the historical prohibition of private ownership of biological resources was to be replaced by a new patent law allowing a system of monopoly rights over seeds, with the rights in question almost certain to be held by multi-national corporations.[127] The point is that this was part of US national security strategy for the region.

Five examples from just one year. Many more could be given. We might also note that the following year saw the launch of STOP (Strategy Targeting Organized Piracy), which in turn led to new legislation in the US called the Stop Counterfeiting in Manufactured Goods Act (2006). Launching the Stop Counterfeiting in Manufactured Goods Act, President Bush made the obvious point about accumulation: piracy damages profits. And he made the obvious point about terrorism: 'terrorist networks use counterfeit sales to … finance their operations'. But he also wanted to make a general point about security: piracy 'hurts national security'.[128] Two years later the Prioritizing Resources and Organization for Intellectual Property (PRO IP) Act (2008) was passed. The rationale for the protection of intellectual property was not only because piracy 'hurts businesses [and] innovators', but also because it 'hurts ... our national security'.[129] The same claim is found time and again: the thirteenth 'European Security Conference and Exhibition' held in the spring of 2014 at The Hague discussed intellectual property issues as well as maritime piracy, as these issues together form what it calls the 'full spectrum of topics in security management',[130] while the RAND organisation holds that 'counterfeiting is a threat not only to the global information economy, but also to public safety and ... national security'.[131] The whole problem might be summed up by a passage in the *IP Commission Report* (2013), which argued that the theft of American intellectual property is 'one of the most pressing issues of economic and national security facing our country' and recommended that the national security advisor should be the principal policy coordinator for all actions on the protection of American intellectual property.[132]

Such examples make clear the extent to which the geopolitical problem of securing an accumulation regime increasingly reliant on intellectual property is bound up with the overwhelming hegemonic power of the concern with 'terrorism'. The 'war on terror' and the 'war on piracy' are now one and the same, and this conjunction intensifies over and again as the war rolls on. This is why whenever piracy of intellectual property is now discussed, it is often in terms of *the defence of both capital and security*.

In the political imagination of *capital*, piracy of intellectual property is apparently so profound that it threatens to undermine the whole accumulation regime. In the political imagination of *the state*, piracy of intellectual property is apparently so profound that it threatens to undermine the whole security regime. We are back with a script written in the early days of the systematic colonisation of the world by capital: suffer pirates and the commerce of the world must cease; expel the pirates and the commerce of the world will be restored. But now, in these days of intensified (in)security, we can adjust the script: suffer pirates and the security of the world must cease, expel the pirates and the security of the world will be restored. And as the script reveals, 'the security of the world' means the *security of capital*. The wars on terror, piracy and the working class united as one. *Security mobilised, capital defended*, in a universal war against the Enemy of All Mankind.

This Adversary is not just the Pirate, of course. The implication that we live in a 'fake nation' is that the police power must watch over everything and everyone. The fact that most citizens are now criminalised by some very mundane activities that capital wants to treat as 'piracy' means that those same citizens are in no position to object when security measures carried out in their name are mobilised against them. And the security measures in question are of the highest order, because the acts in question are considered worse than simple crimes or felonies. The acts are treated *as if* they could bring an end to capitalism as we know it and are regarded as so heinous that they are *styled as* piratical. And once styled that way they demand nothing less than the mobilisation of all the powers that the state can muster in its defence of capital, which are precisely the powers the state now likes to muster in the name of security.

In this light, Johnny Teenager and all the rest of us illegally downloading cultural products appear to security and capital as nothing less than a threat beyond all threats: the piratical consumer and the disgruntled Worker rolled together as one, members of the swinish multitude trying to get something for nothing, Zombies unable to understand the new rules of accumulation or, worse, actively rebelling against the rules in such a way that connects us back to the low-level grunts of the war-machine and the industrial machine, the masterless men and women of the early class war, the rebellious and disobedient women (the witches) and men who once appeared as an affront to the strictures imposed by the modern state and who were therefore seen to be working for the Devil. These are the very creatures who emerge when we peer behind the curtain marked 'Universal Adversary'. These are the creatures who are evidence of the extent to which the war on terror and the war of accumulation coincide. These are the creatures whose lives and pleasures must be destroyed in the name of security and capital. These are the creatures whose opposition to security and capital, and to the security of capital, will render them always the Enemy of All Mankind.

Notes

Introduction

1   Thomas Hobbes, *Leviathan* (1651), ed. Richard Tuck (Cambridge: Cambridge University Press, 1991), pp. 70, 89, 91, 93, 102, 138, 139, 452.
2   Hobbes, *Leviathan*, p. 118.
3   Hobbes, *Leviathan*, pp. 42, 75, 76, 77, 78, 83, 99, 207, 270, 274, 444–5.
4   Hobbes, *Leviathan*, pp. 18, 42, 75, 76, 99 314.
5   Hobbes, *Leviathan*, p. 75.
6   Hobbes, *Leviathan*, p. 82.
7   Homeland Security Council, *Planning Scenarios: Executive Summaries: Created for Use in National, Federal, State, and Local Homeland Security Preparedness Activities*, July 2004, p. iv.
8   James Clifford, 'History of Consciousness', in Jerome Neu (ed.), *In Memoriam: Norman O. Brown* (Santa Cruz, CA: New Pacific Press, 2005), p. 48; Joseba Zulaika, *Terrorism: The Self-Fulfilling Prophecy* (Chicago: University of Chicago Press, 2009), p. 91.
9   Alain Badiou, 'Philosophy and the "War Against Terrorism"' (2001), in *Infinite Thought: Truth and the Return of Philosophy*, trans. Oliver Feltham and Justin Clemens (London: Continuum, 2003), p. 146. It is worth noting in this regard that what goes by the name of 'terrorism studies' has generated hundreds of definitions of 'terrorist' and 'terrorism', which themselves have shifted over the three decades since 'terrorism' became a political concern. But also, and worse, terrorism 'experts' are now quite happy to declare that they do not have a working definition of the term and do not wish to have one – see Lisa Stampnitzky, *Disciplining Terror: How Experts Invented 'Terrorism'* (Cambridge: Cambridge University Press, 2013).
10 Ann Laura Stoler, 'Reason Aside: Reflections on Enlightenment and Empire', in Graham Huggan (ed.), *The Oxford Handbook of Postcolonial Studies* (Oxford: Oxford University Press, 2013), pp. 39–66, p. 62.
11 Michael Hardt and Antonio Negri, *Multitude: War and Democracy in the Age of Empire* (New York: Penguin, 2004), pp. 30–1; Carlo Galli, *Political Spaces and Global War* (2002), trans. Elisabeth Fay (Minneapolis: University of Minnesota Press, 2010), p. 168; Slavoj Žižek, *Welcome to the Desert of the Real: Five Essays on September 11 and Related Dates* (London: Verso, 2002), p. 109.
12 Walter Benjamin, 'Critique of Violence' (1920–21), trans. Edmund Jephcott, in *Selected Writings, Vol. 1: 1913–1926*, ed. Marcus Bullock and Michael W. Jennings (Cambridge, MA: Belknap/Harvard, 1996), p. 243. For the extension see Mark Neocleous, *War Power, Police Power* (Edinburgh: Edinburgh University Press, 2014), building in turn on *The Fabrication of Social Order: A Critical Theory*

of State Power (London: Pluto Press, 2000). The book linking the two is *Critique of Security* (Edinburgh: Edinburgh University Press, 2008).

13   George W. Bush, *The Department of Homeland Security* (2002; place of publication not specified).

14   Robert M. Gates, 'Landon Lecture', Kansas State University, 26 November 26, 2007 – www.defense.gov/Speeches/Speech.aspx?SpeechID=1199.

15   *The U.S. Army/Marine Corps Counterinsurgency Field Manual: U.S. Army Field Manual No. 3-24/Marine Corps Warfighting Publication No. 3-33.5* (Chicago: University of Chicago Press, 2006), sections 1–40, 3–115, 5–24, 5–98, 5–114, 5–115. The 2014 update of this document continues the trend: See FM 3-24/ MCWP 3-33.5, *Insurgencies and Countering Insurgencies* (Washington, DC: Dept. of the Army, June, 2014), sections 1–2, 1–18, 7–25, 7–35, 8–3, 10–56, 12–27.

16   Montgomery McFate, 'The Military Understanding of Adversary Culture', *Joint Forces Quarterly*, 38, 2005, pp. 42–48, p. 43. In November 2004 McFate had organized a conference on Adversary Cultural Knowledge and National Security, funded by the Office of Naval Research and the Defense Advanced Research Projects Agency (DARPA). Also see McFate, 'Culture', in Thomas Rid and Thomas Keaney (eds), *Understanding Counterinsurgency: Doctrine, Operations, and Challenges* (Abingdon, Oxon: Routledge, 2010), pp. 189–204, where culture is again argued for as an important mechanism for 'effective targeting of the adversary' (p. 192). Likewise see Christopher J. Lamb *et al.*, *Human Terrain Teams: An Organizational Innovation for Sociocultural Knowledge in Irregular Warfare* (Washington, DC: Institute of World Politics Press, 2013), pp. 6–12, 29.

17   Martin Muckian, 'Structural Vulnerabilities of Networked Insurgencies: Adapting to the New Adversary', *Parameters*, Winter 2006–07, pp. 14–25 – http://strategicstudiesinstitute.army.mil/pubs/parameters/Articles/06winter/ muckian.htm

18   Major General Charles J. Dunlap, *Shortchanging the Joint Fight? An Airman's Assessment of FM 3-24 and the Case for Developing Truly Joint COIN Doctrine* (Maxwell AFB, AL: Air University Monographs, 2008), p. 13. Also see Dunlap, 'Airpower', in Rid and Keaney (eds), *Understanding Counterinsurgency*, pp. 100–113.

19   Frank Hoffman, 'Marine Corps', in Rid and Keaney (eds), *Understanding Counterinsurgency*, pp. 87–99.

20   Cited in Ellen Nakashima and Craig Whitlock, 'With Air Force's Gorgon Drone "We Can See Everything"', *The Washington Post*, 2 January, 2011.

21   George A. Crawford, *Manhunting: Counter-Network Organization for Irregular Warfare* (Joint Special Operations University Report 09-7, 2009), pp. 10–11; also pp. 6–7, 12, 15, 24. Also see John B. Alexander, *Convergence: Special Operations Forces and Civilian Law Enforcement*, Joint Special Operations University Report 10-6, 2010, pp. 4, 15, 72. For the wider argument concerning the manhunt see Mark Neocleous, 'The Dream of Pacification: Accumulation, Class War, and the Hunt', *Socialist Studies/Études Socialistes*, Vol. 9, No. 2, 2013, pp. 7–31.

22   Christos Boukalas, *Homeland Security, its Law and its State* (Abingdon, Oxon: Routledge, 2014), p. 205.

23   Hardt and Negri, *Multitude*, p. 31; Galli, *Political Spaces*, p. 181; Carl Schmitt, *The Concept of the Political* (1932), trans. George Schwab (Chicago: University of Chicago Press, 1996), p. 27.

24   Mark Neocleous, *The Monstrous and the Dead: Burke, Marx, Fascism* (Cardiff: University of Wales Press, 2005).

25   Mark Neocleous, 'The Monster and the Police: *Dexter* to Hobbes', *Radical Philosophy*, 185, 2014, pp. 8–18. For the general issues see Richard Hofstadter, 'The Paranoid Style in American Politics' (1964), in *The Paranoid Style in*

American Politics and Other Essays (New York: Vintage, 1967), pp. 3–40, p. 29; Michael Rogin, *Ronald Reagan, the Movie and other Episodes in Political Demonology* (Berkeley: University of California Press, 1987), pp. xiii, 272; Rodney Barker, *Making Enemies* (Houndmills, Basingstoke: Palgrave, 2007), pp. 114–6.

26   Jacob Taubes, 'Letter to Armin Mohler', 14 February, 1952, in Jacob Taubes, *To Carl Schmitt: Letters and Reflections*, trans. Keith Tribe (New York: Columbia University Press, 2013), p. 26.

27   Barker, *Making Enemies*, p. 117.

28   Darren Oldridge, *The Devil: A Very Short Introduction* (Oxford: Oxford University Press, 2012), p. 97.

29   Andrew Hill, *Re-Imagining the War on Terror: Seeing, Waiting, Travelling* (Houndmills, Basingstoke: Palgrave Macmillan, 2009), p. 108.

30   Gerry Simpson, *Law, War and Crime* (Cambridge: Polity, 2007), p. 160.

31   www.unausa.org/global-classrooms-model-un/model-un-mobile-app# sthash.xzmJDL5z.dpuf

32   Michel Foucault, *On the Government of the Living: Lectures at the Collège de France, 1979–1980*, trans. Graham Burchell (Houndmills, Basingstoke, 2014), p. 8.

33   Only by registering this mobilisation can we begin to make sense of security as a political project of modernity. This is why the oft-cited 'ironies of security', for example that more people are killed in America each year by drowning in their own bathtubs than by acts of terrorism, miss the point. The point is not to succumb to a position along the lines that 'if we really wanted to make people secure we would spend more time and energy on bathroom safety rather than national security'. Such a position presupposes that what is at stake is some kind of 'real' security that is achievable if only we were better organised and had more realistic or sensible targets. The point, rather, is that populations are never going to be mobilised or social transformations achieved through something like 'bathtub security'. More to the point, 'bathtub security' is hardly a political fear on which the state can operate or through which pacification can take place. 'Security', after all, is important not as something which could ever be genuinely achieved but, rather, for the opportunities it offers to get things done in its name, a power for the fabrication of social order, which is precisely why seemingly marginal figures and possibly invisible powers are far more provocative and productive than a 'real' problem such as how to avoid accidentally killing oneself in the bathroom.

34   Michel Foucault, *'Society Must Be Defended': Lectures at the Collège de France, 1975–1976*, trans. David Macey (London: Allen Lane, 2003), p. 33.

35   Boukalas, *Homeland Security*, p. 205.

36   Frederick Engels, 'The 25th of June', *Neue Rheinische Zeitung*, 29 June, 1848, in Karl Marx and Frederick Engels, *Collected Works, Vol. 7* (London: Lawrence and Wishart, 1977), pp. 139–43, p. 139.

37   'I don't believe in explanations. I believe in suggestion, in the obvious quality of the implicit' – Paul Virilio, 'Fragmentation and Technology', in Paul Virilio and Sylvère Lotringer, *Pure War* (1983), trans. Mark Polizzotti (New York: Semiotext(e), 2008), p. 52.

38   Gilles Deleuze and Félix Guattari, *A Thousand Plateaus: Capitalism and Schizophrenia* (1980), trans. Brian Massumi (London: Athlone Press, 1987), p. 422.

39   Deleuze and Guattari, *Thousand Plateaus*, p. 564.

40   Karl Marx, citing Horace, *Satires*, Book 1, Satire 1, in *Capital: A Critique of Political Economy, Vol. 1* (1867), trans. Ben Fowkes (Harmondsworth: Penguin, 1976), p. 90.

1 'The perpetrator has been named the Universal Adversary': on the disgruntled Worker

1 Secretary Rumsfeld, '21st Century Transformation of U.S. Armed Forces', Remarks as Delivered at the National Defense University, Fort McNair, Washington, D.C., 31 January, 2002 – www.au.af.mil/au/awc/awcgate/dod/transformation-secdef-31jan02.htm [accessed 18 Nov. 2015], emphases added.

2 The comment, from the early years of the 'war on terror', is attributed to the then Vice-President Cheney. Faced with the possibility that Pakistani scientists were helping Al Qaeda build a nuclear weapon, the suggestion was that even if there is only a one percent chance that it is true, security demands that 'we have to treat it as a certainty'. See Ron Suskind, *The One Percent Doctrine: Deep Inside America's Pursuit of Its Enemies Since 9/11* (London: Pocket Books, 2007), p. 62.

3 The two comments just cited are from Secretary of State Rumsfeld and Vice-President Cheney. The phrase 'catastrophic and catalyzing event' is from the neoconservative think tank The Project for the New American Century's (PNAC), of which both Rumsfeld and Cheney were members, and appears in a document prior to the events of September 2001 – *Rebuilding America's Defenses: Strategy, Forces and Resources For a New Century* (Washington, DC: Project for the New American Century Report, September 2000), p. 51.

4 See Brian Massumi, 'Fear (The Spectrum Said)', *Positions*, Vol. 13, No. 1, 2005, pp. 31–48; Eric Cazdyn, 'Disaster, Crisis, Revolution', *South Atlantic Quarterly*, Vol. 106, No. 4, 2007, pp. 647–662; Kevin Rozario, *The Culture of Calamity: Disaster and the Making of Modern America* (Chicago: University of Chicago Press, 2007); Brian Massumi, 'The Future Birth of the Affective Act', in Melissa Gregg and Gregory J. Seigworth (eds), *The Affect Theory Reader* (Durham: Duke University Press, 2010), pp. 52–70; Claudia Aradau and Rens van Munster, *Politics of Catastrophe: Genealogies of the Unknown* (London: Routledge, 2011); Stuart Price, *Worst-Case Scenario? Governance, Mediation and the Security Regime* (London: Zed Books, 2011); Patrick S. Roberts, *Disasters and the American State: How Politicians, Bureaucrats, and the Public Prepare for the Unexpected* (Cambridge: Cambridge University Press, 2013); Joseph Masco, *The Theater of Operations: National Security Affect from the Cold War to the War on Terror* (Durham: Duke University Press, 2014).

5 This is the term used in the Homeland Security Presidential Directives (HSPD), starting with HSPD-8, December 2003: http://fas.org/irp/offdocs/nspd/hspd-8.html [accessed 18 Nov. 2015] and then running through the National Preparedness Guidelines and Planning Scenarios to which we shall turn.

6 See Mark Neocleous, 'Resisting Resilience', *Radical Philosophy*, 178, 2013, pp. 2–7; *War Power, Police Power* (Edinburgh: Edinburgh University Press, 2014), chap. 7.

7 See the argument as I have developed it through Mark Neocleous, *The Fabrication of Social Order: A Critical Theory of Police Power* (London: Pluto, 2000), onto the *Critique of Security* (Edinburgh: Edinburgh University Press, 2008), and then in *War Power, Police Power*.

8 Charles Meade, Roger C. Molander, *Considering the Effects of a Catastrophic Terrorist Attack* (Santa Monica, CA: RAND, 2006), p. xv.

9 See here Stuart Croft, *Culture, Crisis and America's War on Terror* (Cambridge: Cambridge University Press, 2006); Klaus Dodds, 'Hollywood and the Popular Geopolitics of the War on Terror', *Third World Quarterly*, Vol. 29, No. 8, 2008, pp. 1621–1637.

10   Homeland Security Council, *National Planning Scenarios: Created for Use in National, Federal, State, and Local Homeland Security Preparedness Activities* Version 21.2: Final Draft, March, 2006, p. ii.

11   One might note here President Bush's comment following the damages caused by Hurricane Katrina: 'it's *as if* the entire gulf coast were obliterated by ... the worst kind of weapon you can imagine'. Faced with such devastation, he could imagine it only in terms of the logic of security and attack. But also note the '*as if*' here, emphasis added, for it is a form of rhetoric to which we shall return. President Bush, 'Remarks on the Aftermath of Hurricane Katrina' Mobile, Alabama, 2 September, 2005.

12   E. P. Thompson, *Customs in Common* (London: Penguin, 1991), p. 46.

13   Tracey Davis, *Stages of Emergency: Cold War Nuclear Civil Defense* (Durham: Duke University Press, 2007), pp. 19, 89. Also see Jon Mckenzie, *Perform or Else: From Discipline to Performance* (London: Routledge, 2001), p. 19; Price, *Worst-Case Scenario?*, p. 100.

14   Homeland Security Council, *Planning Scenarios: Executive Summaries: Created for Use in National, Federal, State, and Local Homeland Security Preparedness Activities* July 2004, p. iv.

15   FEMA, *Universal Adversary Program, Fact Sheet*, no date – www.fema.gov/txt/media/factsheets/2009/npd_univ_adversary_prg.txt [accessed 18 Nov. 2015].

16   Department of Homeland Security, Office of Inspector General, *A Review of the TOP Officials 3 Exercise* (OIG-06-07, November 2005).

17   FEMA, *Universal Adversary Program.*

18   Homeland Security Council, *National Planning Scenarios* Version 21.2.

19   Note the references to 'the nature of the terrorist adversary' in NIPP documents such as DHS, *National Infrastructure Protection Plan: Partnering to Enhance Protection and Resiliency* (2009), and DHS, *NIPP 2013: Partnering for Critical Infrastructure Security and Resilience* (2013).

20   In November 2009 the Department of Homeland Security and FEMA awarded $1.5 million to GLOBAL TAC, for the 'analysis corporation' to 'provide analytical support' for the Universal Adversary [UA] programme. See the Press Release of the Global Strategies Group, 9 November, 2009 – www.soteradefense.com/media/press-releases/global-tac-secures-15m-award-to-support-department-of-homeland-security-universal-adversary-progra/ [accessed 18 Nov. 2015].

21   www.phe.gov/Preparedness/planning/playbooks/rdd/Pages/scenario.aspx [accessed 18 Nov. 2015]. Note the use of the theatrical term: 'playbooks'.

22   New York State Division of Homeland Security and Emergency Services, State Preparedness Training Center, *Indicators of the Terrorist Attack Cycle – Advanced*, 9–10 August, 2014, 'Course Description' – www.dhses.ny.gov/training/courses/ITAC-Advanced-4-14-15.pdf [accessed 18 Nov. 2015].

23   Army, Marine Corps, Navy, Air Force, *Multiservice Tactics, Techniques, and Procedures for Chemical, Biological, Radiological, and Nuclear Consequence Management Operations (FM 3-11.21/MCRP 3-37.2C/ NTTP 3-11.24/ AFTTP(I) 3-2.37)*, April 2008, A-10.

24   Michael J. McMullen, PowerPoint slides for 'Terrorism Prevention Exercise Program (TPEP)', presented at the Training and Exercise Conference, Dept. of Homeland Security/FEMA, 13 April, 2011.

25   See *Vibrant Response 13 FTX: Exercise Plan (EXPLAN)*, June, 2012.

26   Homeland Security Council, *National Planning Scenarios: Created for Use in National, Federal, State, and Local Homeland Security Preparedness Activities* Version 20.2, April 2005, pp. 2–11.

27   Homeland Security Council, *National Planning Scenarios* Version 21.2.

28 Homeland Security Council, *National Planning Scenarios* Version 21.2, p. iii.
29 For example, the U.S. Department of Homeland Security, *Homeland Security Exercise and Evaluation Program, Vol. V: Prevention Exercises* (December 2005) breaks the Universal Adversary down into the anti-globalization movement, domestic right-wing extremism, the environmental/animal rights movement, the global Salafist Jihad movement, and the lone actor/small group Introduction.
30 In *Emergency Politics*, for example, Bonnie Honig mentions the idea of class in passing and only in relation to the Slow Food movement or the *sans papiers*. In Elaine Scarry's *Thinking Through Emergency*, the idea is even less present; that is, it just never appears. See Bonnie Honig, *Emergency Politics: Paradox, Law, Paradox, Democracy* (Princeton, NJ: Princeton University Press, 2009), pp. 118, 153–155; Elaine Scarry, *Thinking Through Emergency* (New York: W. W. Norton, 2011).
31 See my extended argument about *emergency powers* – though not *exceptional powers* – in *Critique of Security*, Chapter 2.
32 My favourite example: 'the disgruntled employee may not be the greatest risk but remains the cause of one out of every 10 workplace homicides' – Eric N. Smith, *Workplace Security Essentials: A Guide for Helping Organizations Create Safe Work Environments* (Waltham, MA: Butterworth-Heinemann, 2014), p. 117.
33 Edmund Burke, *Reflections on the Revolution in France* (1790), ed. Conor Cruise O'Brien (Harmondsworth: Penguin, 1968), p. 173.
34 I have elsewhere suggested that Burke's preoccupation with the multitude coincides with his invocation of the metaphor of the monster as two of the terms developed in ruling class ideology through the eighteenth century as a way of identifying and politically labelling the nascent and thus at that point unnameable proletariat, and I will return in Chapter 2 to the politics of the mob in the form of the 'crowd'. See Mark Neocleous, 'The Monstrous Multitude: Edmund Burke's Political Teratology', *Contemporary Political Theory*, Vol. 3, No. 1, 2004, pp. 70–88, and Chapter 1 of *The Monstrous and the Dead: Burke, Marx, Fascism* (Cardiff: University of Wales Press, 2005).
35 E. P. Thompson, *The Making of the English Working Class* (Harmondsworth: Penguin, 1968), p. 98.
36 Johnson cited in James Boswell, *The Journal of a Tour to the Hebrides* (1786), in *A Journey to the Western Islands of Scotland* and *The Journal of a Tour to the Hebrides* (Harmondsworth: Penguin, 1984), p. 379; Samuel Johnson, *A Dictionary of the English Language* (1755), entries for 'Plantation' and 'Swine'; Martin Marprelate, 'The Epistle', in *The Martin Marprelate Tracts, 1588–1589*, ed. Joseph L. Black (Cambridge: Cambridge University Press, 2008), pp. 10 and 25.
37 Olivia Smith, *The Politics of Language, 1791–1819* (Oxford: Clarendon Press, 1984), p. 81.
38 The poem and 'The Rights of Swine' can be found in Volume II, pp. 39–41 and pp. 97–102 respectively.
39 Thompson, *Making*, p. 98; Don Herzog, *Poisoning the Minds of the Lower Orders* (Princeton, NJ: Princeton University Press, 1998), p. 545.
40 William Cobbett, 'To the Journeymen and Labourers of England, Wales, Scotland, and Ireland, on the Causes of their Present Miseries', *Political Register*, November 1816), reprinted in *Selections from Cobbett's Political Works, Vol. 5* (London: Anne Cobbett, no date), pp. 2 and 9.
41 *Black Dwarf*, 7 July 1819, cited in Herzog, *Poisoning*, p. 538.
42 Herzog, *Poisoning*, pp. 512–4. 526, 537, 540, 545; Thompson, *Making*, p. 98.
43 [No Author], 'L'Envoy', *Blackwood's Edinburgh Magazine*, Vol. 29, Jan. 1831, pp. 141–2, p. 141.

44   [No Author], 'Reformers and Anti-Reformers – A Word to the Wise From Old Christopher', *Blackwood's Edinburgh Magazine*, Vol. 29, May 1831, pp. 721–731, pp. 728–729. Note once again the connection to the Devil.
45   [No Author], 'Edmund Burke', *Blackwood's Edinburgh Magazine*, Vol. 35, Jan. 1834, pp. 27–48, p. 34.
46   Herzog, *Poisoning*, p. 511.
47   Peter Stallybrass and Allon White, *The Politics and Poetics of Transgression* (London: Methuen, 1986), p. 5.
48   Carl Fisher, 'Politics and Porcine Representation: Multitudinous Swine in the British Eighteenth Century', *Lit: Literature Interpretation Theory*, Vol. 10, No. 4, 1999, pp. 303–26, p. 310. Smith, *Politics of Language*, p. 81.
49   Claudine Fabre-Vassas, *The Singular Beast: Jews, Christians, and the Pig* (1994), trans. Carol Volk (New York: Columbia University Press, 1997), p. 5.
50   Stallybrass and White, *Politics and Poetics*, p. 47.
51   Mark Essig, *Lesser Beasts: A Snout-to-Tail History of the Humble Pig* (New York: Basic Books, 2015), p. 182; Stallybrass and White, *Politics and Poetics*, p. 48.
52   Robert Malcolmson and Stephanos Mastoris, *The English Pig: A History* (London: Hambledon, 2001), p. 46.
53   Sir James Kay-Shuttleworth, *The Moral and Physical Condition of the Working Classes Employed in the Cotton Manufacture in Manchester* (London: James Ridgway, 1832), p. 19. Edwin Chadwick, *Report on the Sanitary Condition of the Labouring Population of Great Britain* (1842), ed. M. W. Flint (Edinburgh: Edinburgh University Press, 1965), pp. 88, 89, 100, 103, 111, 112, 115, 196, 328; Frederick Engels, *The Condition of the Working-Class in England* (1845), in Karl Marx and Frederick Engels, *Collected Works, Vol. 4* (London: Lawrence and Wishart, 1975), pp. 295–583, p. 354; *Children's Employment Commission, Sixth Report* (1867), cited Karl Marx, *Capital: A Critique of Political Economy, Vol. 1* (1867), trans. Ben Fowkes (Harmondsworth: Penguin, 1976), p. 842. On American cities see Catherine McNeur, 'The "Swinish Multitude": Controversies over Hogs in Antebellum New York City', *Journal of Urban History*, Vol. 37, No. 5, 2011, pp. 639–660.
54   See Jason Hribal, '"Animals Are Part of the Working Class": A Challenge to Labor History', *Labor History*, Vol. 44, No. 4, 2003, pp. 435–453.
55   Chadwick, *Report on the Sanitary Condition*, p. 328; Sym cited in Christopher Hamlin, *Public Health and Social Justice in the Age of Chadwick: Britain, 1800–1854* (Cambridge: Cambridge University Press, 1998), p. 204; Malcolmson and Mastoris, *English Pig*, p. 63.
56   Stallybrass and White, *Politics and Poetics*, p. 52.
57   Hendrik Hartog, 'Pigs and Positivism', *Wisconsin Law Review*, 899, 1985, pp. 1–26; Keith Thomas, *Man and the Natural World: Changing Attitudes in England, 1500–1800* (Oxford: Oxford University Press, 1996), pp. 64, 95; McNeur, '"Swinish Multitude"', pp. 649–650; Malcolmson and Mastoris, *English Pig*, p. 43.
58   See Mary Midgley, *Man and Beast: The Roots of Human Nature* (Brighton: Harvester Press, 1979), pp. 25–49; Jacques Derrida, *The Beast and the Sovereign, Vol. 1* (2001–3), trans. Geoffrey Bennington (Chicago: University of Chicago Press, 2009) and *The Beast and the Sovereign, Vol. II* (2001–3), trans. Geoffrey Bennington (Chicago: University of Chicago Press, Chicago, 2011); Cary Wolfe, *Before the Law: Humans and Other Animals in a Biopolitical Frame* (Chicago: University of Chicago Press, 2013), p. 10. On the question of security note a CIA document from 1982 but approved for release only in 2014, *Bestiary of Intelligence Writing*, in which the agency gives specimen samples of clichés and overused terms used in intelligence writing; so obsessed is the security state with beasts that even bad writing has to be designated in that way. *Bestiary of*

Intelligence Writing, 1982, approved for release 29 July, 2014 – www.foia.cia.gov/
sites/default/files/DOC_0000619161.pdf [accessed 19 Nov. 2015]

59   In Chapter 41 of *Leviathan* there appears a long passage on goats.

> In the Old Law (as we may read, *Leviticus* the 16.) the Lord required, that
> there should every year once, bee made an Atonement for the Sins of all
> Israel, both Priests, and others; for the doing whereof, Aaron alone was to
> sacrifice for himself and the Priests a young Bullock; and for the rest of
> the people, he was to receive from them two young Goates, of which he
> was to *sacrifice* one; but as for the other, which was the *Scape Goat*, he was
> to lay his hands on the head thereof, and by a confession of the iniquities
> of the people, to lay them all on that head, and then by some opportune
> man, to cause the Goat to be led into the wildernesse, and there to *escape*,
> and carry away with him the iniquities of the people.

Hobbes introduces the goat to make clear the analogy with the messiah: just
as the Sacrifice of one goat was a sufficient price for the ransom of all Israel,
so the death of the Messiah was a sufficient price for the Sins of all mankind.
Christ 'was both the sacrificed Goat, and the Scape Goat':

> *Hee was oppressed, and he was afflicted* (Isa. 53.7.); *he opened not his mouth; he*
> *brought as a lamb to the slaughter, and as a sheep is dumbe before the shearer, so*
> *opened he not his mouth:* Here he is the *Sacrificed Goat.* "He hath born our
> Griefs, (ver.4.) *and carried our sorrows*; And again, (ver. 6.) *the Lord hath laid*
> *upon him the iniquities of us all*: And so he is the *Scape Goat. He was cut off*
> *from the land of the living* (ver. 8.) *for the transgression of my People*: There
> again he is the *Sacrificed Goat.* And again (ver. 11.) *he shall bear their sins*:
> Hee is the *Scape Goat.* Thus is the Lamb of God equivalent to both those
> Goates; sacrificed, in that he dyed; and escaping, in his Resurrection;
> being raised opportunely by his Father, and removed from the habitation
> of men in his Ascension.

Although Hobbes's reference is the Bible, the term 'scapegoat' in fact
emerged in 1530 when John Tyndale used it to interpret what he thought to
be the literal meaning of a Hebrew phrase as he sought to translate the Bible
into English. By the time Hobbes uses the term it had taken on real political
significance (little could Tyndale have realised this when he invented it), and
it is perhaps significant that Hobbes runs the term alongside the idea of a
sacrificial goat, for both goats together point to the core theme of Hobbesian
philosophy: the constitution of order, security and peace. The point is that the
scapegoat is not killed as a sacrifice but sent out into the wilderness carrying
with it the sins, injustices and violations of rights (the 'iniquities') of the
people. The two goats combined remind the subjects of their obligations to
the order and security created for them by the sovereign. One goat is killed
and the other banished: order is reconstituted and security restored.

'According to People for the Ethical Treatment of Animals (PETA), goats
have historically made up an unusually large percentage of the estimated
million or so animals on the receiving end of covert experiments within the
US army', notes Jon Ronson. Most of this goat-related activity is classified, but
sometimes some of it is known to us from leaked documents. When an atomic
bomb was detonated in the sky near Bikini Atoll in the South Pacific in 1946,
most of the animals that had been placed on a boat below the explosion were
goats. More recently, goats have been used in experiments to transform them
into a goat-spider hybrid to see if it can produce a new form of silk that can be
woven into bullet-proof vests. The US military has a 'Goat Lab' at Fort Bragg

in which goats are routinely used for military experiments. See Jon Ronson, *The Men Who Stare at Goats* (London: Picador, 2004), p. 17.

We might also note the association of enemy figures such as Bin Laden with the goat, depicting him either *as* a goat or as a goat *fucker*. This association has for the most part been dismissed as merely derogatory, which it most certainly is, but the link with the goat might well be because of the goat's association with demonic powers and Satanic forces, a point to which we will turn in Chapter 3.

Finally, given all this 'goatiness', we should at least note in passing that the book President Bush was reading to schoolchildren at the moment he was informed of the attacks on 11 September, 2001, was *The Pet Goat*.

60 John Stuart Mill, 'Nature' (1874), in Mill, *Nature, the Utility of Religion and Theism* (London: Watts And Co., 1904), p. 26.

61 James Serpell, *In the Company of Animals: A Study of Human-Animal Relationships* (Cambridge: Cambridge University Press, 1986), pp. 201–202; Harriet Ritvo, *The Animal Estate: The English and Other Creatures in Victorian England* (Cambridge, MA: Harvard University Press, 1989), p. 21; Malcolmson and Mastoris, *English Pig*, pp. 1–4.

62 Boria Sax, *Animals in the Third Reich: Pets, Scapegoats, and the Holocaust* (New York: Continuum, 2000), p. 71.

63 Peter Singer, *Animal Liberation: Toward an End to Man's Inhumanity to Animals* (Wellingborough: Thorsons Publishers, 1976), p. 118.

64 E. P. Evans, *The Criminal Prosecution and Capital Punishment of Animals: The Lost History of Europe's Animal Trials* (1906), (London: Faber and Faber, 1987), pp. 56, 165. Joyce Salisbury, *The Beast Within: Animals in the Middle Ages* (London: Routledge, 1994), p. 27; Brett Mizelle, *Pig* (London: Reaktion, 2011), p. 38.

65 Herzog, *Poisoning*, p. 516.

66 Cited in C. J. Chivers, 'Tending a Fallen Marine', *New York Times*, 2 November, 2006 – www.nytimes.com/2006/11/02/world/middleeast/02medic.html?pagewanted=all [accessed 19 Nov. 2015]

67 Malcolm Young, *An Inside Job: Policing and Police Culture in Britain* (Oxford: Clarendon Press, 1991), pp. 114, 141. These points are developed in Neocleous, *Fabrication*, pp. 87–88.

68 Andrew Levison, *The Working-Class Majority* (New York: Coward, McCann and Geoghegan, 1974), p. 162. The 'blind pig' was also the name for working class 'speakeasies' which, by the 1960s, also became important features of back cultural and political life, the basis of black political organization, and raids on which often started race riots. See Suzanne E. Smith, *Dancing in the Street: Motown and the Cultural Politics of Detroit* (Cambridge, MA: Harvard University Press, 1999), pp. 192–3; Max Herman, 'Detroit (Michigan) Riot of 1967', in Walter Rucker and James Nathaniel Upton (eds), *Encyclopedia of American Race Riots, Vol. 1* (Westport, Connecticut: Greenwood Press, 2007), p. 165.

69 Francis Grose and Hewson Clarke, *Lexicon Balatronicum: A Dictionary of Buckish Slang, University Wit and Pickpocket Eloquence* (London: C. Chappel, 1811).

70 David Duff, 'Burke and Paine: Contrasts', in Pamela Clemit (ed.), *The Cambridge Companion to British Literature of the French Revolution* (Cambridge: Cambridge University Press, 2011), pp. 47–70, p. 62.

71 See Neocleous, *Critique of Security*, chap. 4.

72 Homeland Security Council, *National Planning Scenarios* Version 21.2, pp. 13–1. The same example is found in Homeland Security Council, *Planning Scenarios: Executive Summaries*, July 2004.

73 Homeland Security Council, *National Planning Scenarios* Version 21.2, pp. 5–1, 6–1, 11–1, 12–1.

2   'They work faithfully; they're not afraid of long hours': on the Zombie

1   CDRUSSTRATCOM CONPLAN 8888-11 "COUNTER-ZOMBIE DOMI-NANCE", 30 April, 2011 – www.cubadebate.cu/wp-content/uploads/2014/05/CONPLAN-8888.pdf [accessed 18 Nov. 2015].
2   Félix Guattari, *Molecular Revolution in Brazil* (1986) (Los Angeles, CA: Semiotext(e), 2008), p. 59.
3   Ali S. Khan, 'Preparedness 101: Zombie Apocalypse', *CDC Public Health Matters* blog, 16 May, 2011 – http://blogs.cdc.gov/publichealthmatters/2011/05/preparedness-101-zombie-apocalypse/ [accessed 18 Nov. 2015].
4   www.cdc.gov/phpr/zombies.htm [accessed 18 Nov. 2015].
5   Elaine Pitman, 'Are Zombies and Preparedness a Perfect Match? Agencies are embracing the popularity of the undead to get people thinking about emergency preparedness', Emergency Management, 19 October, 2011 – www.emergencymgmt.com/training/Are-Zombies-Preparedness-Perfect-Match.html [accessed 18 Nov. 2015].
6   www.ksready.gov/default.asp?PageID=3&Tab=3 [accessed 18 Nov. 2015].
7   www.unausa.org/global-classrooms-model-un/model-un-mobile-app#sthash.xzmJDL5z.dpuf.
8   *CSB Background Guide, WHISMUN 2014*, 7–8 February, 2014, Brooklyn, New York – www.whismun.org/uploads/2/4/3/3/24333005/csb_bg.pdf [accessed 18 Nov. 2015].
9   Political science professor Margaret Sankey at the University: 'An event like this, even with a made up crisis, teaches the way in which the Security Council operates, and it throws into the spotlight the different ways each country would approach a problem … In seeing this applied to something like zombies, you can also see why it is difficult for nations to work together on more realistic problems'. Yet the really practical outcome appears less to do with the UNH and more to do with preparing the population. 'Sankey pointed out that it is good to have extra supplies on hand, know first aid, have good situational awareness, know where to get good information and have copies of important documents on hand; all things equally useful for a Fargo flood, blizzard or accident' – Kayla Van Eps, 'Students Stage Zombie Invasion', *The Advocate* [Minnesota State University Moorhead], 22 October, 2013 – http://msumadvocate.com/2013/10/22/students-stage-zombie-invasion/ [accessed 18 Nov. 2015].
10   Hensley Carrasco, 'Zombies overrun campus in class exercise', *The Good Five Cent Cigar* [University of Rhode Island], 27April, 2012 – http://issuu.com/uri_libraries/docs/cigar_v61_is93_04272012 [accessed 18 Nov. 2015].
11   Peter Dendle, 'The Zombie as Barometer of Cultural Anxiety', in Niall Scott (ed.), *Monster and the Monstrous: Myths and Metaphors of Enduring Evil* (Amsterdam: Rodopi, 2007), pp. 45–57, p. 53; Christopher Zealand, 'The National Strategy for Zombie Containment: Myth Meets Activism in Post-9/11 America', in Stephanie Boluk and Wylie Lenz (eds), *Generation Zombie: Essays on the Living Dead in Modern Culture* (Jefferson, NC: McFarland and Co., 2011), pp. 231–47, p. 232.
12   Stefan Dziemianowicz, 'Might of the Living Dead', *Publisher's Weekly*, Vol. 256, No. 28, 13 July, 2009, pp. 20–4. www.publishersweekly.com/pw/print/20090713/11921-might-of-the-living-dead.html [accessed 18 Nov. 2015].
13   Cited in St. John, 'Market for Zombies?'
14   Steven Wells, 'Zombies Come Back from the Dead', *The Guardian*, 2 Jan., 2006 – www.theguardian.com/film/2006/jan/02/usa.world, [accessed 16 July

2014]; Warren St. John, 'Market for Zombies? It's Undead (Aaahhh!)', *New York Times*, 26 March 2006 – www.nytimes.com/2006/03/26/fashion/sundaystyles/26ZOMBIES.html?pagewanted=all&_r=0, accessed 16 July, 2014. Also see Christopher Borrelli, 'It's the dawn of the zombie zeitgeist', *Chicago Tribune*, 4 May, 2009.

15   Cited in St. John, 'Market for Zombies?'

16   Lance Eaton, 'Zombies Spreading Like a Virus', *Publisher's Weekly*, Vol. 253, No. 39, 2 Oct., 2006, p. 57.

17   Amy Odell, 'Some of the These Male Models Look Like They've been Dead for Five Days', *New York Magazine*, 27 Jan., 2009, and Amy Odell, 'Death Themes Still Evident in Fall Menswear', 19 Jan., 2010 – http://nymag.com/thecut/2009/01/death_makeup.html [accessed 18 Nov. 2015].

18   Ulrich Beck, in Don Slater and George Ritzer, 'Interview with Ulrich Beck', *Journal of Consumer Culture*, Vol. 1, No. 2, 2001, pp. 261–277, p. 262.

19   Jennifer Rutherford, *Zombies* (London: Routledge, 2013). The quote is from the Series Editor's Preface to Rutherford's book.

20   P. Muntz *et al.*, 'When Zombies Attack! Mathematical Modelling of an Outbreak of Zombie Infection', in Jean Michel Tchuenche and Christinah Chiyaka (eds), *Infectious Disease Modelling Research Progress* (Hauppauge, NY: Nova Science Publishers, 2009), pp. 133–150; David Stanley, 'The Nurses' Role in the Prevention of Solanum Infection: Dealing with a Zombie Epidemic', *Journal of Clinical Nursing*, Vol. 21, 2011, pp. 1606–1613.

21   Yari Lanci, 'Zombie 2.0: Subjectivation in Times of Apocalypse: A Zombified Cultural Framework', *Journal for Cultural and Religious Theory*, Vol. 13, No. 2, 2014, pp. 25–37, p. 25.

22   Guy Debord, *Comments on the Society of the Spectacle* (1988), trans. Malcolm Imrie (London: Verso, 1990), p. 13.

23   Ronjon Paul Datta and Laura MacDonald, 'Time for Zombies: Sacrifice and the Structural Phenomenology of Capitalist Futures' in Christopher M. Moreman and Cory James Rushton (eds), *Race, Oppression and the Zombie: Essays on the Cross-Cultural Appropriations of the Caribbean Tradition* (Jefferson, NC: McFarland and Co., 2011), pp. 77–92, p. 77.

24   Chris Harman, *Zombie Capitalism: Global Crisis and the Relevance of Marx* (London: Bookmarks, 2009); Ben Fine, 'Development as Zombieconomics in the Age of Neoliberalism', *Third World Quarterly*, Vol. 30, No. 5, 2009, pp. 885–904; Henry Giroux, *Zombie Politics and Culture in the Age of Casino Capitalism* (New York: Peter Lang, 2010); Derek Hall, 'Varieties of Zombieism: Approaching Comparative Political Economy through *28 Days Later* and *Wild Zero*', *International Studies Perspectives*, Vol. 12, 2011, pp. 1–17; David McNally, *Monsters of the Market: Zombies, Vampires and Global Capitalism* (Leiden: Brill, 2011); Kerry-Anne Mendoza, *Austerity: The Demolition of the Welfare State and the Rise of the Zombie Economy* (Oxford: New Internationalist Publications, 2015).

25   Lanci, 'Zombie 2.0', pp. 28, 32; Rikk Mulligan, 'Zombie Apocalypse: Plague and the End of the World in Popular Culture', in Karolyn Kinane and Michael A. Ryan (eds), *End of Days: Essays on the Apocalypse from Antiquity to Modernity* (Jefferson, NC: McFarland and Co., 2009), pp. 349–368; Jon Stratton, 'Zombie Trouble: Zombie Texts, Bare Life and Displaced People', *European Journal of Cultural Studies* Vol. 14, No. 3, 2011, pp. 265–281; Neil Gerlach and Sheryl N. Hamilton, Trafficking in the Zombie: The CDC Zombie Apocalypse Campaign, Diseaseability and Pandemic Culture', *Refractory: A Journal of Entertainment Media*, Vol. 23, June 2014, online at http://refractory.unimelb.edu.au/2014/06/26/cdc-zombie-apocalypse-gerlach-hamilton/ [accessed 18 Nov. 2015].

26   'Identify your own zombies', *Forbes* magazine advised business managers. 'What are the biggest potential threats to your business? What is it about them that reveals your own vulnerabilities? Do the threats exist because of a real weakness in your business model, or because you just don't want to change your business? If you came up with an idea to neutralize the threat, what would that look like? Who would fight you over it? Why?' – David Sturt and Todd Nordstrom, 'A U.S. Government "Zombie" Plan?', *Forbes*, 29 May, 2014 – www.forbes.com/sites/davidsturt/2014/05/29/a-u-s-government-zombie-plan/. [accessed 18 Nov. 2015].The *Journal for Quality and Participation* ran an item by Stephen Hacker, CEO of 'Transformation Systems International', on the subject of 'Zombies in the Workplace': 'In organizations around the world, zombies have infiltrated all levels of the labor ranks. Carrying their messages of victimhood and pessimism, they infect the whole organization at an exponential rate'. As such, Hacker warns, 'Zombies could be undermining the mission, vision, and the very future of your organization' – Stephen Hacker, 'Zombies in the Workplace', *Journal for Quality and Participation*, Vol. 32, No. 4, 2010, pp. 25–28, p. 25.

27   Robert Saunders, 'Undead Spaces: Fear, Globalisation, and the Popular Geopolitics of Zombiism', *Geopolitics*, Vol. 17, No. 1, 2012, pp. 80–104, p. 81. This absence of the worker is a central problem with some of the attempts to think politically about the Zombies within IR. Thus, for example, Daniel W. Drezner in *Theories of International Politics and Zombies* (Princeton, NJ: Princeton University Press, 2011), p. 21, asserts that 'all modern works in the zombie canon are rooted in the kind of ghoul' and that 'it is flesh-eating ghouls that should animate the concern of international politics'. Thus, the zombie as 'the most obedient of laborers' found in the longer history 'do not represent a transnational security threat'. Likewise, the problem of the worker is also absent from Erin Hannah and Rorden Wilkinson, 'Zombies and IR: A Critical Reading', *Politics*, online first 2015.

28   Susan Zieger, 'The Case of William Seabrook: Documents, Haiti, and the Working Dead', *Modernism/Modernity*, Vol. 19, No. 4, 2012, pp. 737–754, p. 740.

29   Hans-W. Ackerman and Jeanine Gauthier, 'The Ways and Nature of the Zombie', *Journal of American Folklore*, Vol. 104, No. 414, 1991, pp. 466–494, p. 489.

30   Maximilien Laroche, 'The Myth of the Zombi', in Rowland Smith (ed.), *Exile and Tradition: Studies in African and Caribbean Literature* (New York: Dalhousie University Press, 1976), pp. 44–61, p. 44.

31   Laroche, 'The Myth of the Zombi', p. 47; Michael T. Taussig, *The Devil and Commodity Fetishism in South America* (Chapel Hill: University of North Carolina Press, 1980), p. 231.

32   Alfred Métraux, *Voodoo in Haiti* (1959), trans. Hugo Charteris (New York: Schocken Books, 1972), p. 282; Ann Kordas, 'New South, New Immigrants, New Women, New Zombies: The Historical Development of the Zombie in American Popular Culture', in Moreman and Rushton (eds), *Race, Oppression*, pp. 15–30, pp. 16–17.

33   Marina Warner, *Phantasmagoria: Spirit Visions, Metaphors, and Media into the Twenty-First Century* (Oxford: Oxford University Press, 2006), p. 358.

34   Laroche, 'The Myth of the Zombi', pp. 52, 55. More generally see Maya Deren, *Divine Horsemen: The Living Gods in Haiti* (1953), (New York: McPherson and Co., 2004), p. 42; Wade Davis, *The Serpent and the Rainbow* (London: Collins, 1986), pp.187; Joan Dayan, *Haiti, History, and the Gods* (Berkeley, CA: University of California Press, 1995), pp. 37–38; Markman Ellis, *The History of Gothic Fiction* (Edinburgh: Edinburgh University Press, 2000), pp. 208 and 218–219; Mimi

Sheller, *Consuming the Caribbean* (London: Routledge, 2003), pp. 145–146; Annalee Newitz, *Pretend We're Dead: Capitalist Monsters in American Pop Culture* (Durham: Duke University Press, 2006), p. 91; Kyle William Bishop, *American Zombie Gothic: The Rise and Fall (And Rise) of the Walking Dead in Popular Culture* (Jefferson, NC: McFarland and Co., 2010), pp. 57, 69; David Inglis, 'Putting the Undead to Work: Wade Davis, Haitian Vodou, and the Social Uses of the Zombie', in Moreman and Rushton (eds), *Race, Oppression*, pp. 42–59, 43 and 46.

35   'Morning Becomes Romero: George Romero interviewed by Dan Yakir', *Film Comment*, Vol. 15, No. 3, 1979, pp. 60–65, p. 60.

36   W. B. Seabrook, *The Magic Island* (London: George C. Harrap and Co., 1929), p. 94.

37   Cited in Grace Hutchins, 'Hayti', *Afro-American*, 20 August, 1932, in Nancy Cunard (ed.), *Negro: An Anthology* (New York: Frederick Ungar Publishing Co., 1970), p. 288.

38   On pacification see Mark Neocleous, 'Security as Pacification', in Mark Neocleous and George S. Rigakos (eds), *Anti-Security* (Red Quill Press, 2011), pp. 23–56; 'The Dream of Pacification: Accumulation, Class War, and the Hunt', *Socialist Studies/Études socialistes*, Vol. 9, No. 2, 2013, pp. 7–31; 'Fundamentals of Pacification Theory: Twenty-six Articles', in Tyler Wall (ed.), *Pacification* (Ottawa: Red Quill, 2016). On Haiti see Hans Schmidt, *The United States Occupation of Haiti, 1915–1934* (New Brunswick, NJ: Rutgers University Press, 1971), pp. 11–12, 100–101, 137; Dayan, *Haiti, History*, p. 37.

39   Dayan, *Haiti, History*, p. 37; Mary A. Renda, *Taking Haiti: Military Occupation and the Culture of U.S. Imperialism, 1915–1940* (Chapel Hill: University of North Carolina Press, 2001), p. 225.

40   René Dépestre, *Change* (1971), cited Laroche, 'Myth of the Zombi', p. 59.

41   Jean Comaroff and John Comaroff, 'Alien-Nation: Zombies, Immigrants, and Millennial Capitalism', *Codesria Bulletin*, 3 & 4, 1999, pp. 1–26, p. 24.

42   Frantz Fanon, *The Wretched of the Earth* (1961), trans. Constance Farrington (New York: Grove Press, 1968), p. 56.

43   Jean Sartre, 'Preface', to Fanon, *Wretched of the Earth*, p. 13.

44   Seabrook, *Magic Island*, pp. 95–96.

45   Schmidt, *United States Occupation of Haiti*, pp. 171, 178.

46   Seabrook, *Magic Island*, pp. 96–102.

47   Zora Neale Hurston, *Tell My Horse: Voodoo and Life in Haiti and Jamaica* (1938), (New York: Harper and Row, 1990), p. 83.

48   Warner, *Phantasmagoria*, p. 363.

49   Kyle Bishop, 'The Sub-Subaltern Monster: Imperialist Hegemony and the Cinematic Voodoo Zombie', *Journal of American Culture*, Vol. 31, No. 2, 2008, pp. 141–152, p. 142; Jennifer Fay, 'Dead Subjectivity: *White Zombie*, Black Baghdad', *CR: The New Centennial Review*, Vol. 8, No. 1, 2008, pp. 81–101, pp. 86, 95; Chris Vials, 'The Origin of the Zombie in American Radio and Film: B-Horror, U.S. Empire, and the Politics of Disavowal', in Boluk and Lenz (eds), *Generation Zombie*, pp. 41–53, p. 48; Gyllian Phillips, '*White Zombie* and the Creole: William Seabrook's *The Magic Island* and American Imperialism in Haiti', in Boluk and Lenz (eds), *Generation Zombie*, pp. 27–40, p. 28; Bishop, *American Zombie Gothic*, pp. 65–66.

50   Tim Armstrong, *Modernism, Technology and the Body: A Cultural Study* (Cambridge: Cambridge University Press, 1998), p. 98; Steve Shaviro, 'Capitalist Monsters', *Historical Materialism*, Vol. 10, No. 4, 2002, pp. 281–290, p. 289; Kevin Alexander Boon, 'Ontological Anxiety Made Flesh: The Zombie in Literature, Film and Culture', in Niall Scott (ed.), *Monster and the Monstrous: Myths and Metaphors of Enduring Evil* (Amsterdam: Rodopi, 2007), pp. 33–43,

pp. 37–39; Sarah Juliet Lauro and Karen Embry, 'A Zombie Manifesto: The Nonhuman Condition in the Era of Advanced Capitalism', *boundary 2*, Vol. 35, No. 1, 2008, pp. 85–108; McNally, *Monsters of the Market*, pp. 213, 260–261; Evan Calder Williams, *Combined and Uneven Apocalypse* (Winchester: Zero Books, 2011), pp. 105, 106.

51   Max Weber, *Economy and Society*, Vol. II, ed. Guenther Roth and Claus Wittich (Berkeley, LA: University of California Press, 1978), p. 975.

52   See the collection of essays on the 'living death' of working in a modern University – Andrew Whelan, Ruth Walker and Christopher Moore (eds), *Zombies in the Academy: Living Death in Higher Education* (Bristol: Intellect, 2013).

53   For this point made in a variety of ways see Christopher J. Arthur, *The New Dialectic and Marx's* Capital (Leiden: Brill, 2004), p. 172; Bishop, *American Zombie Gothic*, pp. 56–57; Datta and MacDonald, 'Time for Zombies', p. 78; Lars Bang Larsen, 'Zombies of Immaterial Labor: The Modern Monster and the Death of Death', *e-flux journal*, No. 15, April 2010, pp. 1–12, p. 8; Rutherford, *Zombies*, p. 32; Slavoj Žižek, *Less Than Nothing: Hegel and the Shadow of Dialectical Materialism* (London: Verso, 2013), p. 341.

54   A point stressed by Romero himself: 'Morning Becomes Romero', p. 62.

55   Robert Kirkman, Charlie Adlard, and Cliff Rathburn, *The Walking Dead, Volume 4: The Heart's Desire* (Berkeley, CA: Image Comics, 2010).

56   Warner, *Phantasmagoria*, p. 360.

57   Žižek, *Less Than Nothing*, p. 341.

58   Calder Williams, *Combined and Uneven*, p. 90. Steven Shaviro, *The Cinematic Body* (Minneapolis: University of Minnesota Press, 1993), p. 83.

59   See Karl Marx, 'Wage Labour and Capital', in Karl Marx and Frederick Engels, *Collected Works, Vol. 9* (London: Lawrence and Wishart, 1977), pp. 213 and 215; *Capital: A Critique of Political Economy, Vol. 1* (1867), trans. Ben Fowkes (Harmondsworth: Penguin, 1976), pp. 289, 342; *Grundrisse*, trans. Martin Nicolaus (Harmondsworth: Penguin, 1973), p. 364.

60   It is this that explains why Marx so enjoys using the vampire image – see Mark Neocleous, 'The Political Economy of the Dead: Marx's Vampires', *History of Political Thought*, Vol. 24, No. 4, 2003, pp. 668–684; *The Monstrous and the Dead: Burke, Marx, Fascism* (Cardiff: University of Wales Press, 2005).

61   Marx, *Capital, Vol. 1*, pp. 548, 989–990; *Grundrisse*, pp. 693, 831.

62   Marx, *Capital, Vol. 1*, p. 302, emphases added. Also p. 503; *Grundrisse*, pp. 693, 831; *Economic and Philosophic Manuscripts of 1844*, in Karl Marx and Frederick Engels, *Collected Works, Vol. 3* (London: Lawrence and Wishart, 1975), p. 278.

63   Marx, *Grundrisse*, pp. 453–454.

64   Marx, *Grundrisse*, p. 470.

65   Marx, *Grundrisse*, pp. 453–454.

66   Marx, *Capital, Vol. 1*, pp. 302 and 481–482; *Grundrisse*, p. 470.

67   David Cunningham and Alexandra Warwick, 'The Ambassadors of Nil: Notes on the Zombie Apocalypse', in Monica Germana and Aris Mousoutzanis (eds), *Apocalyptic Discourse in Contemporary Culture: Post-Millennial Perspectives on the End of the World* (Abingdon, Oxon: Routledge, 2014), pp. 175–189, p. 186.

68   Gilles Deleuze and Félix Guattari, *Anti-Oedipus: Capitalism and Schizophrenia* (1972), trans. Robert Hurley, Mark Seem and Helen R. Lane (London: Athlone Press, 1984), p. 335; *A Thousand Plateaus: Capitalism and Schizophrenia* (1980), trans. Brian Massumi (London: Athlone Press, 1988), p. 425.

69   Dayan, *Haiti, History*, p. 36; Kordas, 'New South, New Immigrants, New Women, New Zombies', p. 17.

70   C. L. R. Kames, *The Black Jacobins* (1938) (London: Allison and Busby, 1980); Peter Hallward, *Damming the Flood: Haiti, Aristide, and the Politics of Containment*

(London: Verso, 2007), p. 11; Michael Denning, *Culture in the Age of Three Worlds* (London: Verso, 2004), p. 26.

71 Laroche, 'The Myth of the Zombi', p. 55.

72 Dayan, *Haiti, History, and the Gods*, p. 37.

73 Robert Southey, *History of Brazil, Vol. III* (London: Longman, 1819), p. 24.

74 Southey, *History of Brazil*, pp. 28–29.

75 Marina Warner, *Fantastic Metamorphoses, Other Worlds* (Oxford: Oxford University Press, 2002), p. 121.

76 Though it is worth noting that the security measures are also often designed to ensure the Zombie's productivity. In the film *Fido* (2006), for example, the Zombie servant class are managed by a corporate-security company called Zomcon. The company's motto plays on one of the central security concepts: 'A Better Life Through Containment', and the motto leads to the company's key selling point, consistent with the defence of capital inherent in the logic of security as the supreme concept of bourgeois order: 'Thanks to Zomcon, we'll all be productive members of society'. The threat to bourgeois order is almost always rolled into a threat to order as a whole and human society per se. George Romero picked up on this in his film *Land of the Dead*, released the year before *Fido*, in which a black working class Zombie leads the other Zombies in an insurrection: developing enough (class) consciousness they learn to shoot guns and use drills and axes as weapons, they leave the place where they live (called, significantly, 'Union Town') and march into the gated security palaces of wealthy America.

77 Travis Linnemann, Tyler Wall and Edward Green, 'The Walking Dead and Killing State: Zombification and the Normalization of Police Violence', *Theoretical Criminology*, Vol. 18, No. 4, 2014, pp. 506–527, p. 513.

78 Jennifer Cooke, *Legacies of Plague in Literature and Film* (Houndmills, Basingstoke: Palgrave, 2009), p. 168; Emma Dyson, 'Diaries of a Plague Year: Perspectives of Destruction in Contemporary Zombie Film', in Leon Hunt, Sharon Lockyer and Milly Williamson (eds), *Screening the Undead: Vampires and Zombies in Film and Television* (London: I.B. Tauris, 2014), pp. 130–147.

79 Mark Neocleous, *Imagining the State* (Maidenhead: Open University Press, 2003), chap. 1.

80 Cheryl Lynn Ross, 'The Plague of *The Alchemist*', *Renaissance Quarterly*, Vol. 41, No. 3, 1988, pp. 439–458, p. 445.

81 René Girard, 'The Plague in Literature and Myth', *Texas Studies in Literature and Language*, Vol. 15, No. 5, 1974, pp. 833–850; Michel Foucault, *Discipline and Punish: The Birth of the Prison* (1975), trans. Alan Sheridan (London: Penguin, 1977), pp. 196–198.

82 Cunningham and Warwick, 'Ambassadors of Nil', p. 180.

83 Daniel Defoe, *Due Preparations for the Plague, As Well for Soul as Body* (1722), in *The Works of Daniel Defoe, Vol. 15* (New York: George D. Sproul, 1904); Janette Turner Hospital, 'Inspiration', in Janette Turner Hospital, *Due Preparations for the Plague* (Sydney: HarperCollins, 2004), p. 8.

84 Colin Dayan, *The Law is a White Dog: How Legal Rituals Make and Unmake Persons* (Princeton: Princeton University Press, 2011), p. 26.

85 Andrew R. Aisenberg, *Contagion: Disease, Government, and the 'Social Question' in Nineteenth-Century France* (Stanford, CA: Stanford University Press, 1999), p. 5.

86 Michael Hardt and Antonio Negri, *Empire* (Cambridge, MA: Harvard University Press, 2000), pp. 135–136.

87 Thomas Hobbes, *Leviathan* (1651), ed. Richard Tuck (Cambridge: Cambridge University Press, 1991), p. 209; Edmund Burke, *Reflections on the Revolution in France* (1790) (Harmondsworth: Penguin, 1968), p. 201; David Hume, *The*

History of England, Vol. VI (1778), (Indianapolis: Liberty Classics, 1983), p. 342, 516; *The Federalist Papers*, (1788), No. 28; Jean-Jacques Rousseau, *Emile; Or, On Education* (1762), trans. Harold Bloom (Harmondsworth: Penguin, 1991), p. 335; Immanuel Kant, *Critique of Pure Reason* (1781), trans. Norman Kemp Smith (Houndmills, Basingstoke: Macmillan, 1929), p. 576.

88 Martin S. Pernick, 'Contagion and Culture', *American Literary History*, Vol. 14, No. 4, 2002, pp. 858–865.

89 Michel de Montaigne, 'On Solitude', in *The Complete Essays* (1580–1592), trans. M. A. Screech (Harmondsworth: Penguin, 1991), p. 267. See also Elias Canetti, *Crowds and Power* (1960), trans. Carol Stewart (London: Victor Gollancz, 1962), p. 275; Priscilla Wald, *Contagious: Cultures, Carriers, and the Outbreak Narrative* (Durham: Duke University Press, 2008), pp. 2, 12, 14; Peta Mitchell, *Contagious Metaphor* (London: Continuum, 2012).

90 Thomas Hobbes, *On the Citizen* (1642), ed. and trans. Richard Tuck and Michael Silverthorne (Cambridge: Cambridge University Press, 1998), pp. 75–77, 94, 118.

91 Gustave Le Bon, *The Crowd: A Study of the Popular Mind* (1895), ed. Robert A. Nye (New Brunswick, NJ: Transaction Publishers, 1995), p. 50.

92 Gustave Le Bon, *The Crowd*, pp. 51–52, 65, 140, 148–151, 154.

93 Gustave Le Bon, *The French Revolution and the Psychology of Revolution* (1912), ed. Robert A. Nye (New Brunswick, NJ: Transaction Publishers, 1980), pp. 103, 174, 178.

94 Gustave Le Bon, *The Crowd*, pp. 35, 106, 206–208.

95 See Mark Neocleous, *Fascism* (Maidenhead: Open University Press, 1997).

96 See www.gov.uk/government/uploads/system/uploads/attachment_data/file/62637/guideforreaders1_0.pdf [accessed 18 Nov. 2015]. For the huge project 'Understanding Crowd Behaviours' see www.gov.uk/government/publications/understanding-crowd-behaviours-documents [accessed 18 Nov. 2015]. In particular, see the document available on that website produced by the Emergency Planning College of the Cabinet Office, *Understanding Crowd Behaviours: Supporting Evidence* (2009), and for Le Bon specifically see pp. 81–84, 125, 165; and the document produced jointly by the Home Office, the Centre for the Protection of National Infrastructure and the National Counter-Terrorism Security Office, called *Protecting Crowded Places: Design and Technical Issues* (London: HM Government, 2012; revised and expanded March 2014). For discussion see Claudia Aradau, '"Crowded Places Are Everywhere We Go": Crowds, Emergency, Politics', *Theory, Culture and Society*, Vol. 32, No. 2, 2015, pp. 155–175.

97 Department of Defense Minerva Initiative, University-Led Research, 2014 Awards – http://minerva.dtic.mil/funded.html [accessed 18 Nov. 2015].

98 Nicholas Christakis and James Fowler, *Connected: The Amazing Power of Social Networks and How They Shape Our Lives* (London: HarperCollins, 2011).

99 The tone, we are told, stems 'from the apocalyptic vision of the terrorists themselves', as Bush's advisors David Frum and Richard Perle put it. But given the debate we shall have in the chapter to follow, the claim is laughable. See David Frum and Richard Perle, *An End to Evil: How to Win the War on Terror* (New York: Ballantine Books, 2004), p. 34.

100 Elana Gomel, 'The Plague of Utopias: Pestilence and the Apocalyptic Body', *Twentieth Century Literature*, Vol. 46, No. 4, 2000, pp. 405–433, p. 406.

101 Louis-Ferdinand Céline, *Féerie pour une autre fois, I*, cited in Julia Kristeva, *Powers of Horror: An Essay on Abjection* (New York: Columbia University Press, 1982), p. 207.

102 Tina Pippin, *Apocalyptic Bodies: The Biblical End of the World in Text and Image*

(London: Routledge, 1999), p. 9.

103 Stephen D. O'Leary, *Arguing the Apocalypse: A Theory of Millennial Rhetoric* (Oxford: Oxford University Press, 1994), pp. 57–58. Also Ruth H. Bloch, *Visionary Republic: Millennial Themes in American Thought, 1756–1800* (Cambridge: Cambridge University Press, 1985), pp. xi–xii.

104 Carl Schmitt, *Political Theology: Four Chapters on the Concept of Sovereignty* (1922), trans. George Schwab (Camb, MA: MIT Press, 1985), p. 36.

105 Jacob Taubes, *Occidental Eschatology* (1991), trans. David Ratmoko (Stanford, CA: Stanford University Press, 2009), p. 9.

106 Hans Magnus Enzensberger, 'Two Notes on the End of the World', *New Left Review*, 110, 1978, pp. 74–80, p. 74.

107 Taubes, *Occidental Eschatology*, pp. 34, 186; Ernest Tuveson, 'The Millenarian Structure of *The Communist Manifesto*', in C. A. Patrides and Joseph Wittreich (eds), *The Apocalypse in English Renaissance Thought and Literature* (Manchester: Manchester University Press, 1984).

108 Respectively: Ernst Bloch, *Atheism in Christianity: The Religion of Exodus and the Kingdom* (1972), trans. J. T. Swann (London: Verso, 2009); Walter Benjamin, 'On the Concept of History' (1940), trans. Harry Zohn, in *Selected Writings, Volume 4: 1938–1940*, ed. Howard Eiland and Michael W. Jennings (Cambridge MA: Belknap/Harvard, 2003), Thesis VIII and XIV.

109 Krishan Kumar, 'Apocalypse, Millennium and Utopia Today', in Malcolm Bull (ed.), *Apocalypse Theory and the Ends of the World* (Oxford: Blackwell, 1995), p. 202; Roland Boer, *Criticism of Heaven: On Marxism and Theology* (Chicago, IL: Haymarket Books, 2009), p. 100.

110 Hans Blumenberg, *The Legitimacy of the Modern Age* (1966), trans. Robert M. Wallace (Cambridge, MA: MIT Press, 1985).

111 O'Leary, *Arguing the Apocalypse*, pp. 80–81.

112 Peter Osborne, 'A Sudden Topicality: Marx, Nietzsche and the Politics of Crisis', *Radical Philosophy*, 160, 2010, pp. 19–26, p. 21.

113 Enzensberger, 'Two Notes', p. 79.

114 Thomas L. Long, *AIDS and American Apocalypticism: The Cultural Semiotics of an Epidemic* (Albany, NY: State University of New York Press, 2005), pp. 8, 9.

115 Boer, *Criticism of Heaven*, p. 100. Also see O'Leary, *Arguing the Apocalypse*, pp. 160, 168, 180; Charles B. Strozier, *Apocalypse: On the Psychology of Fundamentalism in America* (Boston: Beacon Press, 1994); Matthew Avery Sutton, *American Apocalypse: A History of Modern Evangelicalism* (Cambridge, MA: Harvard University Press, 2014), pp. 7, 125, 368.

116 Jacob Taubes, 'Carl Schmitt: Apocalyptic Prophet of the Counterrevolution', in Jacob Taubes, *To Carl Schmitt: Letters and Reflections*, trans. Keith Tribe (New York: Columbia University Press, 2013), p. 13.

117 Richard Dellamora, *Apocalyptic Overtures: Sexual Politics and the Sense of an Ending* (New Brunswick, NJ: Rutgers University Press, 1994), p. 3.

118 Jacques Derrida, 'Of an Apocalyptic Tone Recently Adopted in Philosophy', *Oxford Literary Review*, Vol. 6, No. 2, 1984, pp. 3–37, pp. 23–24.

119 Catherine Keller, *Apocalypse Now and Then: A Feminist Guide to the End of the World* (Boston: Beacon Press, 1996), p. 11.

120 Susan Sontag, *Illness as Metaphor and AIDS and Its Metaphors* (Harmondsworth: Penguin, 1991), p. 173.

3 'The ringleader of Rebellion': on the Devil

1 George W. Bush, 'Address to the Nation on the Terrorist Attacks', Washington, 11 September, 2001.

2   George W. Bush, 'Address before a Joint Session of the Congress on the State of the Union', Washington, 29 January, 2002.

3   George W. Bush, 'Commencement Address at the United States Military Academy, West Point', New York, 1 June, 2002.

4   See George W. Bush, 'Remarks to Federal Bureau of Investigation Employees', 25 September, 2001; 'Remarks to Central Intelligence Agency Employees in Langley, Virginia', 26 September, 2001; 'Remarks at the Department of Defense Service of Remembrance in Arlington, Virginia', 11 October, 2001; 'Remarks at the Thurgood Marshall Extended Elementary School', 25 October, 2001; *The National Security Strategy of the United States of America*, 2002, Preface and p. 1.

5   David Frum, cited in Howard Fineman, 'Bush and God', *Newsweek*, 14 March, 2010; David Frum, *The Right Man: An Inside Account of the Surprise Presidency of George W. Bush* (London: Weidenfeld and Nicolson, 2003), pp. 236–240. Frum's own take on the evil is in David Frum and Richard Perle, *An End to Evil: How to Win the War on Terror* (New York: Ballantine Books, 2004).

6   Peter Singer, *The President of Good and Evil: Taking George W. Bush Seriously* (London: Granta, 2004), pp. 1–3.

7   Adam Phillips, *On Flirtation* (London: Faber and Faber, 1994), p. 64.

8   Simona Forti, *New Demons: Rethinking Power and Evil Today* (2012), trans. Zakiya Hanafi (Stanford, CA: Stanford University Press, 2015), p. 3.

9   Recall that the war was launched initially under the title 'Operation Infinite Justice' before being renamed 'Operation Enduring Freedom' after some people objected that 'infinite justice' could be dispensed only by God.

10   Alexis de Tocqueville, *Democracy in America, Vol. I* (1835), trans. James T. Schleifer (Indianapolis: Liberty Fund, 2010), pp. 474, 475. For Marx's observation see Karl Marx, 'On the Jewish Question' (1844), in Karl Marx and Frederick Engels, *Collected Works, Vol. 3* (London: Lawrence and Wishart, 1975), p. 151.

11   George W. Bush, 'Address to the Nation Announcing Strikes Against Al Qaida Training Camps and Taliban Military Installations in Afghanistan', Washington, 7 Oct., 2001, emphasis added.

12   George W. Bush, 'Remarks to the American Israel Public Affairs Committee', Washington, May 18, 2004.

13   George W. Bush, 'Remarks at MacDill Air Force Base in Tampa, Florida', 26 March, 2003.

14   Condoleezza Rice, 'Remarks at the American Israel Public Affairs Committee's Annual Policy Conference', Washington, DC, 23 May, 2005 – http://2001-2009.state.gov/secretary/rm/2005/46625.htm [accessed 17 Nov. 2015]

15   George W. Bush 'Inaugural Address', Washington, 20 January, 2001. Bush was citing Virginia statesman John Page who, in a letter to Thomas Jefferson just after the signing of the Declaration of Independence, wrote that 'We know the race is not to the swift, nor the battle to the strong. Do you not think an angel rides in the whirlwind and directs this storm?' Bush continued: 'His [God's] purpose is achieved in our duty. And our duty is fulfilled in service to one another. Never tiring, never yielding, never finishing, we renew that purpose today, to make our country more just and generous, to affirm the dignity of our lives and every life. This work continues, the, story goes on, and an angel still rides in the whirlwind and directs this storm'.

16   'Believer Nation', *Public Perspectives*, May-June, 2000 – www.ropercenter.uconn.edu/public-perspective/ppscan/113/113024.pdf [accessed 17 Nov. 2015]; 'The Religious and Other Beliefs of Americans', *Harris Interactive*, 29 Nov., 2007 – www.harrisinteractive.com/vault/Harris-Interactive-Poll-

Research-Religious-Beliefs-2007-11.pdf [accessed 17 Nov. 2015]. Also Singer, *President of Good and Evil*, p. 92; Darren Oldridge, *The Devil: A Very Short Introduction* (Oxford: Oxford University Press, 2012), p. 90.

17 W. Scott Poole, *Satan in America: The Devil We Know* (Lanham, Maryland: Rowman and Littlefield, 2009), p. xiv; Robert Muchembled, *A History of the Devil: From the Middle Ages to the Present* (2000), trans. Jean Birrell (Cambridge: Polity, 2003), p. 266. Also Phillip Cole, *The Myth of Evil* (Edinburgh: Edinburgh University Press, 2006), p. 210.

18 Robert Fuller, *Naming the Antichrist: The History of an American Obsession* (New York: Oxford University Press, 1995), pp. 4–5; Singer, *President of Good and Evil*, p. 208; Bruce Lincoln, *Holy Terrors: Thinking about Religion after September 9/11* (Chicago: University of Chicago press, 2003), p. 32.

19 See Paul Boyer, *When Time Shall Be No More: Prophecy Belief in Modern American Culture* (Cambridge, MA: Harvard University Press, 1992), pp. 275–6; Stephen D. O'Leary, *Arguing the Apocalypse: A Theory of Millennial Rhetoric* (Oxford: Oxford University Press, 1994), pp. 82, 193.

20 Frum, *Right Man*, p. 140.

21 George W. Bush, 'Remarks at the Peace Officers Memorial Service', Washington, 15 May, 2002.

22 Condoleezza Rice, Speech at 'Princeton University's Celebration of the 75th Anniversary of the Woodrow Wilson School of Public and International Affairs', New Jersey, 30 September, 2005.

23 Cited in Richard T. Cooper, 'General Casts War in Religious Terms', *Los Angeles Times*, 16 October, 2003.

24 Cited in Paul Wood, 'Fixing the Problem of Falluja', *BBC News*, 7 November, 2004.

25 Norman Mailer, *Why Are We At War?* (New York: Random House, 2003), pp. 110–111.

26 Christopher Hill, *Antichrist in Seventeenth-Century England* (London: Oxford University Press, 1971), p. 159.

27 Mark Danner, *Torture and Truth: America, Abu Ghraib, and the War on Terror* (New York: New York Review of Books, 2004), p. 227.

28 'Angel Or Devil? Viewers See Images In Smoke' – http://urbanlegends.about.com/library/bltabloid-arch10.htm [accessed 17 Nov. 2015]. http://web.archive.org/web/20030729205919/www.clickondetroit.com/news/962839/detail.html [accessed 17 Nov. 2015].

29 Mark D. Phillips's book on the image discusses some of the debates that took place surrounding its authenticity. The book is also a useful source of material showing the extent to which just how many Americans believe that the attacks were the work of the Devil. See Mark D. Phillips, *Is it Real? Satan in the Smoke* (New York: Mark D. Phillips, 2011).

30 See, for example, 'Devil Face in the Twin Towers', www.youtube.com/watch?v=16bPTlsf1Fc [accessed 17 Nov. 2015].; 'Face of God and Satan on WTC, 9/11', www.youtube.com/watch?v=zsq3LnFv3tk [accessed 17 Nov. 2015].; and 'Evil Faces in Smoke of 9/11', www.youtube.com/watch?v=wmTbe5avjAw [accessed 17 Nov. 2015].

31 'Devil Face in Smoke of 911 at the WTC', www.christianmedia.us/devil-face.html [accessed 17 Nov. 2015].

32 Alexis de Tocqueville, *Democracy in America, Vol. II* (1840), trans. James T. Schleifer (Indianapolis: Liberty Fund, 2010), p. 940.

33 Henri Lefebvre, *Introduction to Modernity: Twelve Preludes, September 1959– May 1961* (1962), trans. John Moore (London: Verso, 1995), p. 58.

34 Henry Ansgar Kelly, *Satan: A Biography* (Cambridge: Cambridge University

Press, 2006). There are different accounts of the history of these terms, along with others such as 'Lucifer'. Interesting as the history is, it is beyond the scope of this chapter. Moreover, generally speaking those who talk of the Devil tend to use the whole gamut of terms interchangeably. Hence the *Malleus Maleficarum* (1486), a major witch-hunting text which we discuss later in this chapter, comments in Part I, Question IV that the Devil is also known as Diabolus, Demon, Belial, Beelzebub, Behemoth and, 'Satan, that is, the Adversary'. The two most common terms that have been used are Devil and Satan; this chapter takes its cue from Revelation 12:9, which references 'that ancient serpent, who is called the Devil and Satan', and thus uses the terms interchangeably while also largely sticking to 'Devil'.

35　Muchembled, *A History of the Devil: from the Middle Ages to the present (2003)*, p. 10.
36　This is the basis on which Freud develops his argument concerning the Devil as father substitute. See 'A Seventeenth-Century Demonological Neurosis' (1923), trans. James Strachey and Anna Freud, in *The Standard Edition of the Complete Works of Sigmund Freud, Vol. XIX* (London: Vintage, 2001), pp. 67–105, p. 86.
37　Kelly, *Satan*, pp. 2, 29, 31, 83; Jeffrey B. Russell, *The Prince of Darkness: Radical Evil and the Power of Good in History* (London: Thames and Hudson, 1989), pp. 5, 28; Gerald Messadié, *The History of the Devil* (1993), trans. Marc Romano (London: Newleaf, 1996), pp. 232–7; Luther Link, *The Devil: The Archfiend in Art from the Sixth to the Sixteenth Century* (New York: Harry Abrams, 1996), p. 19; C. Breytenbach and P. L. Day, 'Satan', in Karel van der Toorn, Bob Becking and Pieter W. van der Horst (eds), *Dictionary of Deities and Demons in the Bible* (Leiden: Brill, 1999), pp. 726–732; Elaine Pagels, *The Origin of Satan* (New York: Random House, 1995), p. 39; Norman Cohn, *Europe's Inner Demons* (London: Granada, 1976), pp. 60–74.
38　Norman C. Habel, *The Book of Job* (Cambridge: Cambridge University Press, 1975), p. 17.
39　Russell, *Prince of Darkness*, p. 28.
40　Pagels, *The Origin of Satan*, p. 8. Also see Messadié, *History of the Devil*, pp. 3, 248, 252–253, 285; Russell, *Prince of Darkness*, p. 37; Cole, *Myth of Evil*, pp. 28–9; Cohn, *Europe's Inner Demons*, pp. 1–15; Darren Oldridge, *The Devil in Early Modern England* (Thrupp, Gloucestershire: Sutton, 2000), p. 15.
41　Christopher Hill, *Reformation to Industrial Revolution* (Harmondsworth: Penguin, 1969), pp. 116–7; Jeffrey B. Russell, *Lucifer: The Devil in the Middle Ages* (Ithaca: Cornell University Press, 1984), pp. 62–7; Russell, *Prince of Darkness*, pp. 56–8, 112.
42　Muchembled, *A History of the Devil: from the Middle Ages to the present (2003)*, p. 11.
43　Kelly, *Satan*, p. 2, emphasis added.
44　Daniel Defoe, *The History of the Devil: Ancient and Modern, in Two Parts* (1726) (London: EP Publishing, 1972), pp. 140, 156, 157, 169, 222, 364.
45　Increase Mather, *Cases of Conscience Concerning Evil Spirits* (Boston: Benjamin Harris 1693), p. A2; Jean Bodin, *On the Demon-Mania of Witches* (1580), trans. Randy A. Scott (Toronto: CRRS Publications, 1995), p. 135.
46　Dan Edelstein, *The Terror of Natural Right: Republicanism, the Cult of Nature, and the French Revolution* (Chicago: University of Chicago Press, 2009), pp. 30–1.
47　C. S. Lewis, *Mere Christianity* (1952) (London: HarperCollins, 2012), p. 45.
48　Bernard McGinn, 'Introduction: Apocalyptic Spirituality', in Bernard McGinn (ed.), *Apocalyptic Spirituality* (Mahwah, NJ: Paulist Press, 1979), p. 12.
49　Respectively: 'The Third Part of the Homily Against Images, and the Worshipping of Them' and 'An Information for Them who Take Offence at

Certain Places of the Holy Scripture, First Part', both in *Certain Sermons or Homilies Appointed to be Read in Churches in the Time of the Late Queen Elizabeth* [1547–62], (Oxford: Oxford University Press, 1840), pp. 206 and 326; theologian Pedro Ciruelo in 1530, cited in Stuart Clark, *Thinking With Demons: The Idea of Witchcraft in Early Modern Europe* (Oxford: Oxford University Press, 1997), p. 80; Cotton Mather, *The Wonders of the Invisible World. Being An Account of the Tryals of Several Witches Lately Executed in New England* (1692) (London: John Russell Smith, 1862), p. 67.

50   Daniel Defoe, *Robinson Crusoe* (1719) (London: Penguin, 1985), p. 220.

51   Neil Forsyth, *The Old Enemy: Satan and the Combat Myth* (Princeton, NJ: Princeton University Press, 1987); Forsyth, *Old Enemy*, pp. 4, 113–114, 124; Pagels, *Origin of Satan*, pp. 13, 47, 89, 91, 182; Russell, *Prince of Darkness*, p. 44; Kelly, *Satan*, pp. 110, 116, Jeffrey Burton Russell, *The Devil: Perceptions of Evil from Antiquity to Primitive Christianity* (Ithaca: Cornell University Press, 1977), pp. 222, 229–31; Nathan Johnstone, *The Devil and Demonism in Early Modern England* (Cambridge: Cambridge University Press, 2006), pp. 41, 51; Oldridge, *The Devil*, p. xiii.

52   Norman Cohn, 'The Myth of Satan and His Human Servants', in Mary Douglas (ed.), *Witchcraft Confessions and Accusations* (London: Tavistock, 1970), pp. 3–16, p. 8.

53   Moore, *Formation of a Persecuting Society*, pp. 44–5, 63, 66; Hill, *Antichrist*, p. 4; Oldridge, *Devil in Early Modern England*, pp. 4, 9; Johnstone, *Devil and Demonism*, pp. 27–9.

54   Muchembled, *A History of the Devil*, pp. 6–7.

55   Martin Luther, *Table Talk*, Entry No. 252, 20 April – 16 May, 1532, in *Luther's Works, Vol. 54*, ed. and trans. Theodore G. Tappert (Philadelphia: Fortress Press, 1967), p. 34; Max Weber, *The Protestant Ethic and the Spirit of Capitalism* (1904–5; revised ed. 1920–1), trans. Talcott Parsons (London: George Allen and Unwin, 1930), p. 111; Michael Walzer, *The Revolution of the Saints: A Study in the Origins of Radical Politics* (Cambridge, MA: Harvard University Press, 1965), pp. 104, 154; Keith Thomas, *Religion and the Decline of Magic* (Harmondsworth: Penguin, 1973), pp. 561, 562; Michael T. Taussig, *The Devil and Commodity Fetishism in South America* (Chapel Hill: University of North Carolina Press, 1980), p. 170; Heiko A. Oberman, *Luther: Man between God and the Devil* (1982), trans. Eileen Walliser-Schwarzbart (New Haven: Yale University Press, 1989), p. 104; Bernard Capp, 'The Political Dimension of Apocalyptic Thought' and Stephen J. Stein, 'Transatlantic Extensions: Apocalyptic in Early New England', both in C. A. Patrides and Joseph Wittreich (eds), *The Apocalypse in English Renaissance Thought and Literature* (Manchester: Manchester University Press, 1984); Ruth H. Bloch, *Visionary Republic: Millennial Themes in American Thought, 1756–1800* (Cambridge: Cambridge University Press, 1985); Laura de Mello e Souza, *The Devil and the Holy Cross: Witchcraft, Slavery, and Popular Religion in Colonial Brazil* (1986), trans. Diane Grosklaus Whitty (Austin, TX: University of Texas Press, 2003), pp. 78–80.

56   Richard Godbeer, *The Devil's Dominion: Magic and Religion in Early New England* (Cambridge: Cambridge University Press, 1992), p. 86.

57   Anthony J. Barker, *The African Link: British Attitudes to the Negro in the Era of the Slave Trade, 1550–1807* (London: frank Cass, 1978), p. 91.

58   Souza, *Devil and the Holy Cross*, pp. 21–25, 32–34; Irene Silverblatt, *Moon, Sun, and Witches: Gender Ideologies and Class in Inca and Colonial Peru* (Princeton, NJ: Princeton University Press, 1987), pp. 159, 170; Fernando Cervantes, *The Devil in the New World: The Impact of Diabolism in New Spain* (New Haven: Yale University Press, 1994), pp. 5–39; Silvia Federici, *Caliban and the Witch: Women,*

The Body and Primitive Accumulation (New York: Autonomedia, 2004), p. 163; Richard Slotkin, *Regeneration Through Violence: The Mythology of the American Frontier, 1600–1860* (Norman, OK: University of Oklahoma Press, 1973), pp. 32, 38, 57, 65, 88, 120.

59 Mather, *Wonders of the Invisible World*, pp. 63–64.

60 Cotton Mather, *Magnalia Christi Americana; or, The Ecclesiastical History of New England, Vol. 1* (1702), (Hartford: Silas Andrew and Son, 1855), pp. xiv, 556.

61 Souza, *Devil and the Holy Cross*, pp. 27–9, 44, 80; Slotkin, *Regeneration Through Violence*, pp.130; James A. Morone, *Hellfire Nation: The Politics of Sin in American History* (New Haven: Yale University Press, 2003), p. 74.

62 Poole, *Satan in America*, p. 4.

63 Cited in James A. Morone, *Hellfire Nation: The Politics of Sin in American History* (New Haven: Yale University Press, 2003), p. 453; also see pp. 9 and 464.

64 Darren Oldridge, *Strange Histories: The Trial of the Pig, The Walking Dead, and other matters of Fact from the Medieval and Renaissance Worlds* (London: Routledge, 2007), p. ix.

65 Oldridge, *Devil in Early Modern England*, p. 39.

66 Elias Canetti, *Crowds and Power* (1960), trans. Carol Stewart (London: Gollancz, 1962), pp. 45–7.

67 When Robert Southey in his *History of Brazil* reports on the word 'zombi' meaning Deity, he adds a little footnote, as follows: 'Rocha Pitta says the word [zombie] means Devil in their language'. Southey then says that he finds this unlikely and that he has no supporting evidence, but the connection is there from the moment 'zombie' enters the English language: the zombie and the Devil are conspiring together – *History of Brazil, Vol. III* (London: Longman, 1819), p. 24.

68 Oldridge, *Strange Histories*, pp. 64–69.

69 Michel Foucault, *Wrong-Doing, Truth-telling: The Function of Avowal in Justice* ('Fourth Lecture, May 6, 1981'), trans. Stephen W. Sawyer (Chicago: University of Chicago Press, 2014), p. 151.

70 Michel Foucault, *On the Government of the Living: Lectures at the Collège de France, 1979–1980*, trans. Graham Burchell (Houndmills, Basingstoke, 2014), p. 124; Federici, *Caliban and the Witch*, p. 134.

71 H. R. Trevor-Roper, *The European Witch-Craze of the Sixteenth and Seventeenth Centuries* (Harmondsworth: Penguin, 1969), p. 12; R. I. Moore, *The Formation of a Persecuting Society: Power and Deviance in Western Europe, 950–1250* (Oxford: Blackwell, 1987); Jon Oplinger, *The Politics of Demonology: The European Witchcraze and the Mass Production of Deviance* (Selinsgrove: Susquehanna University Press, 1990).

72 Messadié, *History of the Devil*, p. 278; Muchembled, *A History of the Devil*, p. 24.

73 See, for example, Souza, *Devil and the Holy Cross*, pp. 181–182; Christina Larner, *Enemies of God: The Witch-hunt in Scotland* (London: Chatto and Windus, 1981), pp. 193–194; Wolfgang Behringer, *Witchcraft Persecutions in Bavaria: Popular Magic, Religious Zealotry and Reason of State* (1987), trans. J. C., Grayson and David Lederer (Cambridge: Cambridge University Press, 1997); Muchembled, *A History of the Devil*, pp. 19, 23, 40. For criticisms see Brian P. Levack, 'State-building and Witch Hunting in Early Modern Europe', in Jonathan Barry, Marianne Hester and Gareth Roberts (eds), *Witchcraft in Early Modern Europe* (Cambridge: Cambridge University Press, 1996), pp. 96–115.

74 Margaret Denike, 'The Devil's Insatiable Sex: A Genealogy of Evil Incarnate', *Hypatia*, Vol. 18, No. 1, 2003, pp. 10–43, p. 13.

75 Carol F. Karlsen, *The Devil in the Shape of a Woman: Witchcraft in Colonial New England* (New York: Norton, 1998); Barbara Ehrenreich and Deidre English,

Witches, Midwives and Nurses: A History of Women Healers (London: Writers and Readers Publishing Cooperative, 1973).

76 Respectively: Trevor-Roper, *European Witch-Craze*, p. 47; Lucien Febvre, 'Witchcraft: Nonsense or a Mental Revolution?' (1948), in Peter Burke (ed.), *A New Kind of History: From the Writings of Febvre*, trans. K. Folca (London Routledge, 1973), p. 211.

77 Jean Bodin, *Six Books of the Commonwealth* (1576), trans. M. J. Tooley (Place of Publication Unknown: Seven Treasures, 2009), p. 65.

78 Bodin, *Six Books*, pp. 106–107.

79 Bodin, *Six Books*, p. 176.

80 J. W. Allen, *A History of Political Thought in the Sixteenth Century* (London: Methuen, 1960), p. 397. Some have sought to defend Bodin by saying that he did not really believe all the stuff about witchcraft and that the book is just a 'cover' to protect himself. But as Henry White pointed out some time ago, at over 600 pages it is some cover – 'Jean Bodin, and the History of Witchcraft', *The Student* [London], Vol. 4, 1870, pp. 327–338.

81 Clark, *Thinking With Demons*, p. 670. Also, Harold Elmer Mantz, 'Jean Bodin and the Sorcerers I', *The Romanic Review*, Vol. 15, Nos. 3–4, 1924, pp. 153–78; Jonathan Pearl, 'Humanism and Satanism: Jean Bodin's Contribution to the Witchcraft Crisis', *Canadian Review of Sociology and Anthropology*, Vol. 19, No. 4, 1982, pp. 541–8.

82 Bodin, *Demon-Mania*, p. 135.

83 Bodin, *Demon-Mania*, pp. 69, 179, 200, 216.

84 Bodin, *Demon-Mania*, p. 204.

85 Bodin, *Demon-Mania*, pp. 35–36. This was an important issue in debates among demonologists and lawyers in the late-sixteenth and early-seventeenth centuries, as Jonathan Pearl has shown – 'French Catholic Demonologists and Their Enemies in the Late Sixteenth and Early Seventeenth Centuries', *Church History*, Vol. 52, No. 4, 1983, pp. 457–467.

86 Bodin, *Six Books*, pp. 43–44, 135.

87 Bodin, *Demon-Mania*, p. 174.

88 Bodin, *Demon-Mania*, pp. 37, 188, 200, emphasis added.

89 See Mark Neocleous, 'The Problem with Normality, or, Taking Exception to "Permanent Emergency"', *Alternatives: Global, Local, Political*, Vol. 31, No. 2, 2006, pp. 191–213; *Critique of Security* (Edinburgh: Edinburgh University Press, 2008), chap. 2.

90 Bodin, *Demon-Mania*, pp. 173–180, 188, 190–191, 195, 200.

91 St Augustine, *City of God*, trans. Henry Bettenson (Harmondsworth: Penguin, 1972), Book 14, Chap. 4, p. 552.

92 Dallas G. Denery II, *The Devil Wins: A History of Lying from the Garden of Eden to the Enlightenment* (Princeton, NJ: Princeton University Press, 2015), pp. 6, 7, 53.

93 Francesco Guicciardini, *Ricordi* (1512–1530), translated as *Maxims and Reflections of a Renaissance Statesman*, trans. Mario Domandi (New York: Harper Row, 1965), p. 54; Francesco Guicciardini, *Dialogue on the Government of Florence* (1521–4), trans. Alison Brown (Cambridge: Cambridge University Press, 1994), p. 159; Niccolò Machiavelli, *The Prince* (1532), in *The Chief Works and Others, Vol. 1*, trans. Allan Gilbert (Durham: Duke University Press, 1958), p. 66; Trajano Bocalini, *I Raggvagli Di Parnasso* (1612–13), in *I Raggvagli Di Parnasso: or, Advertisements from Parnassus: In Two Centuries. With The Politick Touchstone*, trans. Henry Earl of Monmouth (London, 1669), p. 305. For a longer discussion see Mark Neocleous, *Imagining the State* (Maidenhead: Open University Press, 2003), chap. 2.

94   George L. Mosse, *The Holy Pretence: A Study in Christianity and Reason of State from William Perkins to John Winthrop* (Oxford: Basil Blackwell, 1957). Also see Friedrich Meinecke, *Machiavellism: The Doctrine of Raison d'État and Its Place in Modern History* (1957), trans. Douglas Scott (New Brunswick: Transaction Publishers, 1998), p. 39; C. J. Friedrich, *Constitutional Reason of State: The Survival of the Constitutional Order* (Providence: Brown University Press, 1957), pp. 6, 24, 70; William F. Church, *Richelieu and Reason of State* (Princeton, NJ: Princeton University Press, 1972), pp. 11–13, 38, 44, 62–72, 163–5; J. A. Fernández-Santamaría, *Reason of State and Statecraft in Spanish Political Thought, 1595–1640* (London: Lanham Press, 1983), pp. 5–7, 23.
95   Michel de Montaigne, 'On Giving the Lie', in *The Complete Essays* (1580–1592), trans. M. A. Screech (Harmondsworth: Penguin, 1991), p. 756; Machiavelli, *The Prince*, p. 65; Giovanni Botero, *The Reason of State* (1589), trans. P. J. and D. P. Waley (London: Routledge, 1956), p. 48 The finger of Satan comment is from Reginald Pole, *Apologia ad Carolum Quintum* (1539), cited in Peter S. Donaldson, *Machiavelli and Mystery of State* (Cambridge: Cambridge University Press, 1988), p. 9. More generally, see Perez Zagorin, *Ways of Lying: Dissimulation, Persecution and Conformity in Early Modern Europe* (Cambridge, MA: Harvard University Press, 1990), pp. 13, 330.
96   Francis Bacon, 'Of Simulation and Dissimulation' (1625), in *Essays* (London: Dent, 1972), pp. 17–19; Guicciardini, *Maxims and Reflections*, p. 54; *Dialogue*, pp. 61, 99, 163; Botero, *Reason of State*, p. 47; Bocalini, *I Raggvagli Di Parnasso*, p. 11.
97   Jon R. Snyder, *Dissimulation and the Culture of Secrecy in Early Modern Europe* (Berkeley: University of California Press, 2009), pp. 7, 107, 108.
98   Bodin, *Demon-Mania*, pp. 204, 208, 210.
99   Bodin, *Demon-Mania*, p. 218.
100   Bodin, *Demon-Mania*, p. 203.
101   Elaine Scarry, *The Body in Pain: The Making and Unmaking of the World* (Oxford; Oxford University Press, 1985), p. 28.
102   Thomas Hobbes, *Leviathan* (1651), ed. Richard Tuck (Cambridge: Cambridge University Press, 1991), pp. 18–19, 219.
103   Bodin, *Demon-Mania*, pp. 203, 207. Thomas Becon complained in 1554 that 'this plague is worthy to come upon us, that instead of the Lord's supper we have the most wicked and abominable masses set up, invented by the devil, brought in by antichrist' – Thomas Becon, *A Comfortable Epistle to the Afflicted People of God* (1554), cited Johnstone, *Devil and Demonism*, p. 37.
104   Bodin, *Six Books*, pp. 43, 206.
105   Bodin, *Six Books*, pp. 43–48.
106   King James, *Demonologie, in Forme of a Dialogue* (1597), in Donald Tyson, *The Demonology of King James I* (Woodbury, Minnesota: Llewellyn Publications, 2011).
107   See Mark Neocleous, 'The Fate of the Body Politic', *Radical Philosophy*, 108, 2001, pp. 29–38; *Imagining the State*, chap. 1.
108   Stuart Clark, 'King James's *Daemonologie*: Witchcraft and Kingship', in Sydney Anglo (ed.), *The Damned Art: Essays in the Literature of Witchcraft* (London: Routledge and Kegan Paul, 1977), pp. 156–181, p. 177; W. H. Greenleaf, *Order, Empiricism and Politics: Two Traditions of English Political Thought 1500–1700* (Oxford: Oxford university Press, 1964), pp. 126–128; Preston King, *The Ideology of Order: A Comparative Analysis of Jean Bodin and Thomas Hobbes* (London: George Allen and Unwin, 1974).
109   Larner, *Enemies of God*, p. 195.
110   Stephen L. Collins, *From Divine Cosmos to Sovereign State: An Intellectual History*

of Consciousness and the Idea of Order in Renaissance England (Oxford: Oxford University Press, 1989), p. 7.

111 Bodin, *Demon-Mania*, p. 204, emphasis added.

112 Bruno Latour, *An Inquiry into Modes of Existence: An Anthropology of the Moderns* (Cambridge, MA: Harvard University Press, 2013), p. 184.

113 Hobbes, *Leviathan*, p. 128.

114 Oplinger, *Politics of Demonology*, p. 56.

115 Federici, *Caliban and the Witch*, p. 163. Also see Ehrenreich and English, *Witches, Midwives and Nurses*, pp. 23–26.

116 Behringer, *Witchcraft Persecutions*, pp. 411–412.

117 Kamen, *The Iron Century*, p. 249.

118 Federici, *Caliban and the Witch*, pp. 164–165.

119 Federici, *Caliban and the Witch*, p. 165.

120 See Federici's development of her argument in 'Witch-Hunting, Globalization, and Feminist Solidarity in Africa Today', *Journal of International Women's Studies*, Vol. 10, No. 1, 2008, pp. 21–35.

121 Federici, *Caliban and the Witch*, pp. 133, 137, 140–141, 194, 197.

122 Michael E. Tigar and Madeleine R. Levy, *Law and the Rise of Capitalism* (New York: Monthly Review Press, 1977), p. 136.

123 Federici, *Caliban and the Witch*, p. 220; Silverblatt, *Moon, Sun, and Witches*, pp. 159–196.

124 Taussig, *Devil and Commodity Fetishism*, p. xi.

125 Taussig, *Devil and Commodity Fetishism*, p. xi.

126 Taussig, *Devil and Commodity Fetishism*, p. 169.

127 Mark Neocleous, 'International Law as Primitive Accumulation; or, The Secret of Systematic Colonization', *European Journal of International Law*, Vol. 23, No. 4, 2012, pp. 941–962; *War Power, Police Power* (Edinburgh: Edinburgh University Press, 2014), chap. 2.

128 Foucault, *Wrong-Doing, Truth-telling*, p. 221.

129 Samuel Willard, *The Child's Portion* (1684), cited in Godbeer, *Devil's Dominion*, p. 87.

130 Nicholas Breton, *A Murmurer* (1607), cited Lacey Baldwin Smith, *Treason in Tudor England: Politics and Paranoia* (London: Jonathan Cape, 1986), p. 135.

131 'The Second Part of the Homily Against Disobedience and Wilful Rebellion', in *Certain Sermons or Homilies Appointed to be Read in Churches in the Time of the Late Queen Elizabeth* [1547–62], (Oxford: Oxford University Press, 1840), pp. 500–506, p. 504.

132 'Third Part of the Homily Against Disobedience', pp. 506–513, p. 512.

133 The Bible in several places links pigs to the Devil, such as Matthew 8:31. And see Nicholas Remy, *Demonolatry* (1595), trans. E. A. Ashwin (New York: Dover, 2008), Bk. II., Chap. II, p. 88.

134 See, for example, King James, *Demonologie*, pp. 144, 262.

135 Forsyth, *Old Enemy*, pp. 5, 124–146; Johnstone, *Devil and Demonism*, pp. 147, 184; Link, *Devil*, pp. 87, 192.

136 Taussig, *Devil and Commodity Fetishism*, p. 42.

137 Joseph de Maistre, *Considerations on France* (1797), trans. Richard A. Lebrun (Montreal: McGill-Queens University Press, 1974), p. 79.

138 Michel Foucault, *Security, Territory, Population: Lectures at the Collège de France, 1977–1978*, trans. Graham Burchell (Houndmills, Basingstoke: Palgrave, 2007), p. 235.

139 Foucault, *On the Government of the Living*, p. 270.

140 Martin Luther, 'Temporal Authority: To What Extent It Should Be Obeyed' (1523), trans. J. J. Schindel, in *Luther: Selected Political Writings* (Philadelphia:

Fortress Press, 1974), pp. 51–69, p. 51.

141 Thomas Müntzer, Letter to Count Ernst of Mansfield, 22 Sept., 1523, in Thomas Müntzer, *Sermon to the Princes*, trans. Michael G. Baylor (London: Verso, 2010), p. 100. The 'Confession' is also in *Sermon to the Princes*, pp. 96–97.

142 John Calvin, *The Institutes of the Christian Religion* (1536), (Grand Rapids, MI: Christian Classics Ethereal Library, 2002), Book IV, Chap. 20, sect. 31, p. 916.

143 Catherine Keller, *Apocalypse Now and Then: A Feminist Guide to the End of the World* (Boston: Beacon Press, 1996), p. 187; Raffaele Laudani, *Disobedience in Western Political Thought: A Genealogy* (2011), trans. Jason Francis McGimsey (Cambridge: Cambridge University Press, 2013), p. 25.

144 'Whether it be worshipping, whether it be sacrifice, even if it comes to the point where drugs are used, that's Satan. Very definitely it's Satan because it's evil. It's something that can hurt you or harm you ... We're dealing with evil itself'. This comment from a police officer is far from unusual, as Robert Hicks shows at great length. The comment itself was made at a 'Satanic-crime seminar', and Hicks's book is organised around a systematic analysis of the police seminars and the police 'lecture circuit' in which they speak to teachers, parents, and counsellors and therapists on the topic of Satanism and 'satanic cults'. In so doing they peddle myths concerning certain kinds of rock music, film and literature, but also including the kinds of symbols found on jewellery, and these are myths involving a suspension of the very thing we have long been told is the core of police work: evidence. Hicks argues that 'through the cult seminars, and particularly through the attendant handouts, cult cops invent urban legends, rumours, and subversion myths. When handouts cite sources, most often they list conservative Christian ones'. What Hicks calls the cult-cop model, in which police believe simply in the idea of Satanic and a satanic origin of some crimes, is communicated to wide audience, through police seminars on the subject but also through general police media. This obsession with the hunt for Satan amidst the crime is encouraged by the media use of the term. It relies heavily on a fact we noted at the start of this chapter, that large numbers of people still believe that the Devil exists, but this belief is in turn perpetuated by the very power that is said to exist for our protection; one of the consequences of turning fears of Satan into a police rationale is that it simply produces the very fear through which the police like to thrive. As Messadié points out, the police view of Satanism is a problem since it encourages the view that Satan does indeed exist and is indeed responsible for the evil in the world. Moreover, the myth of Satan at work is deeply connected to the subversion myth. Hence the connection between with hunting of the sixteenth and seventeenth centuries and police work today: both rely on a belief that Satan is at large and encouraging subversion. See Robert D. Hicks, *In Pursuit of Satan: The Police and the Occult* (Buffalo: Prometheus Books, 1991), pp. 9, 63, 335–337, 356–357; Messadié, *History of the Devil*, p. 313.

4 'An offence against the universal law of society': on the Pirate

1 *The National Security Strategy of the United States of America*, 2002, p. 4. Compare: 'Like slavery and piracy, terrorism has no place in the modern world' – George W. Bush, 'Remarks to the United Nations General Assembly', New York, 23 September, 2008.

2 See, for example, House of Commons Transport Committee, *Piracy: Government Response to the Committee's Eighth Report of Session 2005–06* (HC 1690) (London: November 2006), pp. 2 and 10.

3   See, as just a few examples, D. R. Burgess, *The World for Ransom: Piracy is Terrorism, Terrorism is Piracy* (Prometheus Books, 2010); Martin N. Murphy, *Contemporary Piracy and Maritime Terrorism: The Threat to International Security* (Abingdon, Oxon: Routledge/International Institute for Strategic Studies, 2007); Peter Chalk, *The Maritime Dimension of International Security: Terrorism, Piracy, and Challenges for the United States* (RAND corporation, 2008); Peter Lehr (ed.), *Violence at Sea: Piracy in the Age of Global Terrorism* (New York: Routledge, 2007). This list could go on as the following five footnotes show.

4   Chris Mooney, 'The Barbary Analogy', *American Prospect*, 19 Dec., 2001 www.prospect.org/article/barbary-analogy [accessed 17 Nov. 2015].

5   Thomas Jewett, 'Terrorism in Early America: The U.S. Wages War Against the Barbary States to End International Blackmail and Terrorism', *Early America Review*, Winter/Spring 2002 – www.earlyamerica.com/review/2002_winter_spring/terrorism.htm, [accessed 2 Dec. 2014]; Joseph Wheelan, *Jefferson's War: America's First War on Terror 1801–1805* (New York: Carroll & Graf, 2003).

6   Oded Löwenheim, '"Do Ourselves Credit and Render a Lasting Service to Mankind": British Moral Prestige, Humanitarian Intervention, and the Barbary Pirates', *International Studies Quarterly*, Vol. 47, No. 1, 2003, pp. 23–48.

7   Mooney, 'Barbary Analogy'; William Langewiesche, 'Anarchy at Sea', *Atlantic Monthly*, Sept., 2003, www.theatlantic.com/magazine/archive/2003/09/anarchy-at-sea/376873/5/ [accessed 17 Nov. 2015]

8   For just a sample: Robert F. Turner, 'State Responsibility and the War on Terror: The Legacy of Thomas Jefferson and the Barbary Pirates', *Chicago Journal of International Law*, Vol. 4, 2003, pp. 121–142; Douglas R. Burgess, 'Hostis Humani Generi: Piracy, Terrorism and a New International Law', *University of Miami International & Comparative Law Review*, Vol. 13, 2005, pp. 293–341; Captain Morris L. Sinor and Commander Robin M Blackwood, 'Confronting Nomadic Terrorism', *Naval Law Review*, Vol. 52, No. 1, 2005, pp. 98–117; Anthony J. Colangelo, 'Constitutional Limits on Extraterritorial Jurisdiction: Terrorism and the Intersection of National and International Law', *Harvard International Law Journal*, Vol. 48, No. 1, 2007, pp. 121–201; Ingrid Detter, 'The Law of War and Illegal Combatants', *George Washington Law Review*, Vol. 75, 2007, pp. 1049–1105; Daniel J. Hickman, 'Terrorism as a Violation of the "Law of Nations": Finally Overcoming the Definitional Problem', *Wisconsin International Law Journal*, Vol. 29, 2011, pp. 447–642; Mark V. Vlasic, 'Assassination and Targeted Killing: A Historical and Post-Bin Laden Legal Analysis', *Georgetown Journal of International Law*, Vol. 43, 2011–12, pp. 259–333. It should be added that the link between terrorism and piracy predates 2001 – see, for example, Malvina Halberstam, 'Terrorism on the High Seas: The Achille Lauro, Piracy, and the IMO Convention on Maritime Safety', *American Journal of International Law*, Vol. 82, No. 2, 1988, pp. 269–310, p. 289.

9   William Blackstone, *Commentaries on the Laws of England, Vol. 4: Of Public Wrongs* (1769), (Chicago: University of Chicago Press, 1979), p. 71.

10 Francis Raymond Stark, *The Abolition of Privateering and the Declaration of Paris* (New York: Columbia University Press, 1897), p. 58.

11 Cited in Stark, *Abolition of Privateering*, p. 51.

12 William Chambliss, 'State-organized Crime: The American Society of Criminology, 1988 Presidential Address', *Criminology*, Vol. 27, No. 2, 1989, pp. 183–208, p. 186; Peter Earle, *The Pirate Wars* (London: Methuen, 2004), pp. 22–5.

13 Christopher Hill, *Liberty Against the Law: Some Seventeenth-Century Controversies* (London: Penguin, 1996), p. 114.

14 Karl Marx, *Capital: A Critique of Political Economy, Vol. 3* (1867), trans. David Fernach (Harmondsworth: Penguin, 1981), pp. 448–9. The literature on this is now huge, but see Anne Pérotin-Dumon, 'The Pirate and the Emperor: Power and the Law on the Seas, 1450–1850', in James D. Tracy (ed.), *The Political Economy of Merchant Empires: State Power and World Trade 1350–1750* (Cambridge: Cambridge University Press, 1991), pp. 196–227, pp. 204, 209; Janice E. Thomson, *Mercenaries, Pirates, and Sovereigns: State-building and Extraterritorial Violence in Early Modern Europe* (Princeton, New Jersey: Princeton University Press, 1994), p. 54; Alfred P. Rubin, *The Law of Piracy* (Honolulu, Hawaii: University Press of the Pacific, 2006), pp. 13–18; Lauren Benton, *A Search for Sovereignty: Law and Geography in European Empires, 1400–1900* (Cambridge: Cambridge University Press, 2010), pp. 35, 113; Claire Jowitt, *The Culture of Piracy, 1580–1630: English Literature and Seaborne Crime* (Farnham, Surrey: Ashgate, 2010), pp. 23–4, 49.

15 Daniel Defoe, 'A Review of the State of the British Nation', 18 October, 1707, in *Defoe's Review, Book 10, June 17, 1707-November 8,* 1707 (New York: Columbia University Press, 1938), pp. 425–426.

16 N. I. Bukharin, 'The Imperialist Pirate State' (1916), in Olga Hess Gankin and H. H. Fisher (eds), *The Bolsheviks and the First World War: The Origins of the Third International* (Stanford, CA: Stanford University Press, 1940), pp. 236–9; Amedeo Policante, *The Pirate Myth: Genealogies of an Imperial Concept* (Abingdon, Oxon: Routledge, 2015); Rubin, *Law of Piracy*, pp. 345–6. Also see Thomson, *Mercenaries, Pirates*, pp. 43, 54; Earle, *Pirate Wars*, pp. 89, 97, 111, 120; Robert C. Ritchie, *Captain Kidd and the War Against the Pirates* (Cambridge, MA: Harvard University Press, 1986), pp. 7, 10; Gerry Simpson, *Law, War and Crime* (Cambridge: Polity, 2007), p. 160; Eric Wilson, '"The Dangerous Classes": Hugo Grotius and Seventeenth-century Piracy as a Primitive Anti-systemic Movement', *Journal of Philosophical Economics*, Vol. 4, No. 1, 2010, pp. 146–183.

17 Carl Schmitt, *The Nomos of the Earth* in the *International Law of the Jus Publicum Europaeum* (1950), trans. G. L. Ulmen (New York: Telos Press, 2003), pp. 180–181.

18 Thomson, *Mercenaries, Pirates*, p. 108.

19 Thomson, *Mercenaries, Pirates*, pp. 117–8. Also Charles Tilly, *Coercion, Capital, and European States, AD 990–1992* (Oxford: Blackwell, 1992), pp. 80–2; Fernand Braudel, *The Mediterranean and the Mediterranean World in the Age of Philip II* (1949), trans. Sian Reynolds (London: HarperCollins, 1992), pp. 624–49.

20 For the story see Augustine, *City of God*, trans. Henry Bettenson (Harmondsworth: Penguin, 1972), Book IV, Chap 4, p. 139.

21 Daniel Defoe, *A General History of the Pyrates* (1724), ed. Manuel Schonhorn (London: Dent and Sons, 1972), p. 26.

22 Fleur Johns, *Non Legality in International Law: Unruly Law* (Cambridge: Cambridge University Press, 2013), p. 11. As she also puts it: 'illegality may, at times, be intensified as extra-legal outlawry' and the example she gives is the designation of perpetrators of international crime as 'enemies of mankind' (p. 69).

23 Peter Linebaugh and Marcus Rediker, *The Many-Headed Hydra: Sailors, Slaves, Commoners and the Hidden History of the Revolutionary Atlantic* (London: Verso, 2000), p. 156.

24 Michel Foucault, *The Birth of Biopolitics: Lectures at the Collège de France, 1978–1979*, trans. Graham Burchell (Houndmills, Basingstoke: Palgrave, 2008), p. 56; Schmitt, Nomos *of the Earth*, p. 44. For extensions of this argument in different though complementary ways see Policante, *Pirate Myth*, pp. xii, 91;

Zoltán Glück, 'Piracy and the Production of Security Space', *Environment and Planning D*, Vol. 33, 2015; and Philip E. Steinberg, *The Social Construction of the Ocean* (Cambridge: Cambridge University Press, 2001).

25 Henry Newton, Comments as member of the Admiralty, in 'The Trial of Joseph Dawson … For Felony and Piracy at the Old Bailey, 19 October, 1696', in *A Complete Collection of State-Trials and Proceedings Upon High Treason, and Other Crimes and Misdemeanours, Vol. V* (London, 1742), p. 2; *Expulsis Piratis, Restituta Commercia* was first declared by Governor Woodes Rogers of the Bahamas, but the slogan remained the motto of the island until independence in 1973.

26 Samuel Johnson, *A Dictionary of the English Language: An Anthology* (1755), entry for 'Pirate'; Harvard Law School Research in International Law, 'Part IV – Piracy', *American Journal of International Law*, Vol. 26, No. 1, 1932, pp. 739–885, p. 770. The others are cited in Edwin D. Dickinson, 'Is the Crime of Piracy Obsolete?', *Harvard Law Review*, Vol. 38, 1924–1925, pp. 334–360, p. 337.

27 Ulrike Klausmann, Marion Meinzerin and Gabriel Kuhn, *Women Pirates and the Politics of the Jolly Roger* (Montréal: Black Rose, 1997), p. 274.

28 Defoe, *General History*, p. 244.

29 Fernand Braudel, *Civilization and Capitalism, Vol. II: The Wheels of Commerce* (1979), trans. Sian Reynolds (London: Collins, 1982), p. 512.

30 Defoe, *General History*, p. 244.

31 The chapter on Roberts is treated here as representative of the same or similar views in other chapters. In his Preface to *The History of the Pyrates* Defoe observes that Roberts's story in the book is longer than the stories of other pirates told in the book, on the grounds that most other stories replicate the same kinds of details. Roberts's account of plenty and satiety, liberty and power, can therefore be taken to apply more generally. Moreover, as Christopher Hill notes, whatever *The History of the Pyrates* lacks in historical accuracy, it nonetheless still offers evidence of what public opinion was prepared to believe about piracy, confirming as it does a good deal of literary evidence for the libertarian sentiments of pirates and the relatively democratic discipline of pirate vessels. For the same reason John Richetti suggests that the popularity of the collection of pirate biographies in *The History of the Pyrates* lies in the fact that the pirate legend derives some of its fascination from these ideas about political rebellion and a demonic independence. See Defoe, *General History*, p. 6; Hill, *Liberty Against the Law*, pp. 115, 117; John J. Richetti, *Popular Fiction Before Richardson: Narrative Patters 1700–1739* (Oxford: Clarendon Press, 1969), pp. 67, 79.

32 Defoe, *General History*, pp. 194–5, 211, 213.

33 Markus Rediker, *Outlaws of the Atlantic: Sailors, Pirates, and Motley Crews in the Age of Sail* (London: Verso, 2014), pp. 67–8. The figures are from Marcus Rediker, *Between the Devil and the Deep Blue Sea: Merchant Seamen, Pirates and the Anglo-American Maritime World, 1700–1750* (Cambridge: Cambridge University Press, 1987), p. 267. Also Hill, *Liberty Against the Law*, p. 117; Klasmann, Meinzerin and Kuhn, *Women Pirates*, pp. 237–9, 256–60; Policante, *Pirate Myth*, p. 43; Peter Earle, *The Sack of Panama: Sir Henry Morgan's Adventures on the Spanish Maine* (New York: Viking Press, 1981), p. 66; J. S. Bromley, 'Outlaws at Sea, 1660–1720: Liberty, Equality and Fraternity among the Caribbean Freebooters', in Frederick Krantz (ed.), *History from Below* (Oxford: Blackwell, 1985), pp. 293–318; Peter Lamborn Wilson, *Pirate Utopias: Moorish Corsairs and European Renegades* (New York: Autonomedia, 2003), pp. 190–196; Erin Mackie, *Rakes, Highwaymen, and Pirates: The Making of the Modern Gentleman in the Eighteenth Century* (Baltimore: Johns Hopkins University Press, 2009), pp. 126–7, 130, 140.

34   Ritchie, *Captain Kidd*, p. 124. Earle, *Pirate Wars*, p. 101: the pirate communities offer 'evidence of a degree of democracy and egalitarianism which ran quite counter to the norm anywhere else in the late seventeenth-century world'.
35   Hakim Bey, *T.A.Z.: The Temporary Autonomous Zone, Ontological Anarchy, Poetic Terrorism* (New York: Autonomedia, 2003).
36   Stephen Snelders, *The Devil's Anarchy* (New York: Autonomedia, 2014), p. 189. Also Wilson, *Pirate Utopias*, pp. 189–90.
37   Captain Bellamy, cited by Defoe, *History of the Pyrates*, p. 587.
38   Rediker, *Outlaws of the Atlantic*, p. 87.
39   See Klasmann, Meinzerin and Kuhn, *Women Pirates*, who make the strongest feminist argument for 'radical piracy' but who also make a compelling case that Bartholomew Roberts, the person widely regarded as 'the most successful pirate' and who we have cited several times in this chapter, was in fact a woman.
40   R. B. Burg, *Sodomy and the Pirate Tradition: English Sea Rovers in the Seventeenth-Century Caribbean* (New York: New York University Press, 1995).
41   Linebaugh and Rediker, *Many-Headed Hydra*, p. 173.
42   Cited in Earle, *Sack of Panama*, p. 66.
43   Rudolphe Durand and Jean-Philippe Vergne, *The Pirate Organization: Lessons from the Fringes of Capitalism* (2010), (Boston, MA: Harvard Business Review Press, 2013), p. 10; also pp. 65, 79.
44   Richetti, *Popular Fiction*, p. 92.
45   Rediker, *Between the Devil*, pp. 107–8, 247–8, 254, 263–4, 286; Rediker, *Outlaws*, p. 70; Linebaugh and Rediker, *Many-Headed Hydra*, pp. 143–73; Do or Die, 'Pirate Utopias: Under the Banner of King Death', *Do or Die Magazine*, 8, 1999, pp. 63–78; Erin Mackie, 'Welcome to the Outlaw: Pirates, Maroons, and Caribbean Countercultures', *Cultural Critique*, 59, 2005, pp. 24–62, pp. 29–30, p. 44; Nick Land, 'Flying the Black Flag: Revolt, Revolution and the Social Organization of Piracy in the "Golden Age"', *Management and Organizational History*, Vol. 2, No. 2, 2007, pp. 169–92, p. 170; Martin Parker, 'Pirates, Merchants and Anarchists: Representations of International Business', *Management and Organizational History*, Vol. 4, No. 2, 2009, pp. 167–85, p. 175.
46   Rediker, *Villains*, p. 5; also pp. 13–14. The same allusion is made by Earle, *Pirate Wars*, p. 10, and Simpson, *Law, War and Crime*, pp. 159–177. See also the references along these lines cited at the beginning of this chapter.
47   Klasmann, Meinzerin and Kuhn, *Women Pirates*, p. 165.
48   Rubin, *Law of Piracy*, p. 30.
49   The struggle against piracy thus became part of the 'civilising mission' of capitalist expansion. Piracy's antagonistic relation to this expansion meant that piracy was 'uncivilised' and therefore needed to be eradicated. When privateering itself was finally formally abolished, with the Declaration of Paris in 1856, it was done in the wider context of the standard of 'civilisation' (though also acted as a spur for the next phase of imperialism). On 'civilisation' as police power see Mark Neocleous, 'The Police of Civilization: The War on Terror as Civilizing Offensive', *International Political Sociology*, Vol. 5, No. 2, 2011, pp. 144–59, and *War Power, Police Power* (Edinburgh: Edinburgh University Press, 2014), chap. 4.
50   Rubin, *Law of Piracy*, p. 202.
51   Mackie, *Rakes, Highwaymen, and Pirates*, p. 126; Jody Greene, 'Hostis Humani Generis', *Critical Inquiry*, Vol. 34, No. 4, 2008, pp. 683–705, p. 686; Joseph N. F. M. à Campo, 'Discourse without Discussion: Representations of Piracy in Colonial Indonesia 1816–25', *Journal of Southeast Asian Studies*, Vol. 34, No. 2, 2003, pp. 199–214; Policante, *Pirate Myth*, pp. 139–50, 170–1.

52   Viscount Palmerston to Lord Howard de Walden, 12 May, 1838, in *Correspondence with the British Commissioners at Sierra Leone, The Havana, Rio de Janeiro, and Surinam, Relating to the Slave Trade, From May 1st 1838 to February 2nd 1839, Inclusive* (London: HMSO, 1839), p. 181; Osborn cited in Alfred P. Rubin, *Piracy, Paramountcy and Protectorates* (Kuala Lumpur: Penerbit Universiti Malaya, 1974), p. 29.

53   Wilhelm G. Grewe, *The Epochs of International Law* (1984), trans. Michael Byers (Berlin: Walter de Gruyter 2000), p. 570.

54   Matthew Tindall, *An Essay Concerning the Law of Nations, and the Rights of Sovereigns: With an Account of what was said at the Council-Board by the Civilians upon the Question, Whether their Majesties Subjects taken at Sea acting by the late King's Commission, might not be look'd on as Pirates?* (1694), in *A Collection of State Tracts, Published During the Reign of King William III, Volume 2* (London: 1706), pp. 462–75, p. 471, emphasis added.

55   Eugene Kontorovich, 'The Piracy Analogy: Modern Universal Jurisdiction's Hollow Foundation', *Harvard International Law Journal*, Vol. 45, 2004, pp. 183–237, p. 235.

56   Michel Foucault, 'Different Spaces', 14 March, 1967, trans. Robert Hurley, in Michel Foucault, *Aesthetics: The Essential Works, Vol.* 2 (London: Allen Lane, 1998), pp. 174–85, p. 185.

57   *The Tryals of Major Stede Bonnet, and Other Pirates* (London: Benjamin Cowse, 1719), p. 8.

58   As was once declared by the bishops of England – Hill, *Liberty Against the Law*, p. 118.

59   Blackstone, *Commentaries, Vol. 4*, p. 71.

60   Montesquieu, *The Spirit of the Laws* (1748), trans. Anne Cohler, Basia Miller and Harold Stone (Cambridge: Cambridge University Press, 1989), Pt. 4, Book 21, Ch. 8 (p. 366).

61   Rubin, *Law of Piracy*, pp. 10–12; Policante, *Pirate Myth*, pp. 10, 15, 184.

62   Both cited Rubin, *Law of Piracy*, p. 11.

63   Schmitt, *Nomos of the Earth*, pp. 52, 87.

64   Foucault, *Birth of Biopolitics*, p. 56.

65   Kenneth C. Randall, 'Universal Jurisdiction Under International Law', *Texas Law Review*, Vol. 66, 1988, pp. 785–841; M. Cherif Bassiouni, 'The History of Universal Jurisdiction and It's Place in International Law', in Stephen Macedo (ed.), *Universal Jurisdiction: National Courts and the Prosecution of Serious Crimes* (Philadelphia: University of Pennsylvania Press, 2004), pp. 39–62; Dickinson, 'Crime of Piracy', p. 338; Simpson, *Law, War and Crime*, p. 161; Joshua Michael Goodwin, 'Universal Jurisdiction and the Pirate: Time for an Old Couple to Part', *Vanderbilt Journal of Transnational Law*, Vol. 39, 2006, pp. 973–1011; Christopher Harding, '*Hostis Humani Generis*' – The Pirate as Outlaw in the Early Modern Law of the Sea', in Claire Jowitt (ed), *Pirates? The Politics of Plunder, 1550–1650* (Houndmills: Palgrave, 2007), pp. 20–1; Kal Raustiala, *Does the Constitution Follow the Flag? The Evolution of Territoriality in American Law* (Oxford: Oxford University Press, 2009), p. 34.

66   Louis Sohn, 'Introduction' to Benjamin B. Ferencz, *An International Criminal Court, A Step Toward World Peace: A Documentary History and Analysis* (New York: Oceana Publications, 1980), pp. xv–xvi.

67   Policante, *Pirate Myth*, p. 169.

68   Carl Schmitt, 'The Concept of Piracy' (1937), *Humanity*, Vol. 2, No. 1, 2011, pp. 27–29, p. 28. Likewise, within the new diplomatic theory that arose with the modern state system, pirates were considered to be the one group with whom one should never negotiate – see Timothy Hampton, *Fictions of Embassy:*

Literature and Diplomacy in Early Modern Europe (Ithaca, NY: Cornell University Press, 2009), pp. 118, 158–159.

69   Dickinson, 'Crime of Piracy', p. 351.

70   Cited in Dickinson, 'Crime of Piracy', pp. 355–6.

71   *The Princeton Principles on Universal Jurisdiction* (2001), p. 23, emphasis added.

72   Hannah Arendt, *Eichmann in Jerusalem: A Report on the Banality of Evil* (1963) (Harmondsworth: Penguin, 1977), p. 261. On this issue we might note the exchange of letters between Arendt and Karl Jaspers in the lead-up to the trial in December 1960, in which the question of treating Eichmann as an 'outlaw – a *hostis humani generis*, the way pirates used to be', is addressed, but that fourteen years previously in discussing the Nazi 'crimes' the language they use is the language we have encountered in the previous chapter: there was a 'demonic' element in Hitler and his colleagues which led to acts of 'Satanic greatness'. See the letters of 19 October, 1946, 17 December, 1946, 23 December, 1960, and 31 December, 1960, in *Hannah Arendt/Karl Jaspers: Correspondence, 1926–1969* (1985), trans. Robert Kimber and Rita Kimber (New York: Harcourt Brace Jovanovich, 1992), pp. 62, 69, 414 and 419.

73   Grewe, *Epochs*, p. 554.

74   Rubin, *Law of Piracy*, p. 343.

75   Harvard Law School Research, 'Part IV – Piracy', pp. 750, 769, 771.

76   'An Abstract of the Civil Law and Statute now in Force, in Relation to Pyracy', in Defoe, *General History of the Pyrates*, p. 377.

77   Schmitt, 'Concept of Piracy', p. 27.

78   Rubin, *Law of Piracy*, p. 344.

79   Harvard Law School Research, 'Part IV – Piracy', p. 760.

80   Rubin, *Law of Piracy*, p. 343, emphasis added.

81   Barry H. Dubner, *The Law of International Sea Piracy* (The Hague: Martinus Nijhoff, 1988), pp. 39, 43; Harvard Law School Research, 'Part IV – Piracy', pp. 754, 760, 769; Pérotin-Dumon, 'Pirate and the Emperor', pp. 198, 202–3; Thomson, *Mercenaries, Pirates*, p. 108; Rubin, *Law of Piracy*, p. 343.

82   Rubin, *Law of Piracy*, pp. 11–13, 83–4, 122, 186–7.

83   Cited in Rediker, *Villains of All Nations*, p. 128.

84   Rubin, *Law of Piracy*, pp. 11–13, 83–4, 122, 186–7; Daniel Heller-Roazen, *The Enemy of All: Piracy and the Law of Nations* (New York: Zone Books, 2009), pp. 29, 176, 177.

85   Heller-Roazen, *Enemy of All*, pp. 28, 176–177.

86   Interview: John Yoo, *PBS Frontline*, 19 July, 2005 – www.pbs.org/wgbh/pages/frontline/torture/interviews/yoo.html [accessed 17 Nov. 2015]

87   Cited in Jane Mayer, 'Outsourcing Torture: The secret history of America's "extraordinary rendition" program', *The New Yorker*, 14 Feb., 2005 – www.newyorker.com/magazine/2005/02/14/outsourcing-torture [accessed 17 Nov. 2015]

88   *Memorandum on Maritime Security (Piracy) Policy*, 13 June, 2007 – www.presidency.ucsb.edu/ws/index.php?pid=75329&st=piracy&st1 [accessed 17 Nov. 2015].

89   Barack Obama, 'Remarks at the Central Intelligence Agency', Langley, Virginia, 20 April, 2009.

90   Greene, 'Hostis Humani Generis', pp. 687–688.

91   Policante, *Pirate Myth*, p. 201.

92   Judge Kozinski, Dissenting opinion in the case of *White v. Samsung Electronics*, US Court of Appeals, 1993 -http://en.wikisource.org/wiki/White_v._Samsung_Electronics_America,_Inc./En_banc_Opinion#Dissenting_Opinion [accessed 17 Nov. 2015].

93   Alan Greenspan, 'Remarks by Chairman Alan Greenspan at the 80th Anniversary Awards Dinner of The Conference Board', New York, 16 October, 1996 – www.federalreserve.gov/boarddocs/speeches/1996/19961016.htm [accessed 17 Nov. 2015].

94   Peter Baldwin, *The Copyright Wars: Three Centuries of Trans-Atlantic Battle* (Princeton, NJ: Princeton University Press, 2014), p. 18.

95   Kevin A. Hassett and Robert J. Shapiro, *What Ideas Are Worth: The Value of Intellectual Capital And Intangible Assets in the American Economy* (Washington: Sonecon, 2011), pp. iv and 3.

96   Michael Perelman, 'The Political Economy of Intellectual Property', *Monthly Review*, January 2003, pp. 29–37.

97   Ayn Rand, *Capitalism: The Unknown Ideal* (New York: Signet Books, 1967), p. 130. Although authorship of the book is attributed to Rand, Greenspan wrote three of the chapters.

98   Michael Perelman, *Steal This Idea: Intellectual property Rights and the Corporate Confiscation of Creativity* (New York: Palgrave Macmillan, 2002), p. 21. The point being made here most obviously refers to capitalist corporations, but to get an idea of the prevalence of intellectual property concerns one might also look at how organisations outside the sphere of direct accumulation operate. Most of the images used in earlier chapters of this book are owned by corporations, and getting permission to use them often resulted in my ending up dealing with the intellectual property department. Take, for example, Figure 2.3. This is an image which had been in the 'public domain' for some time and which had presumably been intended to be seen by as many people as possible. It is claimed as the 'intellectual property' of the Canadian province of British Columbia (BC). Hence to reproduce an image that they wanted as many people to see I had to put in a request to the 'Intellectual Property Program' for BC. Wanting it to be seen by even more people in the context of this book meant that I not only had to ask and be given permission to reproduce it, but I also had to pay the Canadian province for the privilege. But here's the really strange thing: when I first enquired about using the image, the organisation said they could not actually locate an electronic copy, so to make the process quicker and easier I sent them the copy I already had on my own pc, which I had at some point downloaded and saved. (That is, which I already had in my possession and that I 'owned' in some sense of the meaning of the word, though not in the capitalist sense and thus not in any sense that could be defended in a court). They then sent the same version of the image back to me with the IP contract as the version I could use. (I know it was the one I had sent them because it had the same file name that I had given it). In other words, I ended up providing them with the image which they did not really know that they owned until I told them that they did, for which they allowed me the privilege of paying them so that I could use it. I make this point not to be ungracious about BC, since most of the images used in this book have a similar backstory. I make the point simply to point out that: most public bodies now have intellectual property programs to protect their intellectual property; that these bodies often don't know what they already own or even what their programs are really protecting; that anyone else has to pay to use the intellectual property which the bodies themselves want to be placed in the public sphere; and that this constitutes an alternative source of income for those public bodies.

    One final point on this issue. The more radically-minded reader might ask: 'why not just use the image without telling them? After all, it's hardly as though anyone in the government of BC is ever going to pick this book up, find the image and then prosecute you'. This would of course also add a nice touch of piratical radicalism to this text (on which point see Figures 1.1 and 1.2 in Chapter 1). The problem, however, is that publishers are now so sensitive to the legal issues surrounding intellectual property that they are hesitant about publishing anything without full and proper clearance (Figures 1.1 and 1.2 only managed to get into this book after much persuading on my part and with the carefully worded disclaimer at the beginning of the book). One indication of this hesitancy, but also a sign of how important the issue of intellectual property now is, is the fact that publisher's document known as 'Instructions to Authors', given to me by the publisher of the English version of this book when we agreed the contract, consists of 55 pages. The first 17 pages, nearly one-third of the document, concern intellectual property.

99 Baldwin, *Copyright Wars*, p. 278; Perelman, *Steal This Idea*, pp. 35–36.
100 Rosemary J. Coombe, *The Cultural Life of Intellectual Properties: Authorship, Appropriation, and the Law* (Durham: Duke University Press, 1998), p. 285. Also see Adrian Johns, *Piracy: The Intellectual Property Wars from Gutenberg to Gates* (Chicago: University of Chicago Press, 2009).
101 Perelman, *Steal This Idea*, p. 8.
102 Suzannah Mirghani, 'The War on Piracy: Analyzing the Discursive Battles of Corporate and Government-Sponsored Anti-Piracy Media Campaigns', *Critical Studies in Media Communication*, Vol. 28, No. 2, 2011, pp. 113–134, p. 115 and 116.
103 OECD, *The Economic Impact of Counterfeiting and Piracy. Executive Summary* (OECD, 2007), p. 4.
104 OECD, *Magnitude of Counterfeiting and Piracy of Tangible Products: An Update* (OECD, 2009), p. 1.
105 Business Action to Stop Counterfeiting and Piracy, *Estimating the Global Economic and Social Impacts of Counterfeiting and Piracy* (London, February 2011), pp. 5–6, 46, 52.
106 See 'Monsanto's Seed Snitch Hotline', 20 July, 2014 – http://farmwars.info/?p=13217 [accessed 17 Nov. 2015]; Donald L. Barlett and James B. Steele, 'Monsanto's Harvest of Fear', *Vanity Fair*, May 2008 – www.vanityfair.com/politics/features/2008/05/monsanto200805 [accessed 17 Nov. 2015].
107 Durand and Vergne, *Pirate Organization*, p. 7.
108 Lawrence Lessig, *Free Culture: How Big Media Uses Technology and the Law to Lock Down Culture and Control Creativity* (New York: Penguin, 2004), pp. 54–5.
109 Lessig, *Free Culture*, pp. 53, 61.
110 Coombe, *Cultural Life*, p. 63.
111 Brian Larkin, 'Degraded Images, Distorted Sounds: Nigerian Video and the Infrastructure of Piracy', *Public Culture*, Vol. 16, No. 2, 2004, pp. 289–314, p. 297.
112 Ravi Sundaram, *Pirate Modernity: Delhi's Media Urbanism* (Abingdon, Oxon: Routledge, 2010), p. 106.
113 Sundaram, *Pirate Modernity*, pp. 110–111, 128; John Tehranian, *Infringement Nation: Copyright 2.0 and You* (New York: Oxford University Press, 2011), p. xvii,
114 Jessica Litman, *Digital Copyright* (Amherst, NY: Prometheus Books, 2001), pp. 85–6.
115 Lessig, *Free Culture*, p. 199.
116 Trajce Cvetkovski, 'The Farcical Side to the War on Media Piracy: A Popular Case of Divine Comedy?', *Media, Culture and Society*, Vol. 36, No. 2, 2014, pp. 246–257.
117 Jo Bryce and Jason Rutter, *Fake Nation: A Study into Everyday Crime* (Northern Ireland: Organised Crime Task Force, 2005) – www.academia.edu/597794/Fake_Nation_A_Study_into_Everyday_Crime [accessed 17 Nov. 2015]

118 See, for example, Laura C. Nastase, 'Made in China: How Chinese Counterfeits are Creating a National Security Nightmare for the United States', *Fordham Intellectual Property, Media and Entertainment Law Journal*, Vol. 19, No. 1, 2008, pp. 142–178.

119 IFPI, *Music Piracy: Serious, Violent, and Organised Crime* (London: IFPI, no date), p. 3 – www.ifpi.org/content/library/music-piracy-organised-crime.pdf [accessed 17 Nov. 2015].

120 IACC, *The Negative Consequences of International Intellectual Property Theft: Economic Harm, Threats to the Public Health and Safety, and Links to Organized Crime and Terrorist Organizations* (Washington, DC: 2005), pp. 23–24 – www.iccwbo.org/Data/Documents/Bascap/Why-enforce/Links-to-organized-crime/The-Negative-Consequences-of-International-Intellectual-Property-The ft/ [accessed 17 Nov. 2015]

121 IACC, *Negative Consequences*, pp. 26 and 29. As Marieke de Goede notes, such claims 'often rely on a few badly documented examples that are frequently (re)circulated' – *Speculative Security: The Politics of Pursuing Terrorist Monies* (Minneapolis: University of Minnesota Press, 2012), p. 227.

122 See Kristina Groennings, 'An Analysis of the Recording Industry's Litigation Strategy Against Direct Infringers', *Vanderbilt Journal of Entertainment Law and Practice*, Vol. 7, 2005, pp. 389–398.

123 Nitin Govil, 'War in the Age of Pirate Reproduction', in Sarai Editorial Collective (ed.), *Sarai Reader 2004: Crisis/Media* (Delhi: Centre for the Study of Developing Societies, 2004), p. 379.

124 R. Rangaraj, 'Music Piracy and Terrorism', 2003, available at: www.holoflex.com/media/chennaionline.html [accessed 17 Nov. 2015]

125 US Dept. of Transportation, *Transit Security Newsletter*, No. 36, 2003.

126 *Counterfeit Goods: Easy Cash for Criminals and Terrorists*, Hearing before the Committee on Homeland Security and Governmental Affairs, 109 Congress, 25 May, 2005 – www.gpo.gov/fdsys/pkg/CHRG-109shrg21823/html/CHRG-109shrg21823.htm [accessed 17 Nov. 2015]

127 GRAIN, *Iraq's New Patent Law: A Declaration of War Against Farmers*, 15 October, 2004, – www.grain.org/article/entries/150-iraq-s-new-patent-law-a-declaration-of-war-against-farmers [accessed 17 Nov. 2015]

128 George W. Bush, 'Remarks on Signing the Stop Counterfeiting in Manufactured Goods Act', Washington, 16 March, 2006. Also see *Fact Sheet: President Bush Signs the Stop Counterfeiting in Manufactured Goods Act*, March 16, 2006 – www.presidency.ucsb.edu/ws/index.php?pid=83060&st=piracy&st1= [accessed 17 Nov. 2015]

129 *Fact Sheet: Protecting American Innovation*, 13 October, 2008 – www.presidency.ucsb.edu/ws/index.php?pid=84712&st=piracy&st1= [accessed 17 Nov. 2015]

130 See www.unodc.org/unodc/en/piracy/index.html?ref=menuside [accessed 17 Nov. 2015]and http://business.panasonic.co.uk/security-solutions/13th-european-security-conference-exhibition#sthash.yqwf1LaC.dpuf [accessed 17 Nov. 2015]

131 Gregory F. Treverton, *et al.*, *Film Piracy, Organized Crime, and Terrorism* (Santa Monica, CA: RAND, 2009), p. xiv.

132 IP Commission Report, *The Report on the Commission on the Theft of American Intellectual Property* (Seattle, WA: National Bureau of Asian Research, 2013), pp. iii and 4.

Index